understanding **Hegelianism**

Understanding Movements in Modern Thought
Series Editor: Jack Reynolds

This series provides short, accessible and lively introductions to the major schools, movements and traditions in philosophy and the history of ideas since the beginning of the Enlightenment. All books in the series are written for undergraduates meeting the subject for the first time.

Published

Forthcoming titles include

understanding **Hegelianism**

Robert Sinnerbrink

ACUMEN

For Eva and Mimi

© Robert Sinnerbrink, 2007

First published in 2007 by Acumen

Acumen Publishing Limited
Stocksfield Hall
Stocksfield
NE43 7TN
www.acumenpublishing.co.uk

ISBN: 978-1-84465-093-4 (hardcover)
ISBN: 978-1-84465-094-1 (paperback)

British Library Cataloguing-in-Publication Data
A catalogue record for this book is available from the British Library.

Typeset by Graphicraft Limited, Hong Kong.
Printed and bound by Cromwell Press, Trowbridge.

Contents

Preface and acknowledgements

This book is intended to introduce one of the richest movements in modern philosophy. Hegelianism presents one possible path into modern European or "Continental" philosophy, which we can understand as a series of complex responses to Hegel. In what follows, I show how Hegelian and anti-Hegelian currents of thought shaped some of the most significant movements in twentieth-century European philosophy, from existentialism, Marxism and phenomenology to critical theory and poststructuralism. I foreground the Hegelian themes of the unhappy consciousness, the master/slave dialectic and the struggle for recognition, which have proven very fertile for German critical theory as well as for postwar French philosophy. I also consider the problem of modernity, theories of recognition, and the deconstruction of dialectic, important themes that are all profoundly indebted to Hegelian thought. On the other hand, Hegel has had a largely negative impact on the development of analytic philosophy; fortunately, this has recently begun to change with the emergence of "analytic neo-Hegelianism" (see Rockmore 2005). While I deal primarily with what I loosely call "German" and "French" appropriations of Hegelian thought, I also make some brief remarks on analytic neo-Hegelianism in my concluding discussion.

The book is structured into three parts. It begins with a brief introduction to key elements of Hegel's philosophy, and an overview of some of the main figures in the competing "Right" and "Left" Hegelian schools. I suggest that two of the most famous critiques of Hegelian thought – Kierkegaard's existentialism and Marx's materialism

– represent the defining poles of subsequent Hegelian and anti-Hegelian movements. These existentialist and Marxist currents comprise a conceptual matrix that can help us understand developments in twentieth-century Hegelian and anti-Hegelian thought.

The second part takes up these themes by looking at the contrasting critiques of Hegel presented by Marxist philosopher Georg Lukács and existential phenomenologist Martin Heidegger. Lukács's theme of reification and Heidegger's critique of Hegel as a Cartesian metaphysician set the stage for the appropriation of Hegelian themes in German critical theory and for the critique of Hegelianism in French poststructuralism. I then consider various Hegelian critiques of modernity – of modern reason, society, culture and conceptions of subjectivity – in the critical theory tradition, focusing on Adorno and Horkheimer's *Dialectic of Enlightenment* and on Adorno's negative dialectics. This is followed by an examination of the role of Hegelian themes in the work of Jürgen Habermas and Axel Honneth, who strongly emphasize the Hegelian concept of *recognition* for developing a critical theory of intersubjectivity and of modern society.

In the third part, I turn to the rich tradition of Hegelianism within twentieth-century French philosophy, beginning with the existentialist Hegelianism of Jean Wahl, Alexandre Kojève's Heideggerian-Marxist reading, and Jean Hyppolite's "hybrid" interpretation, which drew upon both existentialist and Marxist impulses. I then explore the ways in which French existentialism and phenomenology were both marked by a significant engagement with Hegelian thought. Here I focus upon Jean-Paul Sartre's existentialist critique of Hegel, Simone de Beauvoir's ambiguous engagement with Hegelian themes in *The Second Sex*, and conclude with a discussion of Merleau-Ponty's account of Hegelian existentialism and the question of a post-Hegelian "hyperdialectics". Finally, I consider the radical critique of Hegelianism articulated by French poststructuralist thinkers Gilles Deleuze and Jacques Derrida, whose attempts to construct a post-Hegelian philosophy of difference involve a complex critical relationship with Hegel. Can Hegelianism be overcome through an anti-dialectical conception of difference? Or does it require a complex "deconstruction" of its scope and limits? Can the philosophy of difference construct an alternative to Hegelian dialectics?

In conclusion, I gesture briefly towards contemporary thinkers (such as Judith Butler and Slavoj Žižek), whose work productively appropriates Hegelian themes while also integrating the critiques of Hegel found in critical theory and in poststructuralism. Their work, along with the Hegel renaissance in contemporary "post-analytic" philosophy, demonstrates the fertility of Hegelianism for contemporary thought. The argument developed in the book as a whole is that the conflict between much contemporary French and German thought derives from conflicting responses to Hegel: French Hegelianism emphasized the unhappy consciousness, the master/slave dialectic, and attempted to transform Hegelian dialectics into a philosophy of difference; German Hegelianism underscored Hegel's theory of modernity, his defence of an expanded theory of rationality, and his thematizing of recognition as part of a theory of social intersubjectivity. I suggest that a proper understanding of the plural and conflicting nature of Hegelianism might clear a path for a productive *rapprochement* between these two often conflicting perspectives defining modern European philosophy.

There are many people I would like to thank for their contributions towards the genesis of this book. I am greatly indebted to György Márkus for inspiring me with a passion for Hegel and Hegelian thought, and for generously commenting on various chapter drafts; to Elisabeth During for giving me the opportunity as a postgraduate to teach her course on the "Heritage of Hegel"; and to my colleague Jean-Philippe Deranty for many discussions on neo-Hegelianism. I must acknowledge Paul Redding, Robert B. Pippin, Michael Theunissen, Rolf-Peter Horstmann and Stephen Houlgate, who all contributed to my *Bildung* as a reader of Hegelian thought. My students at Macquarie University should also be thanked for allowing me to sharpen my thinking through teaching topics central to this study. I would especially like to thank the Series Editor Jack Reynolds, and Tristan Palmer, Sue Hadden and Elizabeth Teague, for their admirable editorial support, for Jack's excellent critical comments on various chapter drafts, and Tristan's patience regarding the completion of my manuscript. Finally, I am deeply grateful to my wife, Louise D'Arcens, without whose loving support, sound advice and firm encouragement I would never have completed this book.

Abbreviations

SL	G. W. F. Hegel, *Science of Logic* (1969 [1811, 1812, 1816/ 1830])
SNS	Maurice Merleau-Ponty, *Sense and Nonsense* (1964 [1948])
SR	Axel Honneth, *The Struggle for Recognition* (1995 [1992])
SS	Simone de Beauvoir, *The Second Sex* (1953 [1949])
TP	Jürgen Habermas, *Theory and Practice* (1973 [1971])
WD	Jacques Derrida, *Writing and Difference* (1972 [1967])

introduction

Hegel and the Enlightenment

G. W. F. Hegel (1770–1831) is without question one of the towering figures of modern thought. Hegel's philosophy has been both adored and reviled, its notorious difficulty spawning a multitude of Hegel myths. Arthur Schopenhauer denounced Hegel as a charlatan, while Nietzsche praised his profound historical sense. Karl Popper accused Hegel of paving the way for totalitarianism, while Alexandre Kojève took his interpretation of Hegel to have the significance of "political propaganda" (quoted in Roth 1988: 118). Even analytic philosophy emerged in reaction to Hegelianism, or more precisely, British idealism, which included figures such as F. H. Bradley, T. H. Green, and J. M. E. McTaggart; for Bertrand Russell, it represented just the kind of dubious metaphysics that conceptual analysis sought to dispel (see Rockmore 2005: 42–53). Despite this controversy, the complex currents of Hegelianism continued to inspire important developments in modern thought, from Marxism and existentialism to critical theory and deconstruction.

Among the most difficult of all modern philosophers, Hegel is also one of the most demonized. As Robert Pippin has remarked, Hegel appears to be "in the impossible position of being both extraordinarily influential and almost completely inaccessible" (1989: 3). The history of Hegelianism has therefore always been the history of the *partial* appropriation of selected Hegelian themes and concepts, rather than a comprehension or productive development of Hegel's system as a whole. One could even say that there is no such thing as a pure "Hegelian" philosopher in the sense that one talks of "Kantian" or

"Heideggerian" philosophers today. Instead, the historical reception of Hegel has tended to foreground certain texts over others (for example, the *Phenomenology* over the *Logic*), certain themes or concepts (the dialectic, *Aufhebung*, recognition), or even particular passages in Hegel's texts (such as the famous master/slave dialectic). In this sense, Hegel's influence has been based on a *selective appropriation* of certain elements of his philosophical system at the expense of others. This partial appropriation (meaning incomplete as well as motivated) makes the history of Hegelianism a very complex enterprise, full of conflicting but also recurring themes given the widely varying practical and theoretical interests at stake.

As we shall see throughout this book, Hegel has been interpreted from a bewildering variety of perspectives; what I present here is of course another interpretation that foregrounds certain aspects and ignores others. For all that, the aim of this book is to show that much recent European philosophy has been shaped by the simultaneous critique and appropriation of Hegelian thought. One could even understand the history of "Continental" philosophy as a complex series of responses to Hegel. There are of course many recurring themes in the reception of Hegel: the concepts of alienation, the unhappy consciousness, the master/slave dialectic, the struggle for recognition, and the comprehension of modernity, to name a few. All of these themes will be explored throughout the book from different Hegelian – and anti-Hegelian – perspectives. Indeed, understanding Hegelianism as a *plural* tradition of thought, so I shall contend, can contribute to our comprehension of the often antagonistic relationship between French and German stands of European philosophy.

As we shall see, the "French" emphasis on the unhappy consciousness and master/slave dialectic, coupled with the project of transforming Hegelian dialectics into a philosophy of difference, stands in sharp contrast to the "German" critical theory focus on Hegel's theory of modernity and on the Hegelian theme of intersubjective recognition. Having said this, however, I shall also emphasize how a number of post-Hegelian thinkers (Adorno, Merleau-Ponty, Deleuze and Derrida) draw remarkably close to each other in attempting to transform Hegelian dialectics into a non-totalizing thinking of difference. This suggests that something of a dialectical transformation – in the plural, open-ended, individuating manner suggested above – of these conflicting French and German Hegelianisms might be possible today. This remains, in my opinion, one of the more challenging and exciting tasks in contemporary European philosophy, a task that would benefit from renewed attention to the complex history of the plurality of overlapping views gathered together under the rubric of "Hegelianism".

In what follows, I introduce Hegel, as is fitting, by situating his thought within the historical context of the Enlightenment. Hegel is notable, even notorious, for being both a defender of enlightenment reason as well as one its sharpest critics. I consider briefly the complex relationship between Hegel and the critical idealism of Kant and the post-Kantian idealists (Fichte and Schelling). The systems of Fichte and Schelling were the subject of Hegel's first major publication (1801), while Kant figured prominently in his next book, *Faith and Knowledge* (1802). Together these texts showed that the young Hegel was a voice to be reckoned with in the emerging movement of post-Kantian or "German" idealism. They also foreshadowed some of the basic elements of his philosophical system, and the intriguing philosophical method known as Hegel's "dialectic".

The path to Hegel's system

Hegel's philosophy is one of the crowning achievements of the Enlightenment (*Aufklärung* in German), a term encompassing a range of important cultural developments during the late eighteenth and early nineteenth centuries. Put simply, the creed of the Enlightenment was that the path to universal human emancipation could be found in the free exercise of reason. Reason could overcome the debilitating effects of ignorance, fear and superstition; rational self-rule could replace blind obedience to authority in social and political life. Defenders of the Enlightenment held that the autonomous use of reason provided a basis for the expansion of objective knowledge, for the rational grounding of moral action, and for the organization of just social and political institutions. This faith in enlightenment rationality was linked with an ideal of *systematically organized knowledge*, acquired through scientific methods, which could be applied to satisfying human needs and increasing our mastery over nature. It was also characterized by the belief in the possibility of *moral improvement* in humanity, the gradual achievement of universal freedom through the development of rational social and political institutions. The optimistic spirit of the Enlightenment is strikingly captured in Kant's motto: *Sapere aude!* (Dare to know!)

Nonetheless, this enlightenment optimism soon led to probing questions about the relationship between reason and faith, the individual and society, and our relationship to nature. While enthused by the enlightenment promise of rational freedom, many artists, writers and philosophers began to question what sources of meaning and moral value could be reliably found in the modern world once religion was called into question and nature was transformed into a mechanistic domain for the satisfaction of human desires. The Enlightenment thus spawned the "counter-Enlightenment", represented by the various "Romantic" movements in art, literature and philosophy. *Romanticism* could be loosely defined as a cultural protest against certain tendencies within the Enlightenment: against reductive conceptions of reason that privileged the universal over the particular, the objective over the subjective, and that promoted human mastery over nature, including rational control over our subjective and affective life. The Romantic critique of enlightenment reason opened up a philosophical and cultural debate, still important today, in which Hegel remains a key protagonist.

Along with many other young intellectuals, Hegel shared the optimism of the Enlightenment along with a growing sense that radical historical change was in the air. The French Revolution of 1789 ushered in a "new age" that would put the ideals of reason and the principle of universal freedom to the test, an enthusiasm soon tempered by criticism once the Revolution gave way to the Jacobinist Terror. While inspired by the French Revolution (he continued to toast Bastille Day every year throughout his life), Hegel nonetheless remained critical of the limits of enlightenment rationality. Hegel's relationship with the Enlightenment is therefore a complex one. On the one hand, he was committed to its ideals: the unity of reason, the autonomy of the rational subject, and the achievement of human freedom through rational historical progress. On the other, he was also one of its sharpest critics, developing a profound critique of the pernicious social and cultural effects of a too limited conception of rationality.

This critical stance towards the Enlightenment is already evident in Hegel's early works, which contrasted Greek communal ethical life with the modern atomized community of self-interested individuals (see Hegel's *On Christianity: Early Theological Writings* (1948)). This attention to the problem of division and alienation in modernity would remain an abiding concern. Hegel's philosophical aim, very broadly, was to provide an antidote to the instrumentalist account of rationality that he saw at the root of many disturbing modern phenomena (atomization and alienation; the disconnection between science, morality and art; the undesirable side-effects of modern economic and social institutions). Hegel wanted to show how reason could overcome the dichotomies afflicting modern life and thought by dialectically unifying subject and object, particularity and universality, freedom and nature.

This meant, however, that philosophy needed to develop into a genuinely *rational system of thought*, a system capable of doing justice to the dynamism of autonomous thought. This systematic character of Hegel's philosophy is perhaps its most intimidating feature. It is difficult for us today, however, to understand the importance accorded to the idea of "system" during the enlightenment period, since we tend to regard the idea of a "system" of philosophy as outmoded or superseded. Interestingly, not all currents of the Enlightenment favoured the valorization of systematic thought. The French enlightenment thinkers (Diderot, Montesquieu, Rousseau and Voltaire), for instance, were resolutely *anti-system*, advocating, in different ways, an expanded conception of humanity that would embrace reason and emotion, freedom and nature, science and the arts. Nonetheless, the ideal of a rationally structured unity of thought is one that inspired all the great German idealist philosophers from Immanuel Kant (1724–1804), J. G. Fichte (1762–1814), F. W. J. Schelling (1775–1854) to Hegel himself. Like the other idealist thinkers, Hegel began his philosophical career in the aftermath of Immanuel Kant's monumental trilogy: the *Critique of Pure Reason* (1781/1787), the *Critique of Practical Reason* (1788) and the *Critique of Judgement* (1790/1793/1794). Hegel's philosophical system can be regarded, in certain ways, as a radicalization of Kantian idealism, an attempt to appropriate its insights but also to remedy its deficiencies in order to transform it into a genuine speculative system of philosophy ("speculative" meaning here autonomous thought capable of overcoming the dichotomies of the understanding through the unifying power of reason).

Kant's critical philosophy

Kant's importance for modern philosophy can hardly be overestimated. Among other things, Kant challenged the dogmatic metaphysics of the seventeenth century (Spinoza, Leibniz, Wolff), arguing that the limits of our capacity for rational knowledge must be investigated before we can make good the claims of traditional metaphysics to provide *a priori* knowledge (knowledge independent of experience). Kant's critical philosophy thus undertook the task of investigating the scope and limits of both theoretical and practical reason; it performed a *self-critique of reason* that would lay the foundation for a rationally grounded system of knowledge.

Kant thus sought to demolish traditional metaphysical speculation and replace it with *critical philosophy*: the critical investigation of our capacity for knowledge through concepts within the bounds of human cognitive experience. His aim was to show how rationally grounded knowledge is compatible with both natural science and moral freedom. Against sceptical empiricism (Hume) and dogmatic rationalism (Wolff, Leibniz, Spinoza), Kant aimed to develop a *rational philosophy of freedom* guided by the principle of *autonomy* (rational self-rule or self-legislation). Reason, in its theoretical and moral–practical versions, *can legislate for itself*; it thus provides us with a firm basis for organizing our knowledge, moral action and political institutions. A comprehensive unity of autonomous reason would provide an antidote to scepticism, fulfilling our desire to find a secure foundation for knowledge and values.

Kant's revolutionary "Copernican" turn in metaphysics reversed the traditional assumption that we have direct cognitive access to things in the world. Instead of assuming that knowledge conforms to objects as "things in themselves", Kant proposed that our knowledge of objects, considered as *appearances*, conforms to the necessary *a priori* (independent of experience) conditions of cognition for us as finite subjects. In other words, we do not have unmediated access to things in the world; objects are never just "given" to us immediately in experience. Rather, we have knowledge of objects of experience, what Kant called "appearances", which means anything about which we can make a cognitive judgement.

Such objects of experience, Kant argued, are structured according to three "subjective" conditions of cognition:

- that all experience presupposes the pure forms of intuition (space and time);
- that the categories of the understanding (for example, substance and causality) structure our cognition of objects; and
- that we must organize the application of these concepts, within experience, under principles of pure reason.

The problem that Kant confronted, however, was to explain how we could have objective knowledge of the world on the basis of concepts that we do not derive from experience. If the categories of the understanding make possible our objective knowledge, how do we know that these categories have "objective validity", that is, actually apply to the world? Answering this question became the task of Kant's notoriously difficult "transcendental deduction" (justification of the conditions of our knowledge): to show that the categories of the understanding are subjective conditions of possibility for objective knowledge; and to show that their transcendental ground or condition was to be found in what Kant called the "transcendental unity of apperception". By this Kant meant the pure (formal) principle of *self-consciousness* that makes possible ordinary empirical experience: a "logical" principle necessary for the unification of cognitive judgements as all belonging to one and the same subject.

We need go no further here into the complexities of Kant's critical philosophy. It is enough to point out that Kant's transcendental idealism made *pure self-consciousness* the grounding principle of our experience and knowledge of the world. Kant's hope in developing the critical philosophy was to demonstrate how human reason evinces a complex unity in diversity. The critique of *pure* (non-empirical) *reason* aimed to show how we could have objective knowledge of the world even though our experience is conditioned by subjective conditions of cognition. The critique of *practical reason* aimed to show that, thanks to the "fact" of moral freedom, we could exercise moral judgement as rational beings even though we are also bound, as phenomenal beings, by natural laws and conditions. And finally, the critique of (aesthetic and teleological) *judgement* aimed to show that theoretical and practical reason could be united through the aesthetic experience of beauty in nature and in art. The aesthetic experience of beauty thus became a symbol of the hope for a harmonious moral order and a human realization of freedom.

The young Hegel

Following the euphoria generated by the French Revolution of 1789, the young Hegel expected a similarly dramatic revolution to follow from the Kantian philosophy. This excitement was nicely summed up in the young Schelling's statement in a letter to Hegel (dated 17 January 1795): "Philosophy is not yet at an end. Kant has given us the results; but the premisses are still lacking. And who can understand results without premisses? Only a Kant! . . .". In fact, what historians of philosophy call "German idealism" – the late eighteenth to early nineteenth-century flourishing of philosophy in Germany from Kant, Fichte and Schelling to Hegel – can be regarded as a series of intersecting attempts to supply these "missing premises" and thus to complete the unfinished project of Kant's critical philosophy (see Beiser 1988).

At the same time, however, we should note that post-Kantian idealism was motivated by a sense that the Kantian critical philosophy had *failed* to make good its claims to have achieved the unity of reason; it failed to overcome the fundamental dichotomy between *theoretical* and *practical reason*. There are numerous examples of this failure in Kant's philosophy. On the one hand, Kant argued for a comprehensive unity of autonomous reason; on the other, he needed to solve the difficulty of a postulated but unrealized subject–object unity. The latter refers to the gulf, evident at various points in Kant's philosophy, between the claims of theoretical reason to know the world empirically, and the claims of practical reason to legislate what we should do morally. The principle of autonomy, for instance, is the ground of practical philosophy and of practical reason more generally, but only in the form of a *postulate* of reason that can be *posited* but not actually proven. There are supposed to be obligatory laws always operating in morality, but it is clear that we can always fail to do our duty and to follow our inclinations instead. The supposedly autonomous Kantian moral subject is at the same time subject to nature in the form of desires, passions, emotions and so on.

These tensions in Kant's philosophy created a profound gulf between *theoretical* and *practical* reason that Kant then attempted to bridge via our power of aesthetic judgement (or at least to provide the hope that such a unity might be possible). The aesthetic experience of beauty in nature gives us reason to hope for reconciliation between theoretical and practical reason; but once again, this is a postulation that cannot be proven. German idealist philosophy can thus be defined as the attempt to overcome the gulf between the theoretical and practical dimensions of reason, an attempt to create their unity motivated by the conviction that Kant's philosophy only demonstrated their lack of unity. In the end, Kant could only show that there is *no necessary contradiction* between freedom and nature; but he could not show that they *actually are in agreement* in experience, and thus vindicate his claim to have rationally justified the unity of reason. That was the task taken up by post-Kantian idealism, articulated in the extraordinarily rich works of Fichte, Schelling and Hegel.

The project of surpassing Kantian idealism via Fichte and Schelling is apparent in Hegel's earliest published work, *The Difference between Fichte's and Schelling's System of Philosophy* (1801). This difficult essay, which critically compares Fichte's "subjective idealism" with Schelling's "objective idealism", foreshadows Hegel's mature project: to overcome the dichotomies in the Kantian critical philosophy by developing a speculative system of reason that unifies the dichotomies between subject and object, universal and particular, freedom and nature. In this early text, often just called the *Differenzschrift*, Hegel argues that Fichte's idealism, like that of Kant, remains a "subjective" idealism because it fails to generate a speculative identity, through reason, between subject and object. While Fichte maintains this identity of subject and object on the theoretical plane, on the practical plane he posits a separation between reason and the world. In our practical–moral action we remain, Fichte claims, condemned to an "endless striving" in attempting to realize the principles of morality. The result is an intractable dichotomy between *theory and practice* that, like Kant's dichotomy, contradicts Fichte's claim to have articulated a speculative unity of reason (unifying theory and practice).

Schelling's philosophy marks an advance on Fichte's, according to Hegel, since it develops a genuinely "objective" idealism that encompasses the unity between subject and object (self-consciousness is what allows us to comprehend nature, while nature is the ground of the development of self-consciousness). Subject and object are no longer in opposition, but represent different degrees of organization of a dynamic, self-developing whole. Indeed, the opposition between subject and object could be overcome by pointing to their originary unity at the level of what Schelling called "intellectual intuition", an experience disclosed, for example, in the "fusion" of reflection and intuition, freedom and nature, subjectivity and objectivity experienced in the work of art. Radicalizing Kant's turn towards aesthetic experience, the young Schelling elevated art to the highest level of knowledge; the intellectual intuition of subject and object in their dynamic interplay would provide the key to the long-sought-for unity of subject and object. Impressed by Schelling's (Romantic) solution to the problem of overcoming the Kantian dichotomies, the young Hegel briefly shared Schelling's position that the identity of reason and intuition ("intellectual intuition") enables us to gain speculative knowledge of the whole (the unity of subject and object).

Hegel soon broke with Schelling, however, over the primary role of *reason*. Philosophy strives for a rational intuition of the whole, but for the young Schelling this requires an intellectual intuition – an identity of subject and object – that is no longer comprehensible through reason alone. Hegel came to reject this view on a number of grounds.

First, how can intellectual intuition be demonstrated or verified in comparison with other claims to knowledge? Secondly, if we maintain with Kant that all knowledge is discursive, requiring the synthesis of intuitions and concepts, then non-discursive, non-conceptual intuition becomes incommunicable. Thirdly, Schelling's claim to know the absolute by intellectual intuition had the effect of dissolving sensuous particularity into a vast undifferentiated whole, what metaphysicians such as Spinoza called "the Absolute". As Hegel quips in the *Phenomenology of Spirit* (1807), this Schellingian Absolute is like "the night in which all cows are black" (PhS: §16). The problem, in Hegel's view, was rather to *know* and *preserve* these finite particulars within the articulated, rational whole.

The challenge for Hegel, therefore, was to find a discursive method through which we could come to know the Absolute: a philosophical or "speculative" knowledge accessible to all rational subjects that could be demonstrated against the claims of ordinary knowledge. By arguing for such knowledge, however, Hegel seemed to challenge Kant's strictures on knowing the Absolute. At the same time, Hegel maintained that this speculative knowledge was possible for us if we could properly overcome the dichotomy between theory and practice in Kant's critical philosophy. Hegel's task was thus to show that *conceptual knowledge of the Absolute was possible within experience*, without lapsing into Kantian dualism, Fichtean "subjectivism", or Schellingian Romanticism. Hegel took to this task by developing a series of sketches (while in the German town of Jena) outlining the metaphysics and the dialectical "logic" that would ground his speculative system of philosophy, encompassing *speculative logic*, the *philosophy of nature*, and the *philosophy of spirit* or mind [*Geist*] (these texts have come to be known as the "Jena manuscripts").

At this point, however, Hegel started to ponder the question of how one should *begin* along the path of speculative knowledge. He thus turned to the problem of providing an introduction to his system, one that did not presuppose an absolute "Cartesian" foundation nor presume that we can have esoteric "Schellingian" intuition of the whole. What we required, as Kant himself had argued, was an account of how such speculative knowledge was possible: a critical "justification" of our rational knowledge, of our cognitive experience of the world in all its variety and richness.

This task was undertaken in Hegel's path-breaking *Phenomenology of Spirit*, published in 1807, which presents his *phenomenological* justification of our knowledge or cognitive experience. Hegel shows in the *Phenomenology* how ordinary consciousness, in its attempts to know reality, ends up in contradiction, which motivates the movement to ever more complex and inclusive patterns of knowing. Hegelian phenomenology means the *self-examination of knowledge* in which the claims of consciousness to know the world are tested against its own standards of knowledge, and these standards of knowledge are in turn tested against the experience of consciousness. This (dialectical) movement continues until a standard of knowledge is reached that is adequate to the whole historical experience of (Western) consciousness, from the origins of Greek philosophy to post-revolutionary enlightenment culture. Once we attain this standard, we have arrived at the standpoint of "absolute knowing", Hegel's speculative version of the famous subject–object identity sought by Fichte and Schelling. Hegel's *Phenomenology* thus depicts the odyssey of consciousness in its journey towards philosophical and historical self-knowledge. It is a tragic drama in which "we", the philosophical audience, observe a character ("consciousness") whose journey begins in ignorance, passes through sceptical despair, but ends in philosophical wisdom. *Our* wisdom emerges when we recognize that this dramatic journey is in fact our own.

part I

The adventures of Hegelianism

one

Introducing Hegelian idealism

For all his formidable difficulty as a philosopher, Hegel was also a committed teacher concerned to introduce his students to philosophy no matter what their level of expertise. Hegel was for a time a teacher at Nürnberg Gymnasium, presenting high-school students with a simplified outline of his philosophical system (see his *Philosophical Propaedeutic*). In this chapter I attempt to do something similar, though less formidable, namely to present a very brief introduction to important themes in some of Hegel's most famous works. I begin with an overview of Hegel's *Phenomenology of Spirit*, focusing on his account of the "dialectical experience of consciousness", and providing a brief explication of his famous master/slave dialectic. I then turn to a very schematic account of the basic idea of Hegelian logic: the analysis of the systems of basic categories of thought that structure our experience of the world. Some important aspects of Hegel's philosophy of history are then explored, including the influential idea of an "end of history". I also present some key elements of Hegel's political philosophy, his account of the conditions necessary for the exercise of modern freedom. In conclusion, I look briefly at so-called British idealism, an important turn-of-the-century movement that generated the strong anti-idealist turn – particularly with Moore and Russell – that paved the way for the emergence of analytic philosophy.

From consciousness to spirit: Hegel's *Phenomenology of Spirit*

Legend has it that Hegel was hastily completing the final pages of his manuscript just as the first cannon-shots rang out announcing the battle of Jena in 1806. Under such dramatic circumstances, even the title of his master work remained uncertain. Originally, Hegel had selected *Science of the Experience of Consciousness* before opting at the last moment for *Phenomenology of Spirit*. Hegel thereby made the term "phenomenology" famous, not to mention *Geist* or spirit, Hegel's transfigured conception of what Kant called *Vernunft* or "reason". "Phenomenology" comes from the Greek term *phainomena*, meaning that which appears or shows itself, and *logos*, meaning reasoned account. It was a term first used by Kant's friend Lambert in 1764, but Kant also used it in his *Metaphysical Foundations of Natural Science* of 1786 to refer to an account of perception and its limits (see Rockmore 1993: 86 ff.).

It was Hegel, however, who made phenomenology famous as a philosophical approach in its own right. The concept of phenomenology was to have a fascinating career in modern thought, being later transformed in quite different directions by Edmund Husserl (1859–1938), Martin Heidegger (1889–1976), Jean-Paul Sartre (1905–80) and Maurice Merleau-Ponty (1908–61). But what did Hegel mean by this term? Hegelian phenomenology is a philosophical method that describes and interprets interconnected patterns of *knowledge as an appearance* (knowledge-claims that make an appearance in our historical world). Our objects of enquiry are not "truth" or "meaning" but rather *configurations of consciousness*. These are figures or patterns of knowledge, cognitive and practical attitudes, which emerge within a definite historical and cultural context in a variety of guises (for example, the figure of "sense-certainty", which can be found in ancient scepticism, Humean impressions and Russellian sense-data).

Hegel's *Phenomenology* depicts certain configurations of consciousness, describing how knowledge and experience conflict in the subject's various attempts to know the world. It shows how consciousness resolves this conflict between its assumed form of *knowledge* and its *experience*, that is, the result of its attempt to know the world in such and such a way. Consciousness, in Hegel's terms, thus undergoes a *dialectical experience* – the movement from a conflict between knowledge and truth to a more complex configuration of consciousness that presents a new relationship between subject and object – a process that "we", the philosophical readers, can observe in its unfolding. Hegel's *Phenomenology* will attempt to demonstrate how the various cognitive attitudes that have emerged in Western thought and culture are interconnected in a conceptually articulated sequence – a sequence culminating in Hegel's own phenomenological enquiry. From this point of view, Hegel's phenomenological exposition can be understood as "the path of natural consciousness which presses forward to true knowledge" (PhS: §77), namely, to the experiential knowledge of itself as spirit.

What about "spirit"? The meaning of this famous Hegelian term only becomes clear during the course of Hegel's exposition, but here we must say something by way of introduction. Spirit or *Geist* is Hegel's term for self-conscious reason, for socially and culturally articulated relations of meaning, or shared forms of social and cultural intersubjectivity. Spirit refers to forms of collective "mindedness" encompassing not only individual self-consciousness but also forms of knowledge and shared meaning in a culture, from sensuous representations in art, symbolic representations in religion, to conceptual comprehension in philosophy. At the same time, spirit also designates social and political institutions as "objective" embodiments of the shared rational norms of knowledge and practice that define human communities. Taken together, these institutionally embodied forms of shared meaning and situated knowledge comprise the historical spirit and self-understanding of a rationally organized human community.

The phenomenological exposition begins, however, not with spirit, but with "consciousness". For Hegel, "natural consciousness" describes a kind of common-sense realism that is the presupposed background of philosophical enquiry. What the phenomenological enquiry explores is the development of natural consciousness into philosophical knowledge. "Consciousness", for Hegel, describes a bipolar cognitive structure relating a knower with something known: a *knowledge-claim* with what is taken as *truth*. In the *Phenomenology of Spirit*, each instance of knowledge involves a relation between a subject and an object (what Hegel calls the poles of "knowing" and "truth") in which consciousness compares its claims to knowledge with its experience of whether these claims remain coherent. If a contradiction emerges between the experience of consciousness and its claim to knowledge, consciousness reconstructs the relationship between knowledge and object so as to correspond with its experience. Consciousness overcomes any disparity that emerges between knowing and truth by cancelling the inadequate aspects of their original configuration, and by incorporating the positive aspects into a more complex unity of consciousness and its object. What emerges is thus a new relation between knowledge and its object, a new configuration of knowing and truth. This is what Hegel called the "dialectical experience" of consciousness: the movement from an initial pattern of consciousness, its inversion into an opposing position, and the reconfiguration of both within a more complex unity.

Lordship and bondage: the struggle for recognition

The most famous passage in Hegel's *Phenomenology* is undoubtedly the section describing the proto-social relationship between dependent and independent subjects – the celebrated "master/slave dialectic". This passage is famous for many reasons. It is a dramatic phenomenological account of the origin of sociability, Hegel's critical version of the "state of nature" fiction familiar from social contract theories in Hobbes, Rousseau and Locke. It provided an inspiration for the tradition of left-wing Hegelians, from the young Karl Marx (1818–83) to Alexandre Kojève (1902–68), who derived much of their social and political philosophy from Hegel's account of the dialectical relationship between master and slave. Yet for Hegel it was only one brief episode in the transition from consciousness of the world to rational forms of theoretical and practical self-consciousness.

Given the enormous influence of this section of Hegel's *Phenomenology*, it is worth elaborating a compressed version of this "struggle for recognition" (see PhS: 111–19). Hegel's dialectic of independent and dependent consciousness, as it is called, is a description of various inadequate conceptions of freedom. It emerges out of the experience of *desire*, the fact that our first experience of self-consciousness, so to speak, is as living, desiring beings immersed in a natural environment. In satisfying our animal desires we gain a fleeting sense of self-identity, for once our desire (for food, drink, sex) is satisfied, it disappears, only to return and demand further satisfaction. By incorporating a desired object into myself, I gain a temporary and unstable sense of my self-identity, which is disrupted as soon as I am once again in the grip of the desire for another object. Although there are traditionally a number of moral and ethical responses to the problem of controlling desire (Epicureanism, Stoicism, and so on), Hegel will argue that it is only in desiring recognition or acknowledgement from *another living, desiring subject* that we can gain genuine satisfaction and a lasting sense of self-identity.

In Hegel's "state of nature", however, the first experience of desiring proto-subjects ("proto-subjects" because we are dealing with pre-rational, not-yet-autonomous beings) is one of *conflict*, even violence. Each desiring subject attempts to assert its independence and self-identity by negating the other desiring subject; the result is a "life-and-death struggle" in which each proto-subject seeks to destroy the other. But to achieve this aim (destroying the other subject) would be self-defeating, victory over a corpse rather than acknowledgement from a living being. So one of the protagonists in the struggle must capitulate, renouncing his independence and submitting to the will of the other; the other thereby succeeds in having his independence acknowledged, albeit under duress. The victorious protagonist, who risked his life in order to prove his independence, becomes *the master*, while the vanquished party, who remained "tethered" to mere life, becomes *the slave*, the dependent consciousness who recognizes only the master's will.

Here is where Hegel's famous "dialectical reversals" come into play. The master's victory is hollow, for he is in fact dependent upon the slave, who works for the master in order that the master may satisfy his desires. The master has extorted acknowledgement of his independence from an utterly dependent being, reduced to the dehumanized status of a "living tool" (Aristotle). The slave, by contrast, will turn out to be the "master of the master", so to speak, for the slave has experienced his own limits, his *finitude* (through encountering the threat of death), the power that negates all his attributes; he is thus negatively aware of his mortal limits and of his capacity for freedom. The slave thus chooses life, curbs his desire, learns self-discipline, develops his abilities and skills in labouring for the master, and slowly comes to recognize his power to transform the objective world through work or collective labour. In the long run, Hegel intimates, the slave will arrive at a truer conception of freedom, recognizing the interconnection between dependence and independence, and developing a sense of self-identity through work and contribution to the social community.

Nonetheless, both master and slave remain locked in an unhappy relation of domination: the master cannot gain recognition of his independence, for the slave remains a dependent being. The slave, meanwhile, remains enslaved to the master, and denied proper recognition of his humanity and freedom. Indeed, the experience of mastery and slavery teaches consciousness that not only life but freedom is essential to it. The question now is how this freedom is to be understood and realized, a question addressed in the next configuration of self-consciousness, which Hegel calls the "unhappy consciousness". This is the experience of the *alienated subject*, and its various attempts to deal with the consequences of an inadequate conception of freedom.

Following the master/slave dialectic, the first strategy is to find freedom in pure thought, a strategy evident in *Stoicism*: I may be enslaved in reality, yet my rational mind remains free and universal, even though my empirical ego (and perhaps also my body) is alienated and dominated. This is a rather stylized presentation of Stoicism, which, to speak generally, advocated detachment from excessive forms of passion through the exercise of reason and rational self-control. Nonetheless, Hegel emphasizes the centrality of free rational thought in his account, and even argues that Stoicism, in the end, can only offer truisms and platitudes that ultimately result in boredom! Hence the next strategy is to radicalize this freedom of thought, turning it against *all* claims to knowledge. This is *scepticism* as the freedom of pure thought, which denies all claims to knowledge in the name of the radical freedom of the rational thinking subject. Yet this thinking subject remains an embodied, living, desiring being, existing in a social world with others. One can really be a sceptic only in theory, for acting in the world requires that we assume the truth of those very concepts that are rejected in the name of sceptical doubt.

Once the subject becomes aware of its separation into a radically free thinking self and unfree empirical self, it becomes an "unhappy consciousness". This is the alienated, religious subject, who struggles against his own internal self-contradictoriness (as both divine and profane), and strives in vain to unite these *universal* and *particular* dimensions of selfhood. The universal aspect is projected outwards into an eternal unchanging essence (God), while the particular aspect remains bound to the degraded body, senses and ego of the individual. The unhappy consciousness thus embarks on ever more radical attempts to unite the unchanging and particular aspects of its alienated subjectivity, first through religious devotion, then in the performance of good works, and finally via utter self-abnegation. But the unhappy consciousness can only overcome its worsening alienation once it realizes that it cannot forcibly unify the universal aspect of its selfhood with its particular bodily experience. Rather, the universal and the particular are contrasting dimensions of self-consciousness, which will eventually be united in the embodied rational individual. My rational subjectivity is always mediated by my relations with others, by my being recognized within an intersubjective context of rational interactions. This is the moment when self-consciousness begins to transform itself into *reason*, the rational unity of universal and particular, the subject that is conscious of itself in being conscious of its *universality*. What lies ahead for self-conscious reason are the conflicting experiences of *theoretical* and *practical reason*, a dichotomy that is overcome only in the more complex unity-in-difference of "spirit": "the We that is I and the I that is We" (PhS: §177), the intersubjective unity that is the true nature of realized freedom.

From spirit to idea: Hegel's *Logic*

Hegel's *Phenomenology* is a "science" of the experience of consciousness that is also a reconstruction of our historical–philosophical experience as members of a modern rational community. The phenomenological experience of consciousness passes through self-consciousness, theoretical and practical reason, and different historical versions of spirit, from Greek antiquity, medieval Christianity, to Enlightenment culture and modern bourgeois society. The phenomenological journey culminates with what Hegel calls "absolute knowing" – a knowing encompassing this whole (circular) movement from consciousness and self-consciousness to reason and self-knowing spirit. We attain absolute knowing when we recognize that immediate intuition – the "sense-certainty" with which we began – presupposes the whole complex phenomenological history of spirit coming to know itself. It is in this sense that the *Phenomenology of Spirit* was intended as an introduction to Hegel's speculative system. Once we have traversed this phenomenological path, we attain a level that enables us to embark upon speculative philosophy proper. Phenomenology thus enables us to move to the level of *pure conceptual* thinking: speculative logic that articulates the basic categories of thought.

Hegel's logic is forbiddingly difficult. Nonetheless, Hegel intended it to be intelligible in principle to all rational individuals who desire philosophical comprehension of the categorical structure of self-conscious subjectivity ("subjective spirit"), of the different kinds of modern social and political institutions ("objective spirit"), and of the three cultural forms of "absolute spirit" providing our cognitive self-reflection (art, religion, philosophy). While debate still rages over the true meaning of Hegel's logic, the simplest way to describe it is as an analysis of interconnected *systems* of basic categories of thought (see Kolb 1986; Pinkard 1988). Unlike formal logic, which considers the logical relations between propositions and the formal rules of valid argumentation, Hegelian logic analyses the system of basic categories of thought as ways of conceptualizing reality as a coherent and intelligible whole.

In this sense, Hegel radicalizes Kant's "transcendental logic", which aimed to describe the logical relations between categories that provide the conditions of possibility for our subjective cognitive experience. For Hegel, this transcendental logic must be transformed into a *speculative logic* that shows the immanent development of categories in a logical sequence or interconnected pattern. These categories are articulated within three interconnected systems, each displaying its own sequence of development. The three major categorial systems Hegel describes are the logic of *being* (*Sein*), which functions via a logic of transition between categories; the logic of *essence* (*Wesen*), which displays a logic of reflection, of opposition and dichotomy, between its categories; and the logic of the *Concept* (or conceptuality) (*Begriff*), which evinces a logic of immanent self-development between interconnected categories – a logic that in turn integrates elements of the previous two categorial systems. This movement from the logical systems of being, to essence, to Concept, comprises the whole of speculative logic, which also provides a "logical" version of the history of metaphysics from Greek ontology (Plato and Aristotle), through substance metaphysics (Spinoza), to modern subject-metaphysics (Kant) and speculative philosophy (Hegel).

This enormously ambitious philosophical project remains contentious, and is even frequently disregarded in contemporary readings of Hegel (see Wood 1990). Nonetheless, Hegel's logic is supposed to provide the underlying framework for all his "*Realphilosophie*" or philosophy of the real, that is, his philosophy of nature and philosophy of subjective spirit. Indeed, the categories of speculative logic also remain at play within Hegel's philosophy of the social world, of art, of history and of politics. A few words introducing the most familiar part of Hegel's extraordinary work must therefore suffice, after which I shall turn briefly to some of the main themes in Hegel's philosophy of history and political philosophy.

Aristotle famously defined logic as "thought thinking itself". Hegel takes this insight – along with Kant's transcendental logic, the logic of categories that make possible our experience – and develops an account of the basic categories of thought in their immanent relations and sequential development within distinctive categorial systems. But where would such a speculative logic begin? It must be with the most basic category of thought, the one that allows us to begin "without presuppositions" (see Houlgate 2005). Why without presuppositions? Because Hegel wants to move beyond the ungrounded character of Kant's "deduction" or justification of the categories, since Kant was criticized for simply taking over Aristotle's table of categories without justifying these or showing their logical interconnection. Moreover, Hegel avoids presupposing without immanent justification the laws of thought presupposed by formal logic, namely that all thought must obey the laws of identity (A = A) and non-contradiction (A cannot simultaneously be not-A in one and the same respect). Even the most basic laws and principles of thought must be grounded and justified in respect of an absolutely minimal presupposition (which will turn out to be *pure being*). Speculative logic will therefore attempt to present a self-grounding system of categorial relations, without presuppositions, that will develop into a rationally connected totality of thought-determinations.

This first category is the category of pure being: "the indeterminate immediate", immediate being free from any determinateness or distinction. Pure being is another term simply for "what is"; whatever is thought about in some sense *is*, that is, presupposes the category of "pure being", being without any definite content. The verb "to be" is an immediate indeterminate presupposition of thought as such. But this pure indeterminateness is also what makes "being" indistinguishable from "nothing". Both being and nothing are defined by pure indeterminateness; yet being and nothing are categories that are at the same time distinct in meaning. We obviously mean different things by "being" and "nothing" but this difference cannot really be articulated by means of these categories themselves: "Let those who insist that being and nothing are different tackle the problem of stating in what the difference consists" (SL: 92). The conflict between these categories – as indistinguishable yet opposed in meaning – can only be resolved by moving to a "higher", more complex category that encompasses the movement between being and nothing. This category is *becoming*, which incorporates the vanishing of being into nothing and nothing into being, as "suspended" (cancelled yet preserved) moments or aspects of its movement.

Becoming itself, however, is an unstable category that undergoes a transformation in its meaning. The instability between the moments of coming-to-be and ceasing-to-be must be stabilized within a more complex category, one that incorporates the negative difference between being and nothing within a "higher" unity. This is achieved in the category of *determinate being*. Hegel calls this movement from the categories of being and nothing to becoming and determinate being an exemplary case of the movement of *Aufhebung* (supersession or sublation). This is one of Hegel's signature concepts, a defining concept of Hegelian speculative thought. The German word *aufheben* is in common usage, yet it expresses opposing meanings: *to cancel, to do away with*, but also *to preserve or take up to a higher level*. In this case, the moments of being and nothing are *both* cancelled *and* preserved as aspects of becoming, and these "suspended" moments of becoming are in turn transformed into the moments of *something* and *other* within the more complex unity of *determinate being*.

Hegel continues the dialectical development of the categories in the transition from the logic of being to the logic of essence. We have seen how there is a simple *transition* or *passing over* from "being" to "nothing": being passing into nothing, both of which are superseded by the category of *becoming*, the latter being superseded by *determinate being*, and so on. Here the categories of being attempt, yet fail, to resolve the conflict between *immediacy* and *determinateness* (which is why pure being ends up transformed into determinate being).

The logic of essence, by contrast, operates with correlated pairs of categories in hierarchical opposition (such as essence and appearance, identity and difference, cause and effect). The categories of essence deal with substructure/superstructure relations, the familiar "two-world" model of metaphysics, which establishes the sensible world of appearance as distinct from the supersensible world of essence. The logic of essence, however, remains bound within an oppositional framework of thought; it is unable to conceptualize properly the unity of universal and particular – essential to the unity of genuinely autonomous reason – without subordinating the particular to the universal, which therefore remains formal and abstract (in the sense of an empty form that abstracts from definite content). Both systems of being-logic and essence-logic, therefore, remain unable to conceptualize the threefold unity of universal and particular within the individual, and so must be superseded by the logic of the *Concept* or *Begriff*.

What does Hegel mean by "Concept" or *Begriff*? (see Pinkard 1988; Kolb 1986). For our purposes it is enough to say that Hegel's term "Concept" in general refers to the dialectical totality of categories or "thought-determinations" that make up the intelligibility of the whole. At the same time, "Concept" also refers to the threefold structure comprising the interrelated aspects of universality, particularity and individuality within any rational whole. By way of example we can consider the Hegelian Concept of self-consciousness. This embraces the aspect of *universality* (the formal unity of self-consciousness, the Fichtean "I" = "I"); the aspect of *particularity* (the desiring aspect of self-consciousness, my own particular desires and appetites); and the aspect of *individuality* (the individuated self-conscious subject who acquires his/her identity through relations of mutual recognition with other subjects). Hegel will then examine this threefold logic of conceptuality in its self-developing movement toward the *Idea*, defined as the *unity of concept and reality*. Hegel's Idea is far from being merely an intellectualist abstraction; on the contrary, it is the unity-in-difference of thought and being that expresses the very rationality of the real.

The ultimate aim of Hegel's logic is to supersede the oppositional logic of the analytic or formal *understanding* (*Verstand*), which grounds the categorial systems of substance- and subject-metaphysics. The speculative logic of the Concept overcomes this dichotomous thinking in favour of a logic that articulates the threefold unity of universal, particular and individual, a logic that Hegel claims belongs to genuinely free, self-developing thought. For all its arcane character, Hegel's logic nonetheless provides essential background for understanding his celebrated analyses of modern history, society, culture and politics. As we shall see, it also provided the impetus, mainly via the work of French Hegelian Jean Hyppolite (1907–68), for the turn against Hegel defining the French philosophy of difference that emerged in the 1960s (especially with Deleuze and Derrida).

History, freedom, modernity

Hegel's entire system is supposed to be grounded through the categorial relations within the different parts of Hegelian logic. This is also true of well-known specific parts of his philosophy (such as the master/slave relationship, the notion of *Geist*, and his famous theses on reason in history and the realization of freedom in the modern world). While the relationship between Hegel's logic and the other parts of his system remains a burning issue for Hegel scholars, for our purposes a brief consideration of how speculative logic informs some of Hegel's best-known analyses of social, cultural and political phenomena will help introduce themes from his philosophy of history, and key aspects of his most important work of political philosophy, the *Philosophy of Right*.

One of Hegel's most significant contributions to modern thought lies in his emphasis on the *historicity* of knowledge and experience. For Hegel, we not only exist in historical time but our knowledge and social experience are historical in character: they are shaped by the history of which we are a part, and which we contribute to shaping in turn. But history, for Hegel, is not simply the chronicling of events, nor is it the seemingly blind succession of conflictual struggles over land, power, wealth or resources. When viewed from a philosophical perspective, Hegel argues, history evinces a *rational progress*, even though the empirical course of history often seems irrational, violent and bloody. (As Hegel notoriously remarks, history is a "slaughterbench" on which individuals, even whole communities, are "sacrificed" in the advancement of freedom.) Although historical agents act largely on the basis of short-term, irrational and egoistic motivations (desire for glory, wealth, power), philosophically comprehended history displays, on the contrary, a "realization of the Idea of freedom" in action. Hegel has been criticized ever since for maintaining a view that seemed to make philosophy an apologia for the status quo. Some critics even claimed that Hegel regarded the contemporary Prussian state as the incarnation of the Idea of freedom!

These criticisms, however, overlook the fundamentally *normative* character of Hegel's philosophy of history. The rationality of a historical community can only be judged by considering the degree to which this community advances the development of the Idea of freedom ("Idea" having here the Hegelian meaning of a "unity of Concept and actuality", that is, a *unity of theory and practice*). An Idea that remains an intellectual abstraction or mere "ought" is no Idea at all; we must be able to point to actualizations of the Idea in historical and social experience (thus works of art are embodiments of the Idea of beauty in historical and cultural experience; social and political institutions are instantiations of the Idea of freedom in history). To cite Hegel's famous story, the career of the Idea of freedom (genuine self-determination and self-realization within a self-grounding rational community) begins in the East, with so-called Oriental despotism, where *one* individual (the Emperor) is free while all others remain unfree. The spirit of freedom moves West, emerging into self-consciousness in ancient Greece, where *some* are free (the male Athenian citizens), while the majority of individuals remain unfree (non-citizens, foreigners, women, slaves). Finally, the Idea of freedom comes to self-realization in the Christian context of the post-revolutionary West, where *all* are recognized as free (at least in principle, if not always in practice), where freedom finally becomes universal and individuals are understood as deserving of recognition as rationally free just in virtue of their status as human beings.

As historical evidence of the realization of universal principles of freedom, Hegel pointed to the philosophical significance of the French Revolution; he also pointed to the emergence of universal principles of morality and justice enshrined within modern constitutional states governed by the rule of law. This philosophical self-understanding of ourselves as free means that we come to realize that our individual freedom is made possible, indeed sustained by, the social, economic and political institutions of the modern world. This historical realization of the Idea of freedom through recognition of the enabling conditions provided by modern social and political institutions has come to be known as Hegel's controversial "end of history" thesis.

The "end of history"?

This idea would prove to have a very long life in the aftermath of Hegel's thought. It provided the impetus for the Marxist model of the realization of freedom through the revolutionary establishment of communism. It provided the inspiration for Alexandre Kojève's influential Marxist–Heideggerian reading of Hegel, which anticipated some of the themes of the "post-historical" condition of postmodernism. It was also recently taken up by Francis Fukuyama (1992), who cited (Kojève's) Hegel in order to claim that Hegel's "end of history" thesis could be applied to the post-1989 spread of free market capitalism and increasing dominance of Western liberal democracy across the globe. Hegel's "end of history" thesis remains controversial and unresolved, to say the least.

Despite the common myth (Hegel as apologist for the Prussian state), the "end of history" does not mean that the social and political arrangements of Hegel's day represented, for him, the pinnacle of realized freedom. What Hegel attempts to articulate is the Idea that history *does* show a rational progression, and that there is a "goal" or "end" discernible in relation to the vast labour of "world history": namely, the *realization of the Idea of freedom*. Hegel's controversial claim is that the conditions for the realization of universal freedom are now established, at least in principle, within the self-reforming social and political institutions of the modern world, and that our historical self-consciousness has in turn reached a stage where we now recognize the universal freedom and dignity of human beings as such (an idea of Christian provenance, as Hegel observes). This means that major transformations in the basic principles and systems of modern societies would be unlikely, which is not to say that crises, wars and struggles will not continue to play a significant role as incentives to the internal reform of the institutional structure of modernity. Hegel is convinced, however, that a philosophical comprehension of history will reveal that there is a rational progression in the realization of freedom, and that the conditions for this realization are now institutionally articulated and philosophically comprehended in the modern world.

As we shall see, Hegel's historical optimism and rationalism have come under serious attack in light of twentieth-century historical events. To name but one critic, Theodor Adorno (1903–69) argued that the horrors of the Nazi attempt to exterminate the Jews of Europe refutes Hegel's historical optimism: Auschwitz condemns Enlightenment rationality in principle. Many postmodernist critics of Hegel, such as Jean-François Lyotard, have followed Adorno's criticism. Hegel was the first philosopher, however, to really force us to consider history itself as a philosophical problem; to consider how our very self-understanding and our horizons of knowledge are part of an ongoing process of historical transformation and philosophical self-reflection. He was also the first philosopher to take very seriously the history of philosophy and to construe philosophy historically. The history of philosophy becomes inseparable from understanding the meaning and context of supposedly "timeless", "eternal" philosophical problems.

Modern freedom

Similarly contentious claims and counterclaims have surrounded Hegel's *Philosophy of Right* (1821), one of the most profound works in political philosophy within the Western tradition. This last major work of Hegel's (published during a repressive turn in German political life) has been accused of providing an apologia for the Prussian state, even a philosophical rationalization for political totalitarianism. Yet it is a work of extraordinary depth and breadth, encompassing Greek ethics and Roman law, Enlightenment morality and Romantic subjectivity, the relationship between economic and political freedom, and the grounding of individual right and universal morality in the rational structure of the modern political state. In brief, the project of the *Philosophy of Right* is to reconstruct the *normative conditions for the realization of freedom* in the modern world. Here I shall only indicate a few central themes that have proven influential, not only for the Hegelian schools that emerged immediately after Hegel's death, but also for the complex currents of twentieth-century Hegelianism that are the subject of this book.

The *Philosophy of Right* can seem a baffling work unless we understand its fundamental task: a philosophical description and comprehension of the *normative conditions* required for the realization of freedom in the modern world. In other words, the *Philosophy of Right* examines the conditions that make possible the freely willing modern subject, who believes him or herself to freely determine the options among which he or she chooses a definite way of life. This "atomized" conception of freedom – atomized in the sense of taking each individual as an isolated "atom" disconnected from other individuals or from shared social practices – will be shown to be deficient as an account of the complex interaction between autonomous individuals, universal principles of morality, and the complex social, economic and political institutions of the modern world. Indeed, Hegel's task is to perform a critical presentation of the limitations of the atomized conception of the freely willing subject. The *Philosophy of Right* aims to show how individualistic conceptions of freedom found in the sphere of "abstract right" and "morality" are grounded in the complex normative context of "ethical life". It is only within the context of modern social and political institutions that we find the conditions that make possible the modern subject's "right to subjective freedom", the familiar liberal notion of the freedom to choose one's own way of life without undue interference.

Hegel thus proceeds to reconstruct the grounds or conditions of the freely willing subject who wills freedom as such. The most basic conception of freedom is the power to abstract from any given determination one might have: whatever attributes I might possess, I am free to withdraw these attributes as I see fit, rejecting any definite or fixed content of my identity as a restriction of my freedom (for example, that I happen to live in a certain city, or have a certain job, or mix with certain people). But this *negative freedom* that I exercise by negating my given determinations, my commitments, without interference by others, must also involve a *positive freedom* to do certain things, to engage in various activities. Freedom is not just the ability *to reject* but also the power *to choose* definite options (I could live elsewhere, get a different job, or find new friends). But in choosing this or that concrete possibility I am at the same time preserving my freedom to withdraw if I so choose. What of the options or possibilities among which I can choose? If these are externally imposed options upon which I am dependent, then it would imply that I cannot be truly self-determining.

For in that case I am beholden to whatever options happen to be given in my current context. So this basic conception of freedom as the free will willing its own freedom runs into contradiction. It claims to be autonomous or self-determining, yet is dependent upon external content for the options among which it must choose.

The only way to resolve this contradiction is to integrate both aspects (negative and positive) of freedom and to make the ends or options I choose *self-chosen* ends or options. Whatever I choose from is no longer simply given to me externally: I do not simply freely choose among given options; rather, I freely create or determine the options themselves, the range of possibilities that I can take up and act upon. On this view of freedom, therefore, what I will is *my own freedom to determine possibilities for action*: my freedom both to accept or to reject these possibilities, or to affirm or deny features of my own way of being. Freedom is no longer simply a matter of personal choice but a matter of recognizing the *right* of individuals to determine their own possibilities for action, a right that must be formally enshrined – for example, through law – within a definite social and political order.

What makes possible this freedom to determine my options for action? In the first instance, it is the fact that I *own* my own actions, that I possess my own body as an original form of "property"; my actions in turn, through work, allow me to make a claim concerning the products of my labour. This observation provides the basis for Hegel's move to the sphere of *property relations*. This right to choose freely among various options within the social–legal order of property relations provides the starting point of Hegel's analysis of the sphere of *abstract right*: the right of individuals to own property protected under law, and to engage in contractual and economic exchanges with others. Such freedom is essentially a right, namely an entitlement recognized by others, anchored in social–political institutions and enforced by law. Within the sphere of abstract right, the individual is merely a "legal subject", a self-interested agent endowed with certain recognized legal entitlements. Since such agents choose according to their own self-interest, there is no guarantee that their choices will also be moral (from an individual point of view) or ethical (from a collective or communal point of view). Some freely willing agents will endeavour to gain an advantage at the expense of others, denying the latter's freedom within the sphere of abstract right. The sphere of right must therefore also encompass that of *crime* and *wrong*. The freely willing subject, who wills freedom, must also will the *conditions* of freedom, which means here the sphere of *abstract right* bounded and enforced by law.

But this conception of freedom as right implies a broader conception of the individual than being a mere property owner or legal person. It also implies a subject who wills that right be upheld while also refraining from the violation of the rights of others. It implies that one has the right of freedom in a universal sense as *a moral subject*. The freely willing subject must also have the capacity to govern, and where necessary limit, its merely self-interested action in the name of universal principles. My right to own property as a legal person, a right protected by law, is grounded in the recognition of me as a *moral being* rather than as a mere "legal person". This transition from abstract right brings us to the sphere of *morality*: the recognition of my freedom as an autonomous moral subject endowed with reason and subject to freely acknowledged universal moral principles.

Hegel's exposition of the sphere of morality encompasses the Kantian–modern conception of morality as grounded in universality but also as embracing individual conscience. It defines a distinctly modern sphere of right that underpins the sphere of abstract right ("abstract" in the sense of being reduced to the most formal level of the right to free exchange and the self-interested pursuit of one's ends). Among other difficulties, Hegel points out that the moral subject who wills the universal according to the unconditional demand of conscience can end up doing "evil": asserting the absolute rightness of his/her conscience and thereby rejecting the possibility of dialogue with others. Such inherently individualistic morality that attempts to ground itself in or to articulate the universal once again runs into contradiction.

The sphere of individual morality must therefore be contrasted with the sphere of what Hegel calls *Sittlichkeit* or "ethical life" (the lifeworld of custom, shared practices and social normativity). The conditions that genuinely ground the sphere of morality are to be found in the normative context of social institutions and the political state. This sphere of ethical life also has three aspects or dimensions: the immediate form of ethical life represented by *the family*; the opposing sphere of *civil society*, the formal mechanisms and institutions regulating economic exchange in the marketplace; and the sphere that encompasses and thus grounds both, namely the rational institutions of the *political state*. In very schematic form, the movement between these levels or aspects proceeds from the natural sphere of intersubjective recognition within the family, the dissolution of the family (once the educated child becomes an adult citizen) and entry into social and economic independence (civil society), and the resulting expansion, dynamism, but also atomization and alienation generated by civil society (notably the creation of inequalities of wealth and an alienated social underclass or "rabble" [*Pöbel*] as an inevitable by-product of an efficient free market).

The alienation generated by the modern social and economic order can be counteracted, Hegel claims, by cultivating in citizens a sense of ethical orientation towards the common good. Hegel's proposal was that modernity could achieve this through fostering a renovation of mediating institutions (the professional "corporations", combining traits of the medieval guild with those of the modern trade union) that would foster a sense of solidarity, a commitment to *communal*, rather than merely personal, interest. Such mediating institutions would enable citizens to connect their personal and professional concerns with the social and political aims of the community, and to mesh their communally oriented will with the successful functioning of the political state. In short, the sphere of ethical life finds its realization and ground in the rational community and self-reforming institutions of the modern political state. It is in this sense that Hegel claimed that the political state is the "Idea of freedom realized in the world", even the "march of God" across the face of the earth.

These remarks, however, along with his critique of liberalism and apparently "communitarian" orientation, earned Hegel the reputation of being an apologist for Prussian conservatism. At the same time Hegel has been hailed as a thoroughly modern defender of liberal democratic society, one who affirms the basic principles of modern autonomy and the principle of subjective freedom, which all rational states must uphold on pain of lapsing into unsustainable dissension. Whatever one's view, it is undeniable that Hegel criticizes the normative inadequacy of contemporary constitutional political states, which suffer from an abstract, atomized conception of freedom and alienating imbalance in the relationship between civil society and state.

British idealism and post-analytic philosophy

Chapter 2 will explore the complex relations between competing "Left" and "Right" Hegelian schools. Before turning to this story, however, it is worth saying a few words about what was perhaps the most significant Hegelian-inspired school at the turn of the century: "British idealism", which included figures such as J. M. E. McTaggart (1866–1925), T. H. Green (1836–82), F. H. Bradley (1846–1924) and Bernard Bosanquet (1848–1923). It might seem strange to think that Hegelianism was thriving at Oxford and Cambridge at the turn of the century.

As Tom Rockmore remarks, however, we forget today that a hundred years ago analytic philosophy "was emerging in a struggle to the conceptual death for the soul of philosophy in England through mortal combat with British idealism" (2005: 31–2). This battle was resoundingly won by analytic philosophy; what was mistakenly labelled "Hegelian idealism" was utterly vanquished. Today, however, things are not so clear cut, for there are signs of a revival of Hegelianism in contemporary post-analytic philosophy. For this reason it is worth presenting something of the thought of the British idealists, particularly because it inspired the anti-idealist revolt that lead to the rise of analytic philosophy.

British idealism, while not strictly *Hegelian* in the sense of interpreting Hegelian texts in depth, can safely be said to have drawn inspiration from Hegel for its own version of metaphysical idealism. The British turn to idealism in the second half of the nineteenth century (that is, when Hegelianism was declining in Germany) emerged in conjunction with a defence of religion and the general revival of metaphysics reacting against the then dominant currents of traditional British empiricism (Rockmore 2005: 34). The Hegelian defence of Christianity, for example, was central to J. H. Stirling's well-known book, *The Secret of Hegel* (1865), which championed the traditional metaphysical themes of God, the immortality of the soul, and freedom of the will (Rockmore 2005: 34). The later generation of British idealists also rejected empiricism, and embraced a conception of organic totality; reality was an absolute whole in which everything was to be conceived as a manifestation of spirit (*ibid.*: 35). Nonetheless, wide divergences remained between individual philosophers on specific points of idealist doctrine. Bradley and Bosanquet highlighted the significance of the Absolute, whereas McTaggart was an atheist; others, such as Green, were far from faithful to Hegel's texts, using idealist themes as a springboard for their own metaphysical speculations; Bradley even denied being a Hegelian, and questioned whether there was such thing as a British Hegelian school (*ibid.*). Hence it would be more accurate for us to say that there were various metaphysical idealists, inspired by Hegel, who shared a critical attitude towards reductive empiricism, a commitment to metaphysical holism and a valorization of moral freedom.

The next few paragraphs say something about some of the key figures. Green engaged in a criticism of empiricism in which he rejected the possibility of direct empirical knowledge in a manner reminiscent of Kant and Hegel, even anticipating the later Wittgenstein and Wilfrid Sellars (Rockmore 2005: 36). Following Kant, he argued for an analysis of the conditions of knowledge, but rejected the Kantian thing-in-itself in favour of what he took to be a "Hegelian" conception – very unlike Wittgenstein – of "an eternal subject, or spiritual principle, also called soul or mind" (*ibid.*: 37). Green thus joined Stirling in defending a Right–Christian view of Hegelianism and a metaphysical holism in keeping with his radical anti-empiricism.

Bradley took up Green's anti-empiricist idealism in an eclectic synthesis that made it very difficult for his contemporaries to classify him; his version of idealism embraced a view of immediate knowledge of appearances that would always be relative to what is not given immediately. The Absolute is thus defined by a pervasive "relativism", but ultimate reality, transcendent to appearances, is non-relational (Rockmore 2005: 38). Ultimate reality, in this respect, lies beyond what we can experience, hence cannot be known (*ibid.*: 39). We should note that such metaphysical claims concerning reality beyond human experience are quite at odds with Hegel's own position. Hegel claimed in the *Phenomenology* that the appearance/reality distinction must be suspended, rather, in favour of a more complex conception of reason. In this regard, some of the British idealists were positively un-Hegelian!

McTaggart rejected the religious and metaphysical inclinations to be found in Green and Bradley, and sharply opposed Christianity in any form (even Hegelian). While teaching at Cambridge, he had Russell and G. E. Moore as students, who both briefly flirted with views resembling McTaggart's Hegelian-inspired metaphysical idealism (Rockmore 2005: 39). In *The Principles of Existence*, McTaggart argued that if anything exists, then the universe must exist. He also famously criticized our assumptions concerning the reality of time (the past–present–future axis of time was illusory as compared with the earlier–later axis), and consequently asserted the immortality of the soul (*ibid.*: 40).

The influential role of some of the British idealists at Cambridge and Oxford inspired the revolt against idealism that gave birth to twentieth-century analytic philosophy. Indeed, Russell and Moore took the British idealists to represent precisely the kind of untenable metaphysical speculation that conceptual analysis sought to dispel. Moreover, they took the refutation of the alleged idealist denial of the reality of the external world to be one of their central philosophical tasks, without realizing that this so-called "idealist" claim was one of which Hegel too was critical. Hegel thus came to be associated with the more implausible doctrines of metaphysical idealism that inspired the analytic defence of empiricism, the return to logic and mathematics, and the restoration of the natural sciences as central to philosophical analysis.

The suspicion that Hegelianism is philosophically and politically dubious has persisted in analytic philosophy until very recently. This stigma arose because of suspicions concerning the metaphysical nature of Hegelian thought, its dubious relationship with Marxism, and possibly pernicious political consequences. Happily, this situation has recently begun to change. Hegelianism is no longer taboo, thanks largely to pioneers such as Walter Kaufmann and Charles Taylor. Indeed, Taylor's 1975 Romantic–expressivist reading of Hegel – a reading tinged with metaphysical as well as subtle Left–Christian elements – did much to show the importance of Hegel for overcoming dualistic, disengaged conceptions of the self (see Taylor 1983).

More recently, a whole school of Kantian and "non-metaphysical" readers of Hegel – from Klaus Hartmann to Robert Pippin, Terry Pinkard and Alan Wood – have highlighted Hegel's relevance to contemporary debates on the nature of reason and moral autonomy, on the importance of reason-giving practices, the problem of normativity (epistemological and social) and the meaning of modern freedom. Distinguished philosophers such as Robert Brandom and John McDowell have also drawn explicitly upon Hegelian insights in dealing with the Kantian problem of the concept–intuition and mind–world relationships, and in the vigorous realism/anti-realism debates that have been a feature of much contemporary debate in Anglophone philosophy (Brandom 1994, 2000; McDowell 1996, 1998; Sedgwick 1997). Brandom, McDowell and Richard Rorty have, in different ways, also retrieved the important Hegelian influence on the American pragmatist tradition from John Dewey to Charles Sanders Peirce (Rorty 1982). From being reviled as the enemy of conceptual analysis, analytic neo-Hegelianism has come full circle. This contemporary revival of interest in Hegelian thought – its relevance for debates on epistemological holism, realism and anti-realism, and the concept–intuition problem – has opened up new prospects for productive dialogue between modern European and post-analytic philosophy.

Summary of key points

Hegel's Phenomenology of Spirit

- Hegelian phenomenology is a philosophical method that describes and interprets interconnected patterns of *knowledge* as an appearance.

- Spirit or *Geist* is Hegel's term for self-conscious reason or shared forms of social and cultural intersubjectivity.

Lordship and bondage: the struggle for recognition

- Hegel's "master/slave dialectic" describes the dialectical relationship between dependent and independent subjects. It is a phenomenological account of the origin of sociability, a critical version of the "state of nature" fiction.
- The master is dependent upon the slave, since the master has extorted recognition from an utterly dependent being. The slave, by contrast, will turn out to be the "master of the master", for the slave has experienced his *finitude* (via the threat of death) and is thus negatively aware of his mortality and his capacity for freedom.
- The "*unhappy consciousness*" is the alienated, religious subject, who struggles against his/her internal self-contradictoriness, striving to unite the *universal* and *particular* dimensions of his/her selfhood.

Hegel's logic

- Hegel's logic can be described as an analysis of the interconnected *systems* of basic categories of thought; these systems of categories are ways of conceptualizing reality as a coherent and intelligible whole.
- Hegel's term "Concept" refers to the dialectical totality of categories that make up the intelligibility of the whole. "Concept" also refers to the threefold structure of universality, particularity and individuality within any rational whole.

History, freedom, modernity

- Viewed philosophically, history evinces a rational progress, even though empirical history seems irrational and violent; philosophically comprehended history displays the "realization of the Idea of freedom".

The "end of history"

- The idea of the "end of history" is that the vast labour of "world history" does show a rational progression towards the *realization of the Idea of freedom*.

- The conditions for the realization of universal freedom are now established within modern social and political institutions; historical self-consciousness has reached a stage where we recognize the universal freedom of human beings.

Modern freedom

- The *Philosophy of Right* presents a philosophical description and comprehension of the *normative conditions* for the realization of freedom in the modern world.
- The *Philosophy of Right* aims to show how individualistic conceptions of freedom found in the sphere of "abstract right" and "morality" are grounded in the complex normative context of modern social and political institutions.

British idealism

- The British idealists inspired the revolt against idealism, led by Bertrand Russell and G. E. Moore, which gave birth to twentieth-century analytic philosophy.
- Russell and Moore took the thought of the British idealists to represent the kind of metaphysical speculation that conceptual analysis sought to dispel.

two

Adventures in Hegelianism

Now that I have outlined the basic elements of Hegel's philosophical project, it is probably worth making a few terminological clarifications, beginning with the most obvious. In what follows, I shall be defining "Hegelianism" very broadly to mean the history of the reception, productive appropriation and critical transformation of Hegel's philosophy. More specifically, I shall interpret "Hegelianism" to refer to the diverse philosophical movements shaped by a sustained engagement, whether affirmative or critical, with important aspects of Hegel's philosophical project. This would encompass both the explicit followers of Hegel's philosophy, who argue over its true meaning and significance (such as the "Left" and "Right" Hegelians), and those independent movements (such as existentialism and Marxism) that are explicitly critical of, while also drawing upon, Hegelian thought. As we shall see, there are also many individual philosophers whose projects remain at odds with Hegel, but for whom a critical confrontation with Hegelian thought remains essential for comprehending modern philosophy and modernity itself (Heidegger, Adorno, Habermas and many others).

In this chapter, I explore some of the adventures of Hegelianism, in all these senses, starting with the dissolution of the Hegelian school into "Right", "Centre" and "Left" Hegelian camps. The disputes that led to this break-up concerned the relationship between Hegel's philosophy, religion and politics: was Hegelianism in essence an expression of Christian religious truth? Or was religion superseded by philosophy? Did the Hegelian realization of freedom mean that philosophy had to be transformed into practical action? Questions such as these led to the disputes between Right and Left Hegelian schools, and eventually to the transformation of Hegelianism in the opposing directions of existentialism and Marxism. I shall explore in particular the Left Hegelian debates over the question of philosophy and politics: with figures such as David Strauss (1808–74), Ludwig Feuerbach (1804–72) and Bruno Bauer (1809–82), an increasingly radical form of Hegelian humanism emerged that was to lead to the Marxist critique of Hegelianism as mere ideology.

On the other hand, the question of religious faith and the singularity of individual existence prompted Kierkegaard's radical Christian–existentialist critique of Hegelian rationalism. The problem underlying these disputes, I shall suggest, is how to understand the *relationship between theory and practice*: does our theoretical understanding determine our social practices? Or do our shared practices determine our ideas and knowledge? Or is there a more basic sense of existence presupposed by both theory and practice? These questions continued to preoccupy many exponents of twentieth-century Hegelianism, particularly within the French and German traditions.

The dissolution of the Hegelian school

After Hegel became Professor of Philosophy at the University of Berlin in 1818, a fully fledged school developed around him, complete with a philosophical society (the Society for Scientific Criticism) and scholarly journal (*The Yearbook for Scientific Criticism*) dedicated to publicizing the Hegelian philosophy. After a late start to his career, Hegel was now recognized as the foremost philosopher in Germany. Many of his immediate students and followers were convinced that he had indeed achieved the "end" of philosophy, its final and complete form. All that remained was to interpret the true meaning of the master's system, and to elaborate its dialectical method in other areas of enquiry (such as theology, law, aesthetics and political philosophy).

The seeds of dissension, however, were already sprouting among members of the Hegelian school. While Hegelian thought enjoyed considerable institutional prestige, Hegel's many opponents regarded his work as a pernicious and corrupting influence. Schopenhauer, for example, tried rather ineffectually to oppose Hegel's influence by holding (poorly attended) lectures concurrently with Hegel's. The Prussian ministry even recalled Schelling to the University of Berlin in 1841 in an attempt to eliminate, as the ministry put it, "the dragon seed of

Hegelian pantheism" (quoted in Toews 1993: 383). Their efforts must have succeeded, for Hegel's influence went into a decline after the 1850s, replaced by materialist, positivist, scientistic and empiricist trends. So sharp was this turn that by the 1870s his work was regarded as all but superseded.

To understand the significance of the disputes over Hegel's work and the reasons for the dissolution of the Hegelian school, it will be helpful to say something of the historical and political context. During the 1820s, the social and political climate of post-revolutionary Europe was beginning to shift, entering a period known as the Restoration, a conservative political turn following the defeat of Napoleon. This conservative political shift also affected the policies of the Prussian government, markedly altering German cultural life and affecting in particular the University of Berlin where Hegel served as Rector from 1829 to 1830. The relatively liberal political climate of Prussia turned sharply conservative under Frederick Wilhelm IV, whose government introduced repressive measures (the so-called Karlsbad edicts) licensing censorship of education and of the press. This widespread curtailment of intellectual freedom prompted Hegel to modify and disguise the more critical aspects of his political philosophy in his *Elements of the Philosophy of Right* (1821).

With this prudent camouflage, Hegel's already ambiguous philosophical work – combining elements of idealism and realism, absolutism and historicism, conservatism and radicalism – became even more open to conflicting interpretations. The disputes that followed in the Hegelian schools turned primarily on the political implications of the *Philosophy of Right* and on the religious and historical orientation of Hegel's thought. Was Hegel's philosophy ultimately concerned with a (religious–philosophical) reconciliation with contemporary reality? Did Hegel strive to present a dogmatic justification of the conservative Prussian order? Was Hegelian philosophy confined to a comprehension of the past and justification of the present, or was it also oriented towards the future? Would the realization of reason mean the revolutionary transformation of society? Such questions increasingly preoccupied Hegel's disciples and critics alike.

Against the background of this conservative political and cultural shift, the question of the future implications of Hegel's thought became a pressing concern. In what looks suspiciously like a Hegelian dialectics gone wrong, the Hegelian school quickly shattered into opposing camps, vigorously battling each other over the meaning and legacy of Hegel's philosophy. These controversies had overlapping religious, political and historical dimensions. The question initially facing Hegel's disciples was how to understand the proper relationship between philosophy and religion, a quarrel that soon linked up with another thorny problem: the relationship between philosophy and politics. These tumultuous disputes generated competing perspectives of Hegelian thought that would make an important contribution to the development of Marxism and existentialism. As we shall see later in this book, they also provide significant background for understanding the development of critical theory and poststructuralism.

The question of religion, philosophy, politics: Right and Left Hegelianism

Many Hegelians were convinced that Hegel's system had finally achieved what philosophy had been striving for since its Greek origins: a rationally grounded and unified account of the world and of our place within it as rational beings. For many of his disciples, Hegel represented the culmination of philosophy: a comprehensive system of rational thought that integrated key elements of both ancient and modern philosophy, while also comprehending the complexity of modern social and historical experience. While Hegel's disciples were convinced of Hegel's importance, they were divided over the implications of his thought for understanding the role of philosophy, above all in relation to religion and politics.

These issues came to a head following Hegel's death, which precipitated an energetic debate over the true meaning and future possibilities of Hegelian thought. The debate was sparked by the publication of David Strauss's *The Life of Jesus Critically Examined* (in 1835–36), a Hegelian critique of orthodox religion from a historicist point of view, where the terminology of "Right Hegelians", "Centre Hegelians" and "Left Hegelians" (also called the "Young Hegelians") was first introduced (see Rockmore 1993: 139–43). We could gloss these three positions as the *accommodationist, reformist* and *radical* wings of the Hegelian school (see Toews 1993). The Right Hegelians attempted to defend Hegel's system such as it stood at the time of Hegel's death; this proved difficult, however, as the relationship between religion and philosophy in Hegel's system remained ambiguous and hence controversial. On the one hand, Hegel claimed that religion is a form of absolute spirit in which truth is revealed in symbolic representations; but modernity ushers in the end of the religious community, such that the truth of religion can only be revealed through speculative philosophy. On the other hand, Hegel also claimed that philosophy and religion express the same truth, even describing speculative philosophy at one point as a form of "divine worship"; this suggests that the truth of (Christian) religion might be identical with speculative philosophy. So depending on how one interpreted Hegel, religion either maintained a subordinate role in relation to philosophy; or else it provided the inner core of Hegel's imposing philosophical system, which ultimately remains a philosophical expression of revealed religious truth.

This, then, was the question at issue: whether Hegel's philosophy successfully achieved a quasi-religious reconciliation with existing social and historical reality (the view of the Right Hegelians); or whether it pointed beyond religious reconciliation (a mystification) towards a social and political transformation of reality in order to realize our rational freedom (the Left Hegelian position). This is why Strauss used the political terminology of "Right", "Centre" and "Left" wings of the Hegelian school: the debate over the relationship between religion and philosophy clearly had direct political implications. If philosophy is grounded in religion and advocates reconciliation with the world, then our task is to understand the world as rational and thereby reconcile ourselves with what exists. If religion is superseded by philosophy, on the other hand, then Hegel's thought becomes open to a couple of possible readings: our task can either be the critical one of testing whether our social and historical reality conforms to reason, or, more radically, it can become the political one of actively transforming our world in the name of realizing reason in historical actuality.

Central to this link between religion, philosophy and politics is one of Hegel's most famous remarks, found in the Preface to the *Philosophy of Right*: "What is rational is actual; and what is actual is rational" (PR Preface: 20). This pithy but ambiguous remark has generated countless interpretations. Marx, for example, took it to be evidence of Hegel's fundamental conservatism, his propensity to provide a philosophical–ideological justification for the (irrational) status quo. Others have taken it as a normative statement, pointing to the way social and historical reality frequently falls short of genuine rationality, and provides an inadequate realization of freedom, which implies that we should transform reality in keeping with the historical progress of reason. In fact, we now know that Hegel's Heidelberg lectures on the Philosophy of Right contained a different formulation: "What is actual must become rational; what is rational must become actual". But this more radical formulation – which remained unpublished in Hegel's day – was markedly toned down by the time Hegel published the text of the

Philosophy of Right in 1821, which was the formulation that exerted such philosophical interest and influence.

The Right Hegelians adopted a conservative reading of Hegel's statement, finding contemporary historical reality (the existing Prussian state) a more or less adequate embodiment of reason. Interestingly, the Right Hegelians were mostly university academics, sympathetic to the apparent coincidence of reason and the institutional status quo, whereas the Left Hegelians generally were more explicitly involved in journalism, public affairs and politics – not surprisingly, they found the Prussian state and its institutions far from being an adequate realization of reason! While some members of the Hegelian Right became increasingly conservative, dogmatically defending the existing Prussian order, most members were anything but reactionaries. Indeed, figures such as Karl Rosenkranz, Johann Eduard Erdmann, Eduard Zeller and Kuno Fischer defended a position closer to a moderate liberalism against the revolutionary Left. Moreover, the Centre Hegelians, such as Karl Ludwig Michelet and Rudolf Haym, argued for the reconciliation between Right and Left tendencies; in good Hegelian fashion, they could be mediated via a synthesis of opposing views.

The Left Hegelians, by contrast, demanded a radical transformation of social and historical reality so that the world could more adequately realize freedom. They rejected the Right Hegelian view that religion provided the truth of philosophy, arguing that religion is not only superseded by philosophy but that the task of philosophical truth was to transform itself into action. They therefore challenged the Hegelian orthodoxy that philosophy can only ever interpret the world retrospectively. As Hegel famously remarked, philosophy arises when a form of life is already in decline: "the Owl of Minerva begins its flight only with the onset of dusk" (PR Preface: 23). As Karl Marx was later to remark, replying to Hegel via his criticism of Feuerbach: "The philosophers have only ever *interpreted* the world, in various ways; the point, however, is to *change* it" (Marx 1978: 145).

Marx represents the radical conclusion to a line of argument that began with a challenge to the relationship between philosophy and religion. David Strauss (1808–74) inaugurated this Left Hegelian humanist perspective by arguing, in his influential *Life of Jesus* (1835), that the traditional content of Christianity could be reconciled with Hegelian philosophy by translating the language of religion into historicist and humanist terms. The philosophical meaning of Christianity, however, could be revealed only by rejecting the claim that the Bible was a literal description of historical truth. Following Hegel, Strauss maintained that the Incarnation did not just occur in a singular individual; rather, the reconciliation between finite and infinite aspects of human spirit takes place within historical time and for the whole human community. Strauss's contention was that the mythical narratives in the Bible were "primitive" cultural expressions of universal truths that could be properly deciphered only by Hegelian philosophy.

This critical account of religion was carried further by Ludwig Feuerbach (1804–72), who developed a more radically "anthropological" version of Hegelian humanism. Feuerbach's confrontation with Hegel can be found in his 1839 "Contribution to the Critique of Hegelian Philosophy", and in his 1839 tract, "Philosophy and Christianity", the precursor to his major work, *The Essence of Christianity* (1841). Feuerbach questioned the Hegelian assumption, common to Strauss and Bauer, that the realization of human essence as spirit implied "the domination of culture over outer and inner 'nature'"; on the contrary, Feuerbach argued, the reconciliation between reason and reality required a reconciliation with the reality of nature, "both nature as external to man and the corporeality of man as part of nature" (Toews 1993: 394–5). Such reconciliation, however, would mean going beyond the framework of Hegelian idealism, which had always underplayed the significance of our sensuous, corporeal nature, attempting to subsume the reality of nature into the edifice of speculative thought. Feuerbach thus deepened the critical humanist and anthropological translation of Hegel, suggesting that Hegel's speculative system disguised the humanistic and historicist meaning of his thought. Indeed, Hegel's metaphysics of absolute spirit was tantamount to a transcendent mystification, an elaborate attempt to deny the limitations of human thinking and the finite character of our sensuous historical existence.

The most influential aspect of Feuerbach's Left Hegelianism, however, was his critique of the relationship between religion and philosophy. Here Feuerbach challenged the Right Hegelian attempt to present Hegel's thought as a reconciliation with actuality. Hegelian philosophy, rather, was a critical demystification of religion, a *religion of humanity* that reversed the alienated representations of religion and thereby revealed its humanistic and anthropological truth. In *The Essence of Christianity*, Feuerbach argued that human beings are not made in the image of God; God is a transcendent projection by human beings who are alienated from their own human essence or "species being" (a view also found in Freud's famous *The Future of an Illusion*). Religious consciousness is an imagistic projection of human alienation from our essential nature as sensuous, emotional, self-conscious beings. Hegel's attempt to supersede or integrate the truth of religion into speculative philosophy, however, was a reductive attempt to overcome this alienated, religious self-consciousness by pathologically attributing human qualities "to a transcendent, superhuman power" (Toews 1993: 395). In doing so, however, Hegel reductively divinized our rational, spiritual nature while at the same time ignoring or demonizing our sensuous, affective and corporeal existence.

Under the influence of Feuerbach's critique of religion, Strauss too went on to claim (in the 1840s) that religion represents "the idea of humanity" in a distorted, alienated form. Religion "objectifies" our human essence as a community of free rational beings by projecting this essence onto a transcendent, supernatural being. Religion thus transposes the truth of the idea of humanity into a transcendent realm instead of prompting us to actualize this truth in the realm of historical experience. Following Feuerbach, Strauss concluded that the humanist content of religion, which is an alienated expression of our human essence as rational beings, should therefore be demystified by Hegelian philosophy and actualized through social and political practice.

Feuerbach's critical account of the truth of religion was challenged and radicalized by Bruno Bauer (1809–92), who argued that Hegel's philosophy, properly understood, results not in theism or pantheism but in *atheism*. Bauer agreed that the truth of Hegelian philosophy was a radical humanism, but rejected Feuerbach's and Strauss's claim that the truth of Christian religion – the identity of finite and infinite spirit – could be translated via the language of the "idea of humanity". For Bauer, the latter was still too religious, containing vestiges of the notion of a transcendent, divine being. Strauss and Feuerbach thus substituted the "idea of humanity" for the idea of God; but in presenting humanity as possessing a substantial "essence", they inadvertently repeated another version of self-alienating religious consciousness (Hegel's "unhappy consciousness"). In reality, everything that was attributed to notions such as "God", "absolute Spirit", "world-spirit" and so on was the work of human self-consciousness in its freedom of thought and conscious activity. Hence the truth of Hegelianism, Bauer argued, was to show that "God is dead for philosophy and only the I as self-consciousness . . . lives, creates, works and is everything" (quoted in Toews 1993: 394). The only power in human history is *self-consciousness*, whose becoming and development was the meaning of all history. This demystification of religion and humanization of history meant that philosophy should become an atheistic practice of liberation from intellectual and social domination rather than a religious reconciliation with what exists. Bauer's Hegelian humanism thus had radical political, even revolutionary, implications: it transformed Hegelianism into "a critical practice of ceaseless emancipation from fixated cultural forms or structures of domination" (Toews 1993: 394).

What followed in the more radical Left Hegelian camp was a critique of the Hegelian humanism that Strauss, Bauer and Feuerbach had so powerfully articulated. Whereas Bauer, in his later work, argued that not "man" but self-developing self-consciousness was the driving force of history, Feuerbach's recourse to an abstract notion of "man" or humanity, our collective species-being, was attacked as yet another metaphysical abstraction. Various attempts were therefore made to conceptualize more concrete notions of "existence", of material reality shorn of any metaphysical illusions. Instead of a Hegelian notion of universal reason imposing itself on reality, the meaning of reality would emerge historically from the concrete historical relations and interactions between existing individuals.

Other important Left Hegelians included Arnold Ruge (1802–80), who edited the *Hallische Jahrbücher*, the Young Hegelian journal, and helped establish Left Hegelianism as a political movement; August von Cieszkowski (1814–80), a Polish count, who reversed the emphasis on history in favour of a view of philosophy oriented towards the future; and Moses Hess (1812–75), who emphasized the possibility of a social revolution arising from the growing contradiction, first identified by Hegel, between the wealthy ruling class and the poverty-stricken "rabble" or *Pöbel* – those who were systemically excluded from participation in bourgeois society. As Marx was later to say of the proletariat, these people belonged to a class *in* civil society without being *of* civil society (1978: 64). In sum, these variations of Left Hegelian humanism, with their progressively more historicist and anthropological translations of Hegelian thought, paved the way for the materialist critique of Hegelian idealism. Together these ideas forged the radical Left Hegelian view that the future of Hegelianism lay in the revolutionary transformation of society that would overcome its contradictory economic and social tendencies, a thesis that was to be famously developed in Marx's revolutionary critique of capitalism.

After Hegelianism: Kierkegaard and Marx

This brief overview of the main tendencies of the Right and Left Hegelian schools suggests two distinct directions of development: a retrieval of religious and theological themes within a philosophy oriented towards reconciliation with actuality, and a humanist, historicist, anthropological overcoming of religion, and of philosophy itself, on the historical plane of social and political practice. For our purposes, these broadly opposed directions, roughly religious and political, could be said to culminate in the work of two thinkers whose work proved enormously influential for twentieth-century thought: the Danish Christian religious thinker Søren Kierkegaard (1813–55), and the German political philosopher Karl Marx (1818–83). Given the rich complexity of their thought, I can only sketch a few key ideas here that will help us understand how Kierkegaard's existential critique of Hegelian rationalism and Marx's materialist critique of Hegelian idealism transformed Hegelian thought in seemingly opposed directions. Despite their superficial opposition, however, Kierkegaard's and Marx's criticisms of Hegel are united at a deeper level: as Karl Löwith observed, the existentialist critique and materialist critique "comprise *one* antithesis to Hegel" (1991: 161). They are united in rejecting the rationality of the existing historical world, and in arguing for a radical confrontation with contemporary reality, whether through individual existential–religious commitment or collective revolutionary social action. We shall explore in Chapter 3 the way that these two competing critiques of Hegelian thought – existentialism and Marxism – provided a matrix for the development of French Hegelian humanism, in its existentialist and Marxist variants.

Kierkegaard's existentialist critique of Hegel

The turn away from reason and universal self-consciousness towards the concrete, singular existence of the self is evident in Kierkegaard's "existentialist" critique of Hegel's system. Unlike the Centre, Right and Left Hegelians, Kierkegaard (like Marx) cannot be called a Hegelian thinker as such; his religious, philosophical and existentialist critique, which emphasizes the singularity of the existing individual, reacts strongly against the rationalism of Hegel's philosophical system. Unlike Marx, who accepted that there was a "kernel of truth" in Hegelian dialectics that needed to be reversed and given its true form, Kierkegaard, like Hegel's rival Schelling, dismissed the Hegelian rationalist system as ignoring the concrete nature of singular existence. Kierkegaard wrote in a highly subjective and literary style, often using authorial pseudonyms, and his Christian existentialism proved very important for a host of diverse twentieth-century existentialist thinkers, often atheistic, such as Karl Jaspers (1883–1973), Martin Heidegger (1889–1976), and Jean-Paul Sartre (1905–80), along with theologians such as Karl Barth (1886–1968) and Paul Tillich (1886–1965). Much of Kierkegaard's work is directed at a critique of the established Christian Church and of other social institutions (including what we would call the mass media), which are taken to be part of a "levelling" process that obliterates genuine subjectivity and individuality. Kierkegaard's critique of the levelling tendencies in the modern world, vividly presented in his pamphlet *The Present Age* (1846), is undertaken in the name of rescuing an authentic sense of Christian faith and a religious commitment to subjective inwardness and existential choice.

Along with such politically significant figures as Friedrich Engels and the political anarchist Michael Bakunin, Kierkegaard attended Schelling's lectures on Hegel at the University of Berlin in the 1840s. In these lectures, the older Schelling presented his critique of Hegel's "negative philosophy": its inability to comprehend concrete singular "existence", and to acknowledge the true significance of religion. In place of Hegel's rationalist conceptual system, Schelling offered his own "positive philosophy", oriented by its relation to a preconceptual ground of Being, and revealed less by philosophical reason than by quasi-religious intuition. This move, as we shall see, was taken over and transformed by Heidegger in his confrontation with Hegel. Impressed by Schelling's criticisms, Kierkegaard developed his own existentialist critique of the fundamental blind spot of Hegel's speculative system: grasping the concrete existence of the individual thinker, and recognizing the primacy of religious subjectivity over the spheres of morality and ethical life. Kierkegaard took Hegelianism, moreover, to be representative of the social and institutional conformity of philosophy as well as its inability to attend to the sphere of inwardness and subjectivity. In constructing the system of absolute knowing, Hegel adopted the "impossible" perspective of pure thought in place of the living subjectivity of the individual human being. The universality of thought, however, Kierkegaard insisted, had to give way to the singularity of existence.

In Kierkegaard's late work, *Concluding Unscientific Postscript* (1846), the pseudonymous author Johannes Climacus criticizes Hegel's system on both conceptual and existential grounds. Conceptually, Hegel's system has the problem of accounting for its presuppositionless beginning; the abstraction from everything required for pure immediacy is unthinkable, and presupposes reflection, while the "movement" that is supposed to be evident in the transition from being to nothing to becoming is a mere abstraction (CUP: 111 ff.). Moreover, from an "existential" point of view, the system itself, paradoxically unfinished, suffers from a fundamental blind spot. In adopting the perspective of speculative thought, of "thought thinking itself", as Aristotle put it, Hegel abstracts from the *concrete subjectivity* and *lived existence* of the individual human being. While there can be a conceptual system, Climacus avers, there can be no system of existence for finite beings like us; contra Hegel, there can only be such a system of existence for God (CUP: 118 ff.). Existence and concept are *incommensurable*: the concept is what synthesizes thought and being, whereas existence is precisely their separation. Concrete existence, the subjective existence of an individual "I" as a synthesis of finite and infinite, remains irreducible to the conceptual system. Hegel thus forgets his own existence, indeed plays God, in presenting the philosophical system from the perspective of pure thought itself.

In place of Hegel's presuppositionless beginning, and the abstract movement of concepts of pure thought, Kierkegaard proposed the "leap": that which brings all abstract reflection to a halt and presses us into a decision. For this is the only way we can return to the concrete subjectivity of the living individual. As Kierkegaard asks, how is the existing "I" related to the "I" = "I" of pure self-consciousness (CUP: 117)? In other words, how can Hegel's system of speculative thought do justice to the concrete, living subject, who demands not just conceptual knowledge but an existential decision about how to live? The attempt to construct a system is impossible for finite human subjects; a system of existence is possible for God but not for finite existing individuals, who are in a dialectical relationship with God as the infinite. With this criticism, Kierkegaard radicalizes the important existential theme of *human finitude* – the finite nature and inherent dependence of human existence – showing the way that Hegel's system attempts to overcome our finite existence by adopting the speculative viewpoint of pure thought. Again, this will be an existentialist criticism repeated by a host of later thinkers, from Heidegger to Sartre and de Beauvoir. The alternative to Hegel's speculative logic, Kierkegaard contends, is an existential *leap of faith* that embraces the unbridgeable abyss between system and existence (CUP: 118 ff.). Kierkegaard's critique concludes by challenging the very notion of "*existence*" in Hegel's logic, arguing that it is an abstract category incapable of capturing the living subjectivity of individual human beings. Kierkegaard's ontologically distinctive notion of existence, peculiar to finite human beings, proved an inspiration for all kinds of existentialist thinkers, returning, now bereft of Christian overtones, in Heidegger's existential analytic of *Dasein* in *Being and Time*.

Marx's materialist critique of Hegel

At the other pole from Kierkegaard's existentialist critique is the young Karl Marx's confrontation with Hegel, which emerges out of the Left Hegelian critique of Hegelianism. (We should note that the young Marx's critique of Hegel was essentially concluded around 1846; after his materialist–socialist turn, Marx became more interested in Hegel's dialectic and his *Logic*.) Nonetheless it remained an inspiration for the various currents of *Hegelian Marxism* that developed especially in the twentieth century. Influenced by the work of Feuerbach (at least before 1843) but also later appropriating what he called Hegel's "dialectical method", Marx inaugurated an independent philosophical tradition that was to rejoin Hegelian thought during the twentieth century (for example in the work of Georg Lukács, Herbert Marcuse and Maurice Merleau-Ponty). Whereas Kierkegaard emphasized the incompatibility of the Hegelian system with individual existence, Marx claimed that Hegel's metaphysics was an *ideological mystification*: a distortion of the relationship between the material sphere of economic and social relations, and the ideal sphere of meaning, of culture, religion and philosophy. For Marx, Hegelian dialectics was a mystification that nonetheless contained an important truth about the material basis of society: what was required was a *radical inversion* of Hegel's "mystifying criticism" in order to eliminate the ideological elements obscuring the material basis of economics, society, politics and history. As Marx famously remarked in *Das Kapital*, his aim was to rescue the "rational kernel" of Hegelian dialectics from its "mystical shell":

> My dialectic method is not only different from the Hegelian, but is its direct opposite. To Hegel, the life-process of the human brain, i.e., the process of thinking, which, under the name of "the Idea", he even transforms into an independent subject, is the demiurgos of the real world, and the real world is only the external, phenomenal form of "the Idea". With me,

on the contrary, the ideal is nothing else than the material world reflected by the human mind, and translated into forms of thought.... The mystification which dialectic suffers in Hegel's hands by no means prevents him from being the first to present its general form of working in a comprehensive and conscious manner. With him it is standing on its head. It must be turned right side up again, if you would discover the rational kernel within the mystical shell.   (Marx 1977: 420)

Marx's relationship to Hegel was therefore not one of mere succession or elaboration. Nor does Marx simply dismiss Hegel's thought as a superseded and discredited form of metaphysical idealism. Indeed, Marx warned against treating Hegel in the way that Spinoza had been treated earlier, to wit as a "dead dog" (1977: 420). On the contrary, Marx radically overturned Hegelianism, while retaining the notion of Hegelian dialectics, transforming the Hegelian philosophical reconciliation with reality into the Marxist revolutionary transformation of society.

In the early 1840s the young Marx wrote a brief critique of Hegel's *Philosophy of Right*, arguing that Hegel's account of the relationship between civil society and the state had to be reversed. Civil society (primarily the economy and its mediating social institutions) was not grounded in the political state, as Hegel had argued; rather, the political state and its mediating institutions were grounded in civil society, which is to say in the economic forces and relations of the society. At the same time (1844), he had been writing his *Economic and Philosophical Manuscripts*, discovered and published in German only in 1932, which drew on the Hegelian concept of "alienation" (*Entäusserung*) in *Phenomenology of Spirit* and applied it to the sphere of wage labour and economic relations. In 1845 Marx penned the posthumously discovered "Theses on Feuerbach", which included Marx's famous aphorism about philosophers needing to *change* rather than merely *interpret* the world; he also wrote *The German Ideology* with Engels in 1845–46, a scathing attack on various Left Hegelian figures and an anticipatory presentation of Marx's materialist philosophy of history. In sum, during the 1840s, a crucial period in his philosophical development, Marx undertook to criticize the ideological dimensions of Hegelianism, analysing what he cuttingly described, in *The German Ideology*, as the "putrescence of the absolute spirit" (Marx 1978: 147). At the same time, Marx applied certain concepts from

Hegel, notably alienation and objectification, to the spheres of economy, society and history.

Although Marx engaged in sustained criticism of aspects of Hegel's logic, it was the *Phenomenology* that remained the focus of his critique. Moreover, it was Hegel's *dialectics* that proved to be the most important theme for the development of his own theory of history and society. In "Contribution to the Critique of Political Economy", Marx pointed out that the Hegelian (particularly Feuerbachian) criticism of religion was already well advanced in his day: this critique showed how religion is an alienated manifestation of human consciousness, both an expression and a protest against real suffering; and that the struggle against religion is therefore also a "struggle against *that world* whose spiritual *aroma* is religion" (Marx 1977: 54). In one of his most famous remarks, Marx describes religion as "the sigh of the oppressed creature, the sentiment of a heartless world, and the soul of soulless conditions. It is the *opium* of the people" (*ibid.*). The critique of religion, however, should not simply be a critique of ideological mystification; it should also be a *critique of the social conditions* that give rise to the need for consolation through religion.

Left Hegelian thought, however, failed to take this step, remaining with the critique of religion and the humanist affirmation of "man as the highest being for man", but without going on to criticize the historical and social conditions that generated the suffering and injustice motivating the turn to religiosity in the first place. Left Hegelianism remained fixed at the level of a critique of religion without proceeding to a *critique of politics* and a transformation of social reality. The historical task of philosophy, according to Marx, is finally "to unmask human self-alienation in its *secular form* now that it has been unmasked in its *sacred* form" (Marx 1977: 54). The Left Hegelians, even Feuerbach, failed to arrive at this next level of critique, and thus inadvertently affirmed the historically regressive and socially inequitable conditions of the German political state. As Marx put it in his "Theses on Feuerbach", philosophically interpreting the world is not enough; the realization of reason demands that we *change* the world through social and political *action*.

The upshot, for Marx, is that Left Hegelianism too reverts to a form of ideological mystification and spurious justification of the unjust status quo. It remains a powerful philosophical–ideological reflection of a form of social and political life that was both historically progressive and regressive at once – the German state of the 1840s. Indeed, for

Marx, Germany could be said to have carried out its revolution in the sphere of thought (in idealist philosophy) rather than in the sphere of social and political action (like the French Revolution): "In politics, the Germans have only *thought* what other nations have *done*" (Marx 1977: 59). The nation that ushered in the Protestant Reformation (with Martin Luther), liberating the individual from the Church, failed to translate this radical change into genuine human emancipation. It remains tethered to the pre-revolutionary *ancien régime* and has not yet entered post-revolutionary modernity.

So is there any possibility of real emancipation, not just for a particular class of people but for the whole society? Marx's answer was that radical transformation can come about only if there is a particular class, the most disenfranchised group in the society, whose emancipation requires the emancipation of society as a whole. Here Marx draws on Hegel's identification, in the *Philosophy of Right*, of the emergence of a social underclass in economic conditions of free market exchange and mass production (an idea developed and elaborated by Moses Hess, an important mediator between Hegel and Marx). Hegel's impoverished "rabble", radically excluded from bourgeois society, suffers a lack of recognition and denial of social value that generates various kinds of anti-social rebelliousness, from petty crime to acts of violence and social insurrection. While Hegel regarded the "rabble" as an unfortunate by-product of modernity, he saw no real solution to the emergence of this alienated underclass, which was to be left to its fate. Hegel's alienated underclass was a dysfunctional result of the workings of the modern economy; their plight could only be ameliorated, in the end, through private charity and emigration (to the colonies!). Marx, by contrast, saw the proletariat as a necessary constituent of bourgeois society, an underclass whose economic existence is based upon its exploitation. Marx's proletariat was thus a class with "radical chains, a class in civil society which is not a class of civil society, a class which is the dissolution of all classes", a class whose particular experience of injustice and loss of humanity represents a general wrong or universal injustice (Marx 1977: 64). Far from being an unavoidable by-product of bourgeois society, the proletariat, for Marx, was the product of the disintegration of the middle classes, the future gravediggers of capitalism.

Marx criticized Hegelian idealism as an ideological mystification concealing the real basis of modern economy, society and politics; yet he also appropriated and transformed Hegel's dialectical method. Hegel's idealist account of the historical realization of rational freedom as spirit needed to be transformed into *historical materialism*, which posited the succession of different modes of production and resultant conflict between social classes as the true motor of history. This critique exerted an enormous influence on the subsequent development of leftist social and political philosophy, which tended to view the *Philosophy of Right* as a theoretically superseded precursor to the Marxist critique of capitalism. Hegelian philosophy – as an ideological expression of the ideas of the bourgeois ruling class – needed to be superseded by "scientific" Marxism, the true account of the underlying economic forces and relations of class struggle determining history and politics. This economic aspect of Marx's theories for a long time obscured the humanist aspect that owed a great deal to Hegel and to the tradition of Left Hegelian thought (for example, to Feuerbach).

Alienation: from Hegel to Marx

One of the reasons for this resurgence of interest in the Hegel–Marx relationship was the surprise discovery of one of Marx's early works, the so-called *Economic and Philosophical Manuscripts* of 1844, which were belatedly published in 1932. Drawing on concepts of human self-alienation and objectification, derived from Hegel and Feuerbach, the young Marx developed his own critical analysis of alienated labour under conditions of modern capitalism. The concept of alienation – roughly speaking the gap between our human essence and our actual existence – was identified by Rousseau and by Hegel as a defining aspect of the history of subjectivity. Rousseau identified our self-alienation of natural freedom as the price for living in modern society; it was a prerequisite for moral progress and individual autonomy but also the source of moral inauthenticity and subjective dissatisfaction. Hegel, for his part, explored the different configurations of alienation in the *Phenomenology of Spirit*, from the experience of unequal recognition in mastery and servitude to the alienated religious consciousness (the "unhappy consciousness"). The latter is an alienated form of subjectivity that is not only confined to modernity (Hegel points, for example, to the Jewish and Christian experiences of religious alienation). As Hegel contends, however, alienation can be overcome only through the rational comprehension of our historical condition and through the social achievement of mutual recognition.

Marx's use of the concept of alienation, by contrast, highlighted the way that individuals are prevented from developing their capacities through free activity by the manner in which economic and social relations are structured under bourgeois capitalism. According to Marx's

1844 manuscripts, the institution of private property and organization of wage labour results in four related dimensions of alienation:

1. *Alienation from the products of one's labour*, which confront one as alien objects rather than as expressions of one's own social activity.
2. *Alienation from the process of production* or from work as a meaningful activity, which is experienced as a diminution and dissipation of our capacities rather than as their enhancement and fulfilment.
3. *Alienation from humanity itself*, from our "species" being as rational social beings engaged in shared forms of meaningful activity.
4. *Alienation from each other*, from our fellow individual human beings, who are experienced as mere instruments for, or else hostile threats to, our individual self-interest (Marx 1977: 74 ff.).

In sum, the products of collective human labour confront us as an *alien objectivity*, dominating rather than liberating us; they represent a source of estrangement from others rather than the free expression of our individual and social being. Moreover, the exchange value of commodities masks the real social relations that gave rise to them, turning the products of human labour into *fetish objects* endowed with "magical" subjective qualities (for instance, a car that satisfies my desire for freedom or for power).

The discovery of Marx's economic and philosophical manuscripts renewed interest in the important role of Hegelian humanism in the early development of Marx's critique of capitalism and philosophy of history. It made the theme of *alienation* a crucial one for understanding Marx but also the Hegelian–Marxist critique of modernity. Hegel was thought to merely counsel a philosophical comprehension of our historical actuality, a philosophical reconciliation with the "end of history" in which rational freedom is finally realized. Kierkegaard and Marx thus both rejected what they perceived to be Hegel's reconciliation with modernity: Kierkegaard rejected on religious grounds the substitution of the system for individual existence. Marx accepted Hegel's dialectical method but rejected the mystificatory idealist elements that obscured the material basis of bourgeois society, the complex dialectics between economic forces of production and social relations of production, which in turn generated the untenable contradictions of capitalism. Hegel's rational reconciliation with reality – the "rosy cross in the heart of the present" – could not overcome, but was rather an expression of, the pervasive alienation endemic to modernity. The Hegelian synthesis of thought and reality thus came apart, dividing into Kierkegaard's world of existential despair, with its subjective demand to overcome alienation through religious commitment, and Marx's world of alienated labour, with its social demand to overcome alienation through revolutionary praxis. Kierkegaard and Marx thus set the stage for the Hegelian disputes of the twentieth century, a period that saw existential and Marxist versions of Hegelianism struggling to comprehend the challenges thrown up by twentieth-century history.

Summary of key points

The dissolution of the Hegelian school

- The disputes in the Hegelian schools turned on the political implications of the *Philosophy of Right* and on the religious and historical orientation of Hegel's philosophy. The key questions were:

  - Was Hegel's philosophy ultimately concerned with a (religious–philosophical) reconciliation with contemporary reality?
  - Or, would the realization of reason mean the revolutionary transformation of society?

Right and Left Hegelianism

- David Strauss coined the terms "Right Hegelians", "Centre Hegelians" and "Left Hegelians". We could gloss these as the *accommodationist*, *reformist* and *radical* wings of the Hegelian school.
- The Right Hegelians maintained that Hegel's philosophy successfully achieved a quasi-religious reconciliation with existing social and historical reality.
- The Left Hegelians argued that Hegel's philosophy pointed beyond religious reconciliation (a mystification) towards a social and political transformation of reality in order to realize our rational freedom.
- David Strauss inaugurated the Left Hegelian perspective by arguing that the traditional content of Christianity could be reconciled with Hegelian philosophy by translating the language of religion into historicist and humanist terms.

- Ludwig Feuerbach developed a radical "anthropological" version of Hegelian humanism, arguing that the reconciliation between reason and reality required a reconciliation with external nature and our own corporeal nature.
- In *The Essence of Christianity* (1841), Feuerbach argued that human beings are not made in the image of God; God is rather a transcendent projection by human beings who are alienated from their own human essence.
- Feuerbach's critical account of religion was radicalized by Bruno Bauer, who argued that Hegel's philosophy results not in theism or pantheism but in *atheism*.
- Bauer argued that the only power in the world and human history is *self-consciousness*, whose development was in truth the meaning of all history.

Kierkegaard and Marx

- Kierkegaard took Hegelianism to be representative of the social and institutional conformity of philosophy as well as its inability to attend to the sphere of radical subjectivity and religious inwardness.
- For Kierkegaard, in constructing the system of absolute knowing, Hegel adopted the "impossible" perspective of pure thought in place of the living subjectivity of the individual human being.
- Karl Marx's confrontation with Hegel emerges out of the Left Hegelian critique of Hegelianism, and remained an inspiration for the various currents of *Hegelian Marxism* in the twentieth century.
- Marx claimed that Hegel's metaphysics was an *ideological mystification*: a distortion of the relationship between the material sphere of economic and social relations, and the ideal sphere of meaning, of culture, religion and philosophy.
- Marx thus overturned Hegelianism while retaining the notion of Hegelian dialectics, transforming the Hegelian philosophical reconciliation with reality into the Marxist revolutionary transformation of society.
- Drawing on the concepts of human self-alienation and objectification, derived from Hegel and Feuerbach, the young Marx developed his own critical analysis of alienated labour under conditions of modern capitalism.

part II

German Hegelianism

three

Reification and metaphysics:
Lukács and Heidegger

Having outlined the basic elements of Hegel's philosophy, and the key moves in the debates between Left and Right Hegelian schools, we can now turn our attention to twentieth-century Hegelianism. The second part of this book focuses on what I am calling "German Hegelianism", by which I mean primarily the tradition of Hegelian Marxism and Frankfurt School critical theory. In the following chapter, I introduce some of the key Hegelian-Marxist ideas of Hungarian political philosopher Georg Lukács (1885–1971), in particular his critique of Hegel's concept of *alienation*, and Lukács's own conception of the process of *reification* in modernity. Lukács's classic work, *History and Class Consciousness* (1923), re-energized the tradition of Hegelian Marxism, and would have a lasting impact on twentieth-century social and political thought. As we shall see, Lukács's concept of reification was decisive for the Frankfurt school of critical theory, above all in Adorno and Horkheimer's seminal text, the *Dialectic of Enlightenment* (written during World War II but not published until 1947).

In the second part of this chapter, I present a brief introduction to the thought of Martin Heidegger, one of the great thinkers of the twentieth century, whose existential phenomenology posed a radical challenge to Hegelianism. Heidegger's various critiques of Hegel – for his metaphysical theory of time, and for his Cartesian metaphysical subjectivism – will be explored in some detail because they have proven very important for postwar French philosophy, particularly for the French poststructuralist critique of Hegel. This analysis of Heidegger's confrontation with Hegel is presented as a counterpoint to the Hegelian

Marxism of Lukács. My suggestion is that these two very different approaches to Hegel present us with a conceptual "matrix" for understanding the intersecting existentialist and Marxist perspectives that characterize the history of French and German Hegelianism.

Although it is an unusual conjunction, taking Lukács and Heidegger as opposing critical approaches to Hegel – roughly speaking, Marxist and existentialist – will provide us with the conceptual background to examine how Hegelian-Marxist themes are interwoven in the work of critical theorists Adorno and Horkheimer, and French Hegelians such as Alexandre Kojève and Jean Hyppolite. Adorno, for example, appropriated Lukács's concept of reification while sharply challenging Heidegger's existential phenomenology (at the same time, Adorno's critique of metaphysics and of modernity resonated with Heidegger's critique). Kojève combined Heideggerian existentialism with Hegel's master/slave dialectic and a Marxist conception of history and politics. Merleau-Ponty too combined elements of Hegelian dialectics with Marxist motifs, and later developed an ontology that appropriated elements of Heidegger's thinking. Finally, much of the poststructuralist critique of Hegel, as we shall see in Chapter 8, derives from Heidegger's confrontation with Hegel's metaphysics of subjectivity. So there are good reasons for contrasting Lukács's Hegelian-Marxist critique of modernity with Heidegger's critique of the Hegelian metaphysics of subjectivity.

Lukács's critique of Hegel

With the exception of British idealism, Hegelianism more generally became dormant in much of Europe in the late nineteenth and early twentieth centuries. It was only during the 1920s that Hegel once again returned to philosophical prominence in Germany and France. This was thanks to various factors, of which I mention three: the efforts of Wilhelm Dilthey, who edited the important volume of Hegel's *Early Theological Writings* in 1907, and whose own brand of radical historicism was indebted to Hegel; an increasingly critical attitude towards the prevailing currents of neo-Kantianism; and the resurgence of the Marxist tradition (largely because of the Bolshevik Revolution of 1917). This last movement found powerful expression in the work of Lukács, whose Hegelian approach to Marxism opened up a new tradition of political philosophy that came to be known (thanks to Merleau-Ponty) as "Western Marxism".

Lukács was probably the first political philosopher to underline the importance of Hegel's knowledge of political economy and its role in Hegel's philosophical understanding of modern life. This was the approach taken in Lukács's later work, *The Young Hegel* (written 1938, published 1947/48), which represented quite a different standpoint from his earlier, more famous, text, *History and Class Consciousness* (1923). In *The Young Hegel*, Lukács argued that we cannot really understand Hegel's conceptions of ethical life, of civil society (which includes the institutional mechanisms of the market) and its relationship with the state without acknowledging the young Hegel's appropriation of modern theories of political economy, along with "communitarian" ideals of shared ethical life (*Sittlichkeit*) drawn from classical (Greek) political philosophy. At the same time, Lukács's emphasis on the economic dimensions of Hegel's development was an anti-orthodox position for a Hegelian Marxist to take. By emphasizing the Hegel–Marx relationship and underlining the concept of alienation, Lukács maintained a critical distance from orthodox Marxism; at the same time, he wrote from a position of internal *resignationism* (even the worst socialism was better than capitalism). This controversial political stance (a resigned defence of "really existing socialism") was to attract a good deal of criticism, Lukács being accused of justifying Stalinism.

In his earlier, better-known work, *History and Class Consciousness*, Lukács adopted a different approach. He radicalized the Hegelian notion of *alienation* (which is also explicitly present in Marx's early writings), transforming it into the concept of *reification* (the process by which human relations and forms of subjectivity become increasingly "thing-like" under conditions of commodity capitalism). Lukács then undertook a Marxist–humanist critique of Hegel's apparent conflation of two key concepts: *objectification* and *alienation*. As Lukács observes, Hegel correctly identified labour or work as one of the key elements in the constitution of modern subjectivity; recall the famous master/slave dialectic, in which the experience of labour, the objectification of our powers through productive work, enabled the "slave" to come to recognize his freedom as reflected in social reality. At the same time, however, Hegel articulated a sophisticated account of the way *alienation* (*Entäusserung*) resulted in the products of our activity taking on a life of their own as part of social objectivity within which we come to recognize ourselves as members of a social community. For Hegel, all my actions, whether through speech or work, become subject to the interpretations and norms shaping my community, and hence are no longer simply "private" expression of my subjectivity or desire.

Lukács's criticism, taken from Marx, is that Hegel identifies "objectification" in general with the specific sense of "alienation" characteristic of modernity. The result was to "ontologise" alienation as an inescapable feature of human activity: alienation is the result of the objectification or humanization of nature through productive labour. More pointedly, Lukács, like Marx, underlined the *negative* dimensions of alienation that Hegel claimed could be overcome through thought or absolute spirit. For Hegel, alienation in its negative sense – expressed in various "pathological" forms of subjectivity and cultural practice – is a structural feature of history; it is only in *thinking* that the divide between subject and object can be completely overcome. For Marx, by contrast, alienation also means an estrangement from our human essence as social and productive beings; and this conflict between subject and object can be overcome only by transforming the social and economic order as such. Against Hegel, Lukács argued that not all objectification can be construed as alienation, either in the sense that describes the subject's estrangement from his or her fundamental human potential, or in the sense that the relationship between subject and object remains fundamentally conflictual. While alienation exists in different historical and social formations, it is the specific form of objectification to be found within bourgeois capitalism that can be said to produce "pathological" alienation.

Hence for Lukács, Hegel's Marxist critics were right to identify the mystifying element in Hegel's idealism, which distorts and conceals the real social relations in society; but they failed to identify the source of this mystification, namely the confusion between objectification and alienation, and the failure to identify the reason why bourgeois society suffers from such pervasive alienation. "Objectification" in the general sense is a fundamental characteristic of human self-conscious rationality, for all forms of human activity involve the "objectification" of human capacities, subjective desires and social ends. Alienation, on the other hand, takes on a particularly debilitating form under the specific historical conditions of bourgeois society, namely the dominance of the commodity form under conditions of modern capitalism.

Like other Marxist critics, Lukács concluded that Hegel's idealist dialectics needed to be given a "historical materialist" foundation; one that would show its practical–political deficiencies (resolving oppositions at the level of theory rather than practice), but also recognize its conceptual insights (showing the inadequacy of prevailing conceptions of freedom enshrined within modern social institutions). Lukács thus introduced the concept of *reification* (*Verdinglichung*) to capture the

Hegelian sense of alienation without taking it to be – as French existential Hegelianism would – a fundamental aspect of human being transcending history and different social formations. There could be no *rapprochement*, for Lukács, between existentialism and Marxism: existentialism would always remain an "ideological" mystification of the material and historical basis of the phenomenon of alienation so well identified by the existentialists.

Reification: Lukács's critique of modernity

Hegel's concept of alienation has had a vigorous afterlife in twentieth-century social and political philosophy. The concept derives from Jean-Jacques Rousseau (1712–78), who famously analysed (in his *Discourse on the Origins of Inequality*) how modernity divides individuals against themselves, pitting the socially recognizable self, dependent upon the gaze and opinions of others, against the private inner self, struggling for natural independence from others. Alienation, for Rousseau, was the price of modern freedom: the complex relations of social dependence in modern life bring forth myriad subjective possibilities, above all, the development of moral autonomy. At the same time, such relations of interdependence "alienate" us from our inner nature, corrupting our natural desire for independence and perverting it through social competition and hierarchies.

Hegel developed this Rousseauian theme, showing how consciousness had to learn historically that its inadequate conceptions of freedom (as isolated independence) are expressions of an alienated form of subjectivity (what Hegel called the "unhappy consciousness"). Indeed, the *Phenomenology of Spirit* can be understood as an analysis of different figures of alienated subjectivity that finally overcomes its alienation through the achievement of *mutual recognition*. Existentialist Hegelians, as we shall see, interpreted alienation as a trans-historical feature of our existential condition as finite mortal beings in the world. Marxists, by contrast, emphasized alienation as a structural feature of historical consciousness, a distorted perception of our relationship to the social order generated by the institutional and economic arrangements of modern society. What of the relation between alienation, philosophy and society? This question stood at the centre of Lukács's highly influential work, *History and Class Consciousness*, the "founding text" of what Merleau-Ponty dubbed "Western Marxism". Roughly speaking, Western Marxism describes non-dogmatic, philosophical (Hegelian) humanist Marxism that emphasized autonomous freedom and individuality within a rationally organized social whole. In doing so, it remained opposed to the orthodox "dialectical materialism" endorsed by the Communist Party and supposedly enshrined within "really existing" socialist states.

Lukács's project, to put it simply, was to return Marxism to its philosophical roots (in Hegel), but also to develop a Marxist *ideology critique* of how the modern philosophical tradition (including Hegel) reflected the phenomenon of reification. By "ideology critique" I mean here a critical analysis of the ways in which forms of discourse and claims to knowledge come to serve specific class or group interests, distorting or obscuring our comprehension of the real economic forces and institutional practices constituting social reality. Extending the Hegelian-Marxist analysis, Lukács argued that *reification* has become the organizing principle of social and cultural life under conditions of commodity capitalism. We might gloss this as a Marxist–materialist interpretation of the Hegelian concept of alienation, an analysis of the process by which social relations, individual subjectivity, and forms of cultural expression are rendered "thing-like" under conditions of modern capitalism. Unlike previous economic and social formations, modern capitalism is unique in positing the *commodity form* as the organizing principle both of objective social institutions and practices as well as their corresponding subjective forms of cultural expression (like art and philosophy).

Lukács drew here on Marx's famous discussion of the "fetishism of commodities" in *Das Kapital*. As Lukács remarks, Marx described the "phenomenon of reification" as the way in which commodities are abstracted from the social process of their production, transforming them into an alien power with an apparent objectivity and independence from us:

> A commodity is therefore a mysterious thing, simply because in it the social character of men's labour appears to them as an objective character stamped upon the product of that labour; . . . It is only a definite social relation between men that assumes, in their eyes, the fantastic form of a relation between things.   (*Capital* I, 72, quoted in HCC: 86)

The real social basis of commodities as products of human activity is transformed into a mysterious process governed by the "objective" laws of the market. The real social relations that organize human labour are obscured by the apparently independent and isolated nature of the object as an *embodiment of value* in general as distinct from its (actual or potential) use – this the definition of the *commodity*. The logic of commodity exchange – as a logic of *equivalence* or of identity – will become the pervasive form of thinking in bourgeois societies, Lukács claims, not only in the economic sphere but in social relations and cultural expressions of meaning.

Lukács extended the analysis of the commodity form – the shift in defining the value of a product by its practical use to defining it by its monetary exchange value – to the sphere of culture and thought. This extension of the logic of commodity exchange to all spheres of social and cultural life had a number of effects, the most important being an increasing reification of experience in both "subjective" and "objective" spheres of social and cultural life. Not just economic relations but all social relations become subsumed under the logic of (monetary) exchange, which is also a logic of formal equivalence, since money renders everything equivalent (everything has its price!). For Lukács, the logic of equivalence between commodities becomes all-pervasive, extending from the economic market to penetrate the realms of culture, thought and subjective experience.

This extension of the commodity form leads to Lukács's critical discussion of what he called "antinomies of bourgeois thought" (HCC: 110–49): the intractable oppositions defining modern post-Cartesian philosophy. His claim, which will be important for Adorno, is that these oppositions defining modern philosophy – between subject and object, freedom and nature, universal and particular, and so on – are conceptual reflections, at the level of thought, of real oppositions in social reality: the "reified" social relations generated by the primacy of commodity production and exchange. The details of Lukács's extensive critique need not detain us here. The important thing to note is Lukács's claim that modern philosophy from Descartes to Hegel should be subjected to an "ideology critique" showing how "bourgeois philosophy" (exemplified by Hegel) articulated these oppositions conceptually but was unable to resolve them in theory or in practice. Rather, from a Marxist perspective, this resolution was to occur on the plane of political action: the overcoming of (Hegelian) philosophy through (Marxist) revolutionary praxis. The proletariat (the excluded class of alienated masses) Lukács further characterized, in Hegelian terms, as the "identical subject–object" of history; the self-conscious makers of history (the revolutionary proletariat) would finally coincide with social and historical reality itself (the new communist society). Although Hegel anticipated this subject–object identity, it was Marx's proletariat – or at least Lukács's ideal or "imputed" proletariat, whose will would be expressed by the Party – that Lukács claimed would realize this "identity" of subject and object in historical reality.

Such utopian visions, however, were shattered by the catastrophic historical experiences of Nazism and totalitarianism. We should note that *History and Class Consciousness* expressed the immediate revolutionary hopes that followed the Russian revolution, hopes that were soon dashed with the oppressive turn of Stalinism. Lukács was strongly criticized for his *revolutionary utopianism*: for having a utopian vision of the inevitability of revolutionary transformation, and more seriously, for underestimating the degree to which the realization of the revolutionary will of the proletariat – "objectively" expressed through the Party – might entail various forms of violence and oppression. This debate would be taken up again in the cold war era between Sartre and Merleau-Ponty during the 1950s. The historical disconfirmation of the Marxist thesis that capitalism would inevitably collapse raised some urgent questions. Why did this revolutionary vision fail? Why did "the masses" choose fascism instead? Were violence and oppression inevitably bound up with modern social and political forms? These questions greatly preoccupied the Frankfurt school critical theorists, who responded by turning to different versions of Hegelian Marxism and by developing an interdisciplinary materialist theory of modern society.

Dialectics and difference: Heidegger's confrontation with Hegel

Before turning to critical theory, as an unorthodox variant of Hegelian Marxism, we should consider the other major current of post-Hegelian thought, the tradition of existentialist thought stemming from Kierkegaard. The most important figure here, for our purposes, is Martin Heidegger, who introduced a radical form of existential phenomenology and deconstruction of modern subject-metaphysics that proved to be profoundly influential for French and German Hegelianism, albeit in different, at times even opposing, ways. Among the figures crucial to Heidegger's confrontation with modern metaphysics (such as Descartes, Kant, Nietzsche) we must also include Hegel, even though Heidegger devoted much longer analyses to Kant and

Nietzsche. Nonetheless, Heidegger's magnum opus, *Being and Time* (1927), contains a sharp critique of Hegel's conception of time. More-over, his 1930–31 lecture courses on the *Phenomenology of Spirit*, cul-minating in his later essay "Hegel's Concept of Experience", developed a critique of Hegelian thought that has proven very significant for postwar French Hegelianism as well as for French poststructuralism. Heidegger argued that Hegel's metaphysics represents the culmination of the Cartesian metaphysics of self-grounding subjectivity (or rather of "subjectness", Heidegger's term for the subject–object framework). Deconstructing the tradition of modern philosophy – the metaphysics of "subjectness" from Descartes through Kant to Hegel – became an urgent task for Heidegger, one that was radicalized by his French followers, notably by Derrida.

Heidegger's analysis of existence (Dasein)

Heidegger's profound influence on modern thought is becoming increasingly palpable today. Heidegger's best-known work, *Being and Time*, was published in 1927 and hailed as a philosophical classic. In that work, Heidegger was concerned to raise the fundamental question of philosophy, a question that has been forgotten in the history of modern philosophy: the *question of Being*. As Heidegger notes, we must presuppose a vague understanding of "Being" (*Sein*) in our everyday experience; we must presuppose the concept of "Being" in our most basic use of language; yet the philosophical concept of "Being" remains obscure or indefinable. What, then, is the sense or meaning of Being? We need to answer this question, Heidegger contends, if we wish to ground the various sciences that deal with particular kinds of beings (mathematical, biological and so on). To answer this question properly, however, we should begin with a phenomenological analysis of the kind of being that we ourselves are: beings capable of questioning our own way of Being. We should avoid the traditional, philosophically loaded concept of the "human being" (with its various definitions such as "rational animal", "speaking being", "consciousness" and so on). Instead, Heidegger proposes that we designate ourselves more neutrally as "*Dasein*", that is, as "existence" or, more literally, as "being-there".

We are beings whose way of Being is defined as "existence" (*Existenz*), which means that we dwell in a meaningful world in a finite, temporal and self-interpreting manner such that our own Being is an issue for us – something about which we care fundamentally. Heidegger analyses *Dasein* in its average everyday existence, describing the complex structure of our temporal existence, which he calls our "being-in-the-world". By analysing the holistic structure of our being-in-the-world, we can show that we are defined by an existential *care* for our own Being; and more originarily, by the experience of *temporality* in our existence as finite beings aware of our own finitude. On the question of temporality, Heidegger rejects the traditional philosophical understanding of time as a succession of "now" moments (the analysis of internal time-consciousness undertaken by Heidegger's teacher, Edmund Husserl, was an important philosophical source as well as a target of Heidegger's critique). In *Being and Time*, Heidegger claims that the phenomenological structure of human temporality involves a primary projection towards a future horizon of possibilities, against an inherited background of past facticities (given circumstances), which together allow the present to be disclosed as a meaningful world in which we can engage in practical activities. We find a critique in *Being and Time* (§82) of the way that Hegel misconstrues the phenomenological structure of human temporality. Heidegger thus contrasts, in a critical manner, his own "existential–phenomenological" description of the temporality of *Dasein* with Hegel's dialectical–historical conception of the relation between time and spirit.

Heidegger's criticism of Hegel on time and spirit

It is significant that Hegel is one of the few figures in *Being and Time* (along with Descartes and Kant) to be singled out for an explicit critique. In this sense, we could regard Heidegger's brief analysis of Hegel's conception of the relation between time and spirit as a contribution to what Heidegger called the task of a "destruction" (*Destruktion*) of the history of ontology – a dismantling of inherited conceptual structures and interpretations in order to reveal their originary and suppressed meaning. This idea will be appropriated and transformed in Jacques Derrida's deconstruction of what he called the "metaphysics of presence". For Heidegger, temporality as such, with the exception of Kant, has remained unthought, or at least distorted and misunderstood within the history of metaphysics (BT: 20). The "metaphysical" understanding of time is based upon the assumption that the definitive dimension of the experience of time is provided by the ordinary perception of beings encountered in *the present*. Hegel is taken to exemplify the "vulgar" metaphysical conception of time as an infinite sequence of discrete "nows" or present moments. Indeed, Hegel's concept of time, according to Heidegger, is "the most radical way in which the vulgar understanding of time has been given form conceptually" (BT: 392). Throughout the philosophical tradition, Heidegger argues, time as "world-time" has been connected with the "soul" or "spirit"; but it is Hegel who explicitly points out the connection between this "present-centred" conception of time and the historical development of spirit. Heidegger's brief critique of Hegel's "metaphysical" conception of time and spirit – that spirit "falls into" historical time from an atemporal origin – is thus presented as a contrast to the *existential–ontological* interpretation of the originary temporality of *Dasein*.

Heidegger begins by pointing out that Hegel's analysis of time, like that of Aristotle, belongs to the "The Philosophy of Nature". Heidegger's analysis of paragraphs 254–8 of Hegel's *Encyclopaedia* aims to establish how Hegel's basic conception of time, defined as "intuited becoming", privileges the punctual moment of the present – as a now-here moment – within the abstract becoming or flux of successive moments. Heidegger argues that Hegel's "logical" conceptualizing of time – construing the "now-moment" as the "negation" of the punctuality of space, or the "now" as "logically" corresponding to the "here" – demonstrates how time, in the rich phenomenological sense of "lived temporality", is here formalized and levelled down to an "unprecedented degree" (BT: 394). This *logical formalization* of time is precisely what allows Hegel to make the connection between spirit and its development through historical time, for both time and spirit share the same formal structure that allows spirit to be realized temporally in history: "Hegel shows the possibility of the historical actualization of spirit 'in time' by going back to *the identity of the formal structure of spirit and time as the negation of a negation*" (BT: 396). This is the decisive point in Heidegger's discussion: the identity of time and spirit as sharing the logical structure of the "negation of the negation" is also their reduction to an empty "formal–ontological" abstraction that obliterates originary temporality. In connecting time and spirit in this manner, Hegel obscures the way our experience of time is rooted in the threefold structure of originary or "ecstatic" temporality: the projecting into the future, against the background of a shared past, in order to disclose the present as a domain of possible action. According to Heidegger, Hegel fails to see that the "logical" conception of time that he presents presupposes a more originary phenomenological account of temporality.

We can certainly ask questions here about the adequacy of Heidegger's interpretation. Why does Heidegger focus on the concept of time taken from the philosophy of nature rather than Hegel's explicit discussions of the historicity of spirit? Moreover, why is Heidegger's discussion in this respect restricted to the most elementary classification of time in the philosophy of nature? In the paragraphs Heidegger discusses from the "Mechanism" chapter of the *Encyclopaedia*, for example, Hegel examines the categorial structure of time and space pertinent not only to Aristotle but to *Newtonian mechanics*. Hegel's discussion, moreover, cannot provide an adequate example of the essential relationship between time and spirit, simply because nature occupies a different categorial level than spirit and thus cannot provide the basis for conceptualizing spirit in its historical development. In §82 of *Being and Time*, Heidegger overlooks this hermeneutic dimension in Hegel's discussion of time within the philosophy of nature. Nonetheless, Heidegger's basic criticism – that Hegel is guilty of conceptual–logical abstraction in his account of time, history, and spirit – will be repeated frequently in twentieth-century critiques of Hegelianism.

Heidegger's reading of Hegel's Phenomenology

Heidegger's next sustained engagement with Hegel occurs in his 1930–31 lecture series on the opening chapters of the *Phenomenology of Spirit*, a reading centred on the problem of *finitude*. This term has proven a major theme in phenomenology, existentialism and in various strands of post-Heideggerian thought. It refers to the *finite* character of human existence, not just our mortality but the inherent limits to our experience as such: not only is my existence inherently contingent and "ungrounded"; human experience and knowledge are also marked by limits beyond which we strive but cannot go. Finite existence means not only that we live and die but that the possibility of my non-existence is inherent in every moment of my temporal existence; finitude colours my experience of time and selfhood in profound ways. This idea of finitude is sharply at odds with many assumptions about human existence within the metaphysical tradition. As Heidegger remarks in *Kant and the Problem of Metaphysics* (1929), the problem of finitude is opened up in modern philosophy by Kant's discovery of the transcendental imagination and of the transcendental horizon of time as temporality. However, according to Heidegger, Kant retreats from this insight (in the second edition of the *Critique of Pure Reason*) by reverting to the primacy of the *understanding* (rather than transcendental imagination) in his account of pure self-consciousness. Hegel follows Kant's lead, restoring the mastery of speculative logic over metaphysics, and thereby foreclosing the problem of finitude by integrating the latter into the infinitude of reason (Heidegger 1997: 171). We must therefore ask what Heidegger means by "the problem of finitude": how does Hegel foreclose genuine access to this central problem of "the inner possibility and necessity of metaphysics"? (*ibid.*).

Heidegger takes up these questions in his 1930–31 lecture series devoted to reading the "Consciousness" and "Truth of Self-Certainty" chapters of the *Phenomenology of Spirit*. He deepens this analysis in his later (1942–3) commentary on the "Introduction" to the *Phenomenology*, an essay entitled "Hegel's Concept of Experience". In these texts Heidegger situates his critical dialogue with Hegel in the context of the post-Kantian project of constructing a metaphysics centred on the finite human subject. The confrontation between Hegel and Heidegger takes place on the terrain of *the problematic of finitude*, the "crossover" between the Hegelian project of thinking the infinity of spirit, and the Heideggerian project of thinking the finitude of Being: "we shall try to *encounter* Hegel on *the problematic of finitude*. This means . . . that through a confrontation with *Hegel's* problematic of infinitude we shall try to create, on the basis of our own inquiry into finitude, *the* kinship needed to reveal the spirit of Hegel's philosophy" (HPS: 38). According to Heidegger, Hegel's *Phenomenology* remains bound to the traditional philosophical conception of finitude, which is integrated into Hegel's speculative concept of infinitude and thus incorporated into reason.

With Hegel, Heidegger claims, infinitude becomes a more significant problem than finitude, since the interest of speculative reason is to supersede all oppositions within the rational totality. In this sense, Heidegger understands the project of post-Kantian idealism to consist in the systematic attempt to overcome the "relative" knowledge of finite consciousness (in the sense of object-dependent knowledge of otherness) in favour of *the absolute knowledge* of speculative reason (in the sense of a no longer "relative" or object-dependent self-knowledge). Heidegger plays on the connection between the term "absolute" and that which "ab-solves" itself of any relation of dependence; Hegel's *absolute* knowledge would thereby be an *ab-solvent* knowledge that *ab-solves* or *detaches* itself from the relativity of consciousness. Because absolute knowledge *detaches* itself from object-dependent knowledge defining consciousness, it becomes self-knowledge or cognition of cognition; object-dependent consciousness thus becomes aware of itself or becomes *self-consciousness*.

In this respect, Heidegger's interpretation of consciousness in the *Phenomenology* rests on the assumption that Hegel's entire phenomenological exposition presupposes the standpoint of absolute knowing in the sense of an *absolvent* knowledge that has absolved itself from any dependence on the consciousness of objects (HPS: 51). The absolvent knowing belonging to the phenomenological observers, that is, to the "we", is entirely detached from the relativity of ordinary human knowing (HPS: 50). Hegelian phenomenology can thus be characterized, Heidegger claims, as "the *absolute self-presentation of reason* (*ratio–logos*), whose essence and actuality Hegel finds in *absolute spirit*" (HPS: 30). Heidegger's emphasis here is on the way Hegel's conception of reason integrates, and thus supersedes, the finitude of the knowing subject. Philosophical or absolute knowing is the standpoint of reason knowing itself, rather than the finite standpoint of the human subject with its limited knowledge of objects.

Heidegger on self-consciousness

We can summarize Heidegger's confrontation with Hegel as having two related aspects:

1. An emphasis on the ontological centrality of the rational, knowing subject.
2. An emphasis on the way Hegelian dialectics reveals Being from the perspective of the dialectical *experience* of self-conscious subject.

As we shall see, Heidegger presents what we could call a "Cartesian" reading of Hegel, situating Hegel in the wake of Descartes's attempt to locate a secure foundation for knowledge in the self-certainty of the thinking subject. Not surprisingly, the limitations of Heidegger's "Cartesian" interpretation become apparent in his discussion of Hegelian self-consciousness. The basic difficulty in Heidegger's reading is that Hegelian self-consciousness is largely equated with a Fichtean version of the Cartesian *ego cogito*. The result is a failure on Heidegger's part to grasp the dialectic of dependence and independence of self-consciousness and the problem of the freedom of self-consciousness in regard to the unhappy consciousness.

Heidegger describes the transition from consciousness to self-consciousness in strongly Fichtean terms: "we can say that by saying I, I is posited as I: I = I". The subject reflects upon itself, differentiates itself from the not-I; but at the same time it also unites with the not-I and thus with itself precisely through this self-differentiation (HPS: 125). Heidegger takes this "Fichtean" formulation of Hegel's conception of self-consciousness to claim that self-consciousness is the condition of the possibility of our consciousness of objectivity in general. For Heidegger, Hegel conceives of the "I" in terms of the *cogito*, and self-being in terms of self-consciousness; but this conception of self-consciousness involves an ontological interpretation of the *Being* of the self (HPS: 136). The problem, Heidegger claims, is that Hegel's Cartesian–Fichtean model of self-consciousness, where Subject = Object, results in an ontologizing of the self, turning the self effectively into an object. The Cartesian–Fichtean model of self-consciousness must therefore be transformed into an account of the essence of self-consciousness "by way of *being-for-another*": a shift away from the model of the self defined by the subject–object relationship (HPS: 138). One would therefore expect here a discussion of the role of *desire* and *recognition* in the constitution of self-consciousness. Instead, according to Heidegger's reading, Hegel develops at this point a new concept of Being as *infinite Life*. To be sure, Heidegger does turn to a very brief consideration of desire, but he omits to extend this discussion to the crucial section on the struggle for recognition.

Heidegger's Cartesian–Fichtean interpretation of Hegel on self-consciousness, however, fails to account for the moment of *concrete individuality* in the Concept of self-consciousness. In the *Phenomenology*, Hegel defines the Concept of self-consciousness as comprising three essential moments: the pure undifferentiated "I" (universality); the mediation through the object of desire (particularity); and the movement of recognition between self-conscious subjects (concrete individuality) (PhS: §176). While Heidegger accounts for the first moment (the abstract self-identity of the "I" as "I" = "I"), and the second moment (the particularity of self-consciousness as desire), he has no account of the third moment (concrete individuality articulated through intersubjective recognition). In this sense, Heidegger's interpretation of Hegel remains at the level of abstract *reflection* (rather than that of speculative reason), conceiving of self-consciousness according to an abstract *formalism*: a deficient conception of self-consciousness that fails to unite all three moments of universality, particularity and the crucial third moment of individuality achieved through intersubjective recognition.

Instead of elaborating how the independence of self-consciousness emerges from the experience of mastery and servitude, Heidegger turns to a discussion of Life as Hegel's new concept of Being. On the basis of this account of Life, Heidegger claims that the phenomenology of spirit is *"the fundamental ontology of absolute ontology*, or onto-logy in general" (HPS: 141). The *Phenomenology* provides the last possible justification of the metaphysics of subjectivity, presumably before Heidegger's own attempt to overcome the latter through the existential analysis of *Dasein*. Another reason for Heidegger's puzzling emphasis on Life soon becomes apparent: it prepares the way for Heidegger's criticism of Hegel's parenthetical remark on Time. In the middle of the exposition of Life, Hegel remarks that Essence is "absolutely restless infinity": it is "the simple essence of Time, which, in his equality with itself, has the pure shape of Space" (PhS: §169). Heidegger returns here to his earlier criticism of the relation between time and spirit, conclud-ing again that this remark provides evidence that "time and space are for Hegel primarily problems of the philosophy of nature" (HPS: 144). As a result, Hegel fails to develop the problematic of time properly in terms of history or spirit (*ibid.*). Indeed, Hegel remains mired within the reification of the temporality and historicity of the subject through an ontologically inappropriate interpretation of the self that remains rooted in the ontology of things. As mentioned, the problem here is that Heidegger restricts Hegel's conception of time to the domain of the philosophy of nature, and misleadingly argues that Hegel transposes a representational notion of time as empty succession into the domain of historical spirit. In doing so, Heidegger's "Cartesian–Fichtean" approach overlooks precisely the themes that are original in Hegel's account of self-consciousness: the role of concrete individuality as *intersubjective recognition*, and the question of the *historicity* of self-conscious spirit.

Hegel's concept of experience

Heidegger's 1942–3 interpretation of the "Introduction" to the *Phenomenology of Spirit* is his most intensive treatment of Hegel's philosophy as a whole. In this concluding section, I shall attempt only a brief analysis of Heidegger's "Cartesian" interpretation of Hegel. The latter remains important because it served as an authoritative reference point for numerous post-Heideggerian critics of Hegelianism, who insisted that Hegel elevates the Cartesian *cogito* to the level of an "abso-lute subject".

Heidegger begins his interpretation by emphasizing the centrality of Descartes for modern metaphysics. Indeed, modern philosophy, for Heidegger, is defined by the search (inaugurated by Descartes) for an absolute foundation for knowledge in "unconditional self-certainty", and an *a priori* or transcendental grounding for this knowledge (argued by Kant). Heidegger thus cites Hegel's famous remark on Descartes in the *Lectures on the History of Philosophy* concerning the discovery of the terrain of self-consciousness:

> Here, we may say, we are at home, and like the mariner after a long voyage in a tempestuous sea, we may now hail the sight of land; with Descartes the culture of modern times, the thought of modern Philosophy really begins to appear, after a long and tedious journey so far. (Hegel 1896: 217)

Heidegger takes this comment to reflect Hegel's endorsement of Cartesianism, without discussing Hegel's criticism of Descartes's equation of thought with the abstract understanding (rather than speculative reason). Hegel, according to Heidegger, inherits and completes this search for an absolute or self-grounding knowledge that is grounded in the unconditional self-certainty of self-consciousness.

Let us consider this point in more detail. Hegel is the first philosopher, Heidegger notes, to fully possess the terrain of self-certain subjectivity. This important event in modern thought occurs once Descartes makes the *cogito ergo sum* the unshakeable foundation of all knowledge; the cogito as "*fundamentum inconcussum*" is thereby elevated to the level of the Absolute. The Absolute, Heidegger explains, is spirit:

> that which is present and by itself in the certainty of unconditional self-knowledge. Real knowledge of beings now means the absolute knowledge of the Absolute in its absoluteness.
> (HCE: 28)

Heidegger's formulations are certainly legitimate in so far as we consider Hegel's claim to develop a system of absolute knowledge. It is in this connection that Heidegger develops his *ontologically* oriented interpretation of the *Phenomenology*, namely that Hegel presupposes the presence or *parousia* of the Absolute to us, and that the Absolute wills to disclose its Being through (absolute) knowledge. Indeed, Hegel's aim from the beginning of the *Phenomenology*, Heidegger claims, is "to point out the Absolute in its advent with us" (HCE: 31). Being or the Absolute is always already present to us as that within which knowledge in general is possible: "This closeness to us (*parousia*) is in itself already the way in which the light of truth, the Absolute itself, casts its ray upon us" (HCE: 30). The Absolute *is* as the ontological horizon of Being through and in which beings are disclosed to us in their intelligible presence.

Heidegger then shifts emphasis in his reading of Hegel in order to develop a thesis that is crucial for his overall project: namely, that in the course of modern philosophy, from Descartes to Hegel and Nietzsche, the meaning of Being is increasingly *subjectivized* until it is in danger of being obliterated altogether (this is the ambiguous challenge posed by the essence of modern technology or what Heidegger will call "enframing" or *Gestell*). This thesis of the *subjectivization of Being* is a central feature of Heidegger's reading of the *Phenomenology* and of Hegel's role in the completion of Western metaphysics. For Heidegger, modern philosophy since Descartes has taken possession of the terrain of subjectivity as "the self-certainty of mental representation in respect of itself and what it represents" (HCE: 33). Hegel in turn takes complete possession of the terrain of subjectivity by transforming it into self-knowing and self-willing spirit. According to Heidegger, philosophy becomes "Science" (*Wissenschaft*) in the absolute metaphysics of Hegel precisely because "it draws its meaning from the nature of the subject's self-certainty which knows itself as unconditional" (*ibid.*). Philosophical science is thus the completion of the Cartesian project of a self-grounding knowledge that has its absolute foundation in the unconditional self-certainty of the knowing subject.

At this point Heidegger articulates the explicit connection between the metaphysics of *subjectness* (resting on the subject–object relation) and the modern understanding of Being as *technology*. It is important to note that by "technology" or "technics" Heidegger does not simply mean machines or technical devices; rather, "technology" is Heidegger's term for the way reality shows up in modernity in an essentially technologically disclosed way – that is, beings are increasingly revealed exclusively as a stock or reserve of resources available for ordering and use. Now, as we have seen, Heidegger argues that the modern understanding of Being discloses itself as *subjectness*. This process of the subjectivization of Being culminates with Hegelian absolute spirit and Nietzschean will to power; it determines modernity, moreover, as the epoch of *technology*. Heidegger thus links his critique of metaphysics with his confrontation with modernity: the critical encounter with technology as completed subject-metaphysics is announced through Hegel's interpretation of Being as subjectness. In Heidegger's terms:

Within subjectness, every being becomes as such an object. . . .
If, in the era of subjectness [i.e., modernity] that is the ground
of the nature of technology, nature *qua* Being is placed in
opposition to consciousness, then this nature is only the sum
total of particular beings taken as the object of that modern
technological objectification which lays hands indiscrim-
inately on the estate of things and men.   (HCE: 132)

What is striking in this analysis is its proximity to Hegel's *own* critique
of the metaphysics of reflection. Hegel too criticizes the practical effects
of the principle of abstract identity and universality that results in the
obliteration of particularity, the domination of otherness, and the
reification of subjectivity. As we saw earlier, similar claims were made
by Lukács, but from a Hegelian-Marxist perspective. Modernity, for
Heidegger, is the era of subjectness and hence of technological
objectification. Modern technology is itself nothing other than natural
consciousness that "accomplishes the unlimited self-assuring feasib-
ility of everything that is through the irresistible transformation of
everything into an object for a subject" (HCE: 62–3). The modern
age of technology is the age of objectifying, instrumental rationality,
the unlimited transformation of beings into resources available for
use.

In this sense, Heidegger's critical remarks have affinities with Hegel's
own critical confrontation with modern metaphysics of the subject
and its moral–practical implications. The fundamental difference
between Hegel and Heidegger turns on their respective relationships
to modernity. Hegel provides a critical legitimation of modernity,
which includes a critique of the anachronistic character of subject-
metaphysics (like Cartesianism) within "fully developed" modernity.
This contrasts with Heidegger's assertion that modern subject-
metaphysics provides the basis for the nihilism of the age of modern
technology.

Heidegger's "Cartesian" reading of Hegel and deconstructive critique of the Hegelian metaphysics of the subject became a decisive reference point for French poststructuralist philosophers such as Deleuze,
Foucault and Derrida. In this respect, what I have been calling the
"existentialist" strain of Hegelian and anti-Hegelian thought would
play a key role in the French appropriation of Hegel. On the other
hand, the Marxist strain of Hegelianism would also prove very important for the Frankfurt school critical theorists, who remained sharply
opposed to Heidegger, primarily for political reasons (Heidegger's

disastrous engagement with National Socialism during the 1930s). As we shall see, Lukács's critique of the process of reification within (capitalist) modernity provided the inspiration for Adorno's appropriation of Hegel. Adorno also developed a sharp critique of Heidegger's thought while at the same time elaborating a critique of metaphysics that paralleled aspects of Heidegger's thinking. It is this intriguing crossover between German and French Hegelianism and anti-Hegelianism that we shall explore in the following chapters.

Summary of key points

Lukács's critique of Hegel

- Lukács mounted an influential Marxist–humanist critique of Hegel's apparent conflation of two key concepts: *objectification* and *alienation*.
- Hegel identifies "objectification" with the specific sense of "alienation" characteristic of modernity: the result was to "ontologize" alienation as an inescapable feature of human activity.

Reification: Lukács's critique of modernity

- Lukács's project was to return Marxism to its philosophical roots (in Hegel), but also to develop a Marxist *ideology critique* of how modern philosophy (including Hegel) reflected the phenomenon of *reification*.
- "Reification" is the process by which social relations, individual subjectivity and forms of cultural expression are rendered "thing-like" under conditions of commodity capitalism.

Heidegger's criticism of Hegel on time and spirit

- Hegel's concept of time, according to Heidegger, is "the most radical way in which the vulgar understanding of time has been given form conceptually".
- Yet Hegel fails to see that the "logical" conception of time that he presents presupposes a more originary phenomenological account of temporality.

Heidegger's reading of Hegel's Phenomenology

- The confrontation between Hegel and Heidegger concerns *the problematic of finitude*, the "crossover" between the Hegelian project of thinking the infinity of spirit, and the Heideggerian project of thinking the finitude of Being.

Heidegger on self-consciousness

- Heidegger presents a "Cartesian" reading of Hegel, situating Hegel in the wake of Descartes's attempt to locate a secure foundation for knowledge in the self-certainty of thinking subject.
- Heidegger's "Cartesian–Fichtean" approach, however, overlooks the role of *intersubjective recognition*, as well as the *historicity* of self-conscious spirit.

Hegel's concept of experience

- Heidegger's reading of Hegel develops the thesis that in the course of modern philosophy the meaning of Being is increasingly *subjectivized*.
- Hegel provides a critical legitimation of modernity, including a critique of the anachronistic character of subject-metaphysics; by contrast, Heidegger asserts that subject-metaphysics culminates in the nihilism of technological modernity.

four

Enlightenment, domination and non-identity: Adorno's negative dialectics

Like other varieties of Hegelian thought, what I am calling "German Hegelianism" is characterized by a selective appropriation of certain concepts or themes, notably the concepts of *alienation* and *reification*. In this chapter and in Chapter 5 I shall explore the ways in which the German tradition of critical theory – from Theodor Adorno to Jürgen Habermas and Axel Honneth – appropriated key elements of Hegel's thought, while at the same time submitting the system of Hegelian metaphysics to various forms of critique. As we shall see, Hegel's critical justification of modernity, his "dialectical method", and elements of his philosophy of history, all played a significant role in the development of Frankfurt school critical theory as well as being central targets of its critique. This chapter will focus on how critical theorists Theodor Adorno (1903–69) and Max Horkheimer (1895–1973) transformed these Hegelian concepts into their own radical critique of modern reason and the domination effects of consumer culture. Their transformation of the Lukácsian concept of reification enabled Adorno and Horkheimer to present a powerful critical diagnosis of the dangers posed by the rule of *instrumental* or *subjective* rationality in modernity ("instrumental" in the sense of employing reason as a means to achieving a given end, and "subjective" in the sense of subjectively chosen ends, above all, self-preservation). It also allowed Adorno to point to ways in which the dominance of calculative "identity thinking" could be overcome through recourse to the aesthetic experience of avant-garde art and the critical form of "non-identity" thinking. Indeed, Adorno's later project of thinking a *negative dialectics* – a dialectic no

longer oriented towards conceptual closure, unity or universality –
is one of many attempts by post-Hegelian European philosophers to
rethink Hegelian dialectics, as we shall see later in the cases of Merleau-
Ponty, Deleuze and Derrida.

Enlightenment, myth and the fate of reason

The oscillation between existentialist and Marxist currents that we
shall track later in French Hegelianism can also be discerned, in a more
attenuated way, in Theodor Adorno's work. Adorno's complex philosophical project combined a Romantic–existentialist suspicion of the
universal and emphasis on the singularity of the individual, with a
Marxist critique of the destructive effects of commodity capitalism on
the possibility of freedom in the modern world. Indeed, we might
describe Adorno's thought as an "anti-Hegelian Hegelianism": a project
that appropriated elements of Hegelian dialectics, while also taking it
to exemplify the kind of "identity thinking" that needed to be overcome.

This complex appropriation of Hegel's thought, moreover, was
also evident in Lukács, who moved from a Romantic–existentialist
perspective in his youth to an explicitly Hegelian-Marxist position
(although he later repudiated his most famous book, *History and Class
Consciousness*, as insufficiently "materialist"). Both Lukács and Adorno
remained indebted, in different ways, to what they took to be the
Hegelian method of "dialectical" thinking. Lukács gave Hegelian
dialectics a *Marxist–materialist* interpretation, using it to diagnose the
way the conceptual oppositions marking modern philosophy from
Descartes to Kant and Hegel (subject and object, freedom and nature,
universal and particular, and so on) were conceptual reflections of
"reified" oppositions in social reality generated by the dominance
of the commodity form. Adorno, by contrast, subverted Hegelian
dialectics into what he called "negative dialectics": a dialectical thinking that refused totality, closure, or sublation into any "higher" conceptual unity, or the subordination of sensuous particularity to
conceptual universality. As we shall see, Adorno's negative dialectics
presented an open yet critical kind of thinking that sought to preserve
the multiform aspects of what he called "non-identity" – sensuous
particularity, the body, nature, difference and so on – that tend to be
obliterated by conceptual thinking.

In the *Dialectic of Enlightenment*, Adorno and Horkheimer developed
a dialectical account of the relationship between enlightenment reason

and mythology in modernity. Their aim was to show how mythology is already a form of enlightenment, while enlightenment reason – with its faith in technical progress, the "rational" organization of society, and the domination over nature – is our modern mythology. As we shall see, Horkheimer and Adorno drew upon, but also transformed, Hegel's dialectic between enlightenment and faith (outlined in the *Phenomenology of Spirit*). They argued that the roots of domination and of the increasing dissolution of autonomous subjectivity evident in modernity were to be found in the rise of instrumental rationality coupled with the dominance of the commodity form as a structuring principle of modern culture. In doing so, Adorno and Horkheimer attempted to diagnose the metaphysical and historical grounds of the catastrophes of twentieth-century history (Nazism, the Holocaust, the emergence of both "hard" and "soft" totalitarianism). Such a bleak diagnosis, however, also raised the question of what kinds of critical resistance or possibilities for social transformation might be available in what they claimed has become a totally reified, "administered society". In what follows, I shall explore Adorno and Horkheimer's quasi-Hegelian account of the dialectic of enlightenment, outlining its effects on morality and culture, while also examining some of the difficulties raised by what some critics (such as Habermas) have called their "totalizing critique" of modernity.

The dialectic of enlightenment

As its subtitle suggests, the *Dialectic of Enlightenment: Philosophical Fragments*, consists of a series of fragmentary philosophical essays that together comprise a radical critique of modern Western culture. Written during the darkest period of World War II, and published as an "underground text" only in 1947, the book's project is summarized by the authors – a "message in a bottle" for future generations – as a response to the burning question facing all twentieth-century political thinkers: "why humanity, instead of entering a truly human state, is sinking into a new kind of barbarism" (DE: xiv). The *Dialectic of Enlightenment*, Adorno and Horkheimer remark, is an enquiry into "the self-destruction of enlightenment" (DE: xvi), a radical self-examination of enlightenment culture and the domineering rule of *instrumental reason* in modernity. Instrumental rationality, let us recall, refers to the deploying of rationality as a means to satisfy certain ends, which Adorno also called *subjective* rationality, in the sense of rationality submitted to the satisfaction of the desire for self-preservation. Their thesis is that both the social and cultural lifeworld and the psychic processes of individual subject-formation have become penetrated by the processes of reification. Reason in the substantive and moral–practical sense has been restricted and deformed into the narrow and contentless form of *instrumental rationality*. This is the dominant form of rationality in modernity expressed in areas as diverse as modern science and technology, modern economy and bureaucracy, advertising and mass culture.

The first essay in the *Dialectic of Enlightenment*, "The Concept of Enlightenment", develops two basic theses: that myth is already enlightenment; and that enlightenment reverts to mythology. This intertwining of enlightenment and myth is analysed from Greek mythic culture to the instrumentalist culture of modernity. Far from opposing the nihilism of modern reason to the tragic wisdom of the Greeks (as Nietzsche did, for example), Adorno and Horkheimer argue that the roots of enlightenment reason are to be found in the emergence of mythic thought. By privileging instrumental rationality over sensuous nature and social freedom, enlightenment culture reverts to a mythic faith in the social and economic machinery of power. Blind faith in the forces of technical efficiency, in technological mastery, the economic market and commodity culture comprise our contemporary forms of societal irrationality.

As with Lukács, Adorno and Horkheimer take up sociologist Max Weber's idea that the processes of societal and cultural *rationalization*, which were supposed to enhance our freedom by extending the formality, calculability and predictability of social practices and institutions, end up destroying our subjective freedom and imprisoning us within an "iron cage" of reason. They then seek to demonstrate these theses further in two long excursus: one on the epic narrative of Odysseus, interpreted as an account of the prehistory of the modern alienated subject; the other on the relation between Kant, de Sade and Nietzsche, which demonstrates the moral nihilism implicit within enlightenment culture; how enlightenment reason, pursued to its extreme conclusion, reverts to (amoral) terror.

What links both these excursus with the essay on enlightenment and myth is the problem of the *domination of nature*: how the development of modern instrumental rationality, directed towards the mastery of *external nature* through science and technology, has also resulted in the domination of our own *internal nature* – sensuousness, affectivity and desire – within a thoroughly reified "administered society". The fate of art in modernity is then considered in Adorno and Horkheimer's famous, and much misunderstood, essay, "The Culture Industry: Enlightenment as Mass Deception". In summary form, Adorno and Horkheimer argue in the latter that the dissolution of social experience brought about by the dominance of *identity thinking* (and underlying this, of the commodity form) undermines the modernist faith that the creative power of art could overcome social reification. On the contrary, the regression of modernist art into commodified entertainment and ideological distraction degrades its critical power, promoting a fetishising of technique, and a resigned affirmation of the prevailing social, cultural and political powers. The *Dialectic of Enlightenment* then concludes with an essay entitled "Elements of Anti-Semitism", which sketches a philosophical prehistory of anti-Semitism and an analysis of the psychological and social roots of the reversion of European civilization to racist violence and nihilistic destruction during World War II.

I would like to focus here on three themes in Adorno and Horkheimer's critique of modernity: (a) the intertwining of enlightenment and myth; (b) the domination of nature through instrumental reason; and (c) the implications of the collapse of autonomous art into commodity culture. All these themes are related, primarily by the thesis that modernity has failed to achieve the enlightenment project of freedom and autonomy because it has restricted reason to *instrumental reason*, whether as science and technology or as commodity culture; and that this instrumental reason has dominated inner and outer nature, whether understood as natural environment or as sensuous appearance, as sensuous embodiment or as unconscious desire. Now it is significant that Adorno and Horkheimer's *negative* critique of Western modernity, the "dark side" of enlightenment reason and culture, was supposed "to prepare a positive concept of enlightenment which liberates it from its entanglement in blind domination" (DE: xviii). Unfortunately, this *positive* conception of non-instrumental reason, what Adorno called an aesthetic thinking of *non-identity*, is missing from the *Dialectic of Enlightenment*. It remains a torso, a fragmentary critique of enlightenment rationality that nonetheless anticipates many themes associated with poststructuralism.

The intertwining of enlightenment and myth

Adorno and Horkheimer's account of the relation between enlightenment reason and mythic thought has striking affinities with Hegel's analysis of the relationship between enlightenment and faith in the *Phenomenology of Spirit*. In the latter, Hegel showed that, although enlightenment reason criticized religious faith, indicating its failure to accord with the precepts of rational knowing, reason could not offer anything substantial to replace it. Instead, reason reverted to the very dogmatism that it criticized in religion; for the enlightenment endorsed a blind faith in a narrowly construed form of instrumental rationality. The result of this empty and formal conception of reason, directed towards mastering nature but empty of ethical and social content, was to elevate *utility* to the highest value of enlightenment culture. Utilitarianism is thus the "truth" of the Enlightenment, which means it is that which also shows up the falsity or inadequacy of its claims to rationality. Worse still, this empty rationality can be readily linked with domination and terror (Hegel analyses in the *Phenomenology* the relationship between "absolute freedom" and political violence in the case of the French Revolution and Jacobinist Terror, which he took to be a "necessary" stage in the development of modern bourgeois society). Because enlightenment reason privileges an empty universality over concrete particularity, it ends up sanctioning violence against particularity in the name of a false universal.

Adorno and Horkheimer's "dialectics" is also drawn from Hegel, but is transformed, in Adorno's "negative dialectics", into an open-ended movement that refuses integration into a "higher unity" (cf. deconstruction). For Hegel, we recall, the historical and cultural experience of consciousness is *dialectical* in the sense of constituting a movement or becoming in which consciousness reverts into its opposite, and then transforms itself by incorporating its opposite at a more complex level. Reason sets itself over against its opposite (non-reason as nature, faith and so on), but finds that this opposition breaks down or self-destructs; it therefore incorporates its opposite into itself, transforming itself into something more complex, both differentiated and unified at a higher level of complexity.

Adorno and Horkheimer take over this Hegelian idea of dialectic but eliminate from it the element of closure and teleological development (namely, that a more complex, rational form of consciousness progressively emerges in history). The movement of Western history, they claim, has not revealed a progress of rationality and realization of freedom. Rather, the project of enlightenment has self-destructed; as Adorno and Horkheimer assert, "the wholly enlightened earth is radiant with triumphant calamity" (DE: 1). The Enlightenment's mastery over nature has resulted not in freedom but in a destructive domination over nature and in the societal reification of modern subjects. Enlightenment reason transforms itself into its opposite: a mythic belief in the reifying forces of instrumental reason.

The domination of nature

The concept of enlightenment reason that Adorno and Horkheimer analyse emerges with the scientific revolution, and with the transition from feudal to capitalist societies. The project of liberating humankind from enslavement to nature was to be guaranteed by the development of scientific rationality and technical expertise, by moral universalism as a rational basis for morality, and by the creation of wealth through industrial development and market economies. The early modern philosopher Francis Bacon is cited for his account of *knowledge as power*: knowledge directed towards the control over natural forces that are to be harnessed for human benefit (DE: 1). The development of scientific rationality, moreover, begins a process that sociologist Max Weber called the "disenchantment of nature": the animistic view of nature as a harmonious living whole gives way, in the modern period, to a scientific understanding of nature as inert matter governed by physical laws. This disenchantment of nature, Adorno and Horkheimer observe, "means the extirpation of animism" (DE: 2). At the same time, this process of rationalization, for Weber, not only disenchants nature but also makes more complex the structure of modern societies into distinct spheres of institutional practice (science, morality and legality, art), each with its own distinctive logic, procedures and norms.

The mythic view of the world, by contrast, regards nature as a dynamic unity, animated by spirits, cosmic energies, divine forces; nature comprises a living, infinite whole of which human beings are finite, connected parts. The modern scientific disenchantment of nature results in the alienation of human beings from the natural world; nature now becomes inert matter to be rationally mastered, harnessed and controlled, a mere source of natural resources to be used for productive purposes. In their analysis, the instrumental rationality of the Enlightenment, whose essence is *technology*, is directed towards one fundamental aim: *domination over nature*, both external and internal to us, which also implies *domination over others*. "What human beings seek to learn from nature is how to use it to dominate wholly both it and other human beings" (DE: 2). The Enlightenment thus raises "computation and utility" into absolute values (an idea we already found in Hegel's analysis of the Enlightenment); whatever is not useful or computable, even in the spheres of art and morality, is deemed irrelevant or irrational. The Enlightenment tests the claims of aesthetic and moral experience by the standards of rational utility, calculability and profitability, and condemns whatever does not conform to these narrow criteria. As Adorno and Horkheimer remark, somewhat hyperbolically, "Enlightenment is totalitarian" (DE: 4).

Whatever we make of this claim, their point is that the Enlightenment progressively destroys its own myths, be they religious, social or political. Much like Nietzsche's analysis of nihilism, their argument is that "the myths which fell victim to the Enlightenment were themselves its products" (DE: 5). Every myth is an attempt to narrate events as arising from an origin (DE: 8). As such, the myths challenged by the Enlightenment were legitimating narratives that sought to interpret both natural and social reality in order to better control them. The most powerful myth, in this sense, is that of enlightenment reason itself: the myth of human emancipation through the rational control and instrumental mastery over nature. Enlightenment rationality is the secular myth of mastering nature through its scientific disenchantment and technical control. "Myth becomes enlightenment and nature mere objectivity. Human beings purchase the increase of their power with estrangement from that over which it is exerted" (DE: 6). The tragedy of enlightenment is that it enables us to gain power over that which supposedly enslaves us, yet further enslaves us in the process of granting us this power of rational control.

What of the other side of the story? Myth is usually held up as the opposite of enlightenment reason. The mythic world-view animates nature; nature is understood as a living whole of divine forces that can, however, be influenced by the rituals of magic and religion. What motivates mythic thought is fear of the unknown, the fear of the natural and supernatural, the erratic, unpredictable, ineluctable forces of nature. So appeasing the gods through magic, ritual and sacrifice becomes a way of influencing nature and overcoming the fear of the unknowable and the unmasterable. In this sense, however, myth shares the same impulse and aim of enlightenment reason: to master, or at least influence, the forces of nature. The mythic interpretation of nature already uses symbol, metaphor and representation to name, classify and narrate the origin of the world. The most graphic instance of the logic of substitution in mythic thought is the practice of *sacrifice*: the sacrificed animal or human individual is a *representative* of the tribe or community, an *exemplary* representative of power and purity *in general* (sacred animal or virgin), who is offered as a gift to the gods to appease them or to offer thanks. In exchange for the sacrifice the community receives protection or favour from the gods against the vicissitudes of fortune and fate.

Adorno and Horkheimer point out here that this practice involves a relation of conceptual generality (the particular sacrificial victim as representing a general concept or universal) and a relation of exchange (the human sacrifice offered is repaid by good fortune from the gods). In this sense, myth is already a form of *rationalization*: a way of attempting to influence or control nature by means of a narrative of origins and a practice of substitution and exchange. Once organized into the symbolic form of religion and ritual, *myth is already a form of enlightenment*: a rational attempt to overcome the fear of unknown natural forces through a conceptual representation of, and practical intervention upon, the world. The magic rituals of the shaman or priest, the ritual sacrifices of the tribal community, anticipate the experimental method of modern science: the sacrifice of faith on the altar of scientific truth for the prize of technical and social control over all of human life. For Adorno and Horkheimer, this is precisely the intertwining of enlightenment and myth: "Mythology itself sets in motion the endless process of enlightenment by which, with ineluctable necessity, every definite theoretical view is subjected to the annihilating criticism that it is only a belief, until even the concepts of mind [*Geist*], truth and, indeed, of enlightenment itself have been reduced to animistic magic" (DE: 7).

Since both myth and enlightenment are rooted in the desire to instrumentally control and dominate nature, they are mutually inter-twined in their social and historical development. "Just as myths already entail enlightenment, with every step enlightenment entangles itself more deeply in mythology" (DE: 8). Mythology of enlightenment has become a faith in technology, progress and efficiency that will deliver us social and individual freedom. The historical result, however, has been the opposite: a deformation of reason and desire, the privile-ging of a false identity between human beings and the world, between mind and body, subject and object, where the deep structures of sub-jectivity have been penetrated by the reifying processes of instrumental rationalization. The course of Western cultural history, then, has been a narrative of the entanglement of myth, domination and labour. The Enlightenment sought social freedom through the domination over nature, but reverted to a mythology that socially dominated the natural within human beings.

What is this colonization of subjectivity by instrumental reason? Adorno and Horkheimer point to the *subject–object relation* as the key element that characterizes the dominance of modern instrumental rationality. The modern cognitive subject, confronted by a world of manipulable objects, strives to order its experience by controlling nature, both external and internal to the subject, through goal-directed rationality and practical action. The subject–object schema is based, they argue, on relations of *social domination* that comprise the source of our conceptual understanding (namely, binary oppositions) and forms of linguistic expression. These conceptual and linguistic forms of domination in turn legitimate and foster societal domination and oppression; taken together, they result in the exclusion of whatever fails to conform to the instrumentalist paradigm of reason. Only the emergence of autonomous art and aesthetic experience presented an alternative space for all that falls outside the rule of instrumental reason. Modern art provided a refuge for the thought of non-identity, and thus an image or experience of the freedom that is foreclosed within modern social reality. Modern art itself, however, is far from free of demands of instrumental rationality, which brings us to the problem of the industrialization and commodification of art.

Art as commodity: the culture industry

In the chapter on the "Culture Industry: Enlightenment as Mass Deception", Adorno and Horkheimer apply their thesis concerning the will to domination inherent in instrumental rationality to the domain of autonomous art and modern culture. The critical potentials of modern art have been neutralized, they argue, through the transformation of art into an organized system of mass cultural commodity production. This is what Adorno and Horkheimer call the "culture industry": an organized economic, industrial and social system embracing not only films, radio, mass media and television but also architecture, sport, leisure industries, tourism, marketing and advertising. Their application of the idea of the dialectic of enlightenment to modern mass culture has been enormously influential, but also frequently misunderstood in the development of cultural studies, media theory and philosophies of culture.

What is their critique of the culture industry? Their basic argument is that the industrialization of cultural production and the correlated replacement of aesthetic autonomy with the values of instrumental and social utility have resulted in the commodification of art. This industrialization and commodification have led to the reduction of autonomous art to entertainment, advertising or propaganda. The possibility of non-identity – the moment of freedom, otherness and experimentation – is thus destroyed; modern art, whether high or low, elite or popular, must now conform to the requirements of various cultural markets. The critical function of culture becomes integrated into the circuits of commodity production and consumption. The commodification of art promotes the autonomy of advertising and marketing, the "social realism" of contemporary consumer culture. The critical potential of art disappears in favour of the satisfaction of consumer desire; these manipulated desires then feed back into the system of the production of cultural commodities: "The culture industry endlessly cheats its consumers out of what it endlessly promises" (DE: 111).

What are the effects of commodity culture on our social experience? For Adorno and Horkheimer, the manipulation of subjective desires serves the ends of cultural industries: it is a technique of social control leading to cultural resignation rather than social resistance. The enlightening power of aesthetic culture reverts to the myth of happiness through cultural consumerism and commodified entertainment. The questioning of our historical actuality degenerates into a resignatory affirmation of the prevailing social powers. The pseudo-liberation promised by the culture industry is coupled with an evacuation of genuine subjectivity, its degeneration into reified *pseudo-individuality*, the end of the autonomous individual: "The most intimate reactions of human beings have become so entirely reified, even to themselves, that the idea of anything peculiar to them survives only in extreme abstraction: personality means hardly more than dazzling white teeth and freedom from body odor and emotions" (DE: 136). Critical theory, as Adorno and Horkheimer bleakly conclude, can do little more than keep the spirit of critical reflection alive in the face of these all-encompassing forces of reification. For the cultural industry has all but liquidated the autonomous individual, thanks to the manipulation of subjective desire at the most basic level of (unconscious) individual subject-formation.

Three problems for Adorno and Horkheimer

1. *The concept of domination.* A central claim of the *Dialectic of Enlightenment* is that enlightenment reason becomes complicit with domination over internal and external nature. But what concept of

"domination" do Adorno and Horkheimer invoke here? It covers everything from concept–formation and linguistic communication; coercion of individual action through social, economic and political control; mastery of natural environment through scientific and technological intervention; to repression of sensuous desires and drives in the constitution of a socialized ego. But how can all of these intellectual, social, and technological processes be called "domination" without some account of how they are supposed to interconnect? Moreover, how can these all be explained via the one overarching principle: the "domination of nature"?

2. *The "totalizing" critique of reason.* For Adorno and Horkheimer, the rule of instrumental reason stymies any viable form of practical or political intervention. As modern subjects, we are colonized by the oppressive forces of instrumental rationality and societal reification. How do Adorno and Horkheimer account, then, for their own critical intervention (and our understanding of it) if all modern subjects are really as dominated as they suggest? Adorno and Horkheimer's answer is that enlightenment culture must be able to accommodate reflection on its own "recidivist elements" – those elements in modernity that revert to mythic faith in instrumentality and that legitimate the forces of domination – in order to *remain true* to the principles of enlightenment thought and thus to keep open the promise of social freedom. But this critical reflection presupposes that the culture of modernity – its language, practices and radical potentials – has not been entirely reified by the forces of instrumental rationality. Adorno and Horkheimer's totalizing critique of enlightenment reason cannot be coherently maintained, for the very intelligibility of their critique presupposes that modern subjects are not utterly reified in the manner that they assert. Their account of cultural modernity is decidedly *one-sided*, as Hegel would say, ignoring the positive aspects of modernization and rationalization processes in modernity.

3. *The ambivalence of cultural commodification.* A parallel with Adorno's colleague and friend Walter Benjamin (1892–1940) is instructive here. For Benjamin, merely criticizing mass culture and the masses' consumption of its products does not explain why these products are desired in the first place. Adorno and Horkheimer assume that the subjective desires of modern individuals can be completely manipulated, but this implies that they are already beyond the reach

of critical thought and reflection. Instead, we should investigate what the hidden truth potential of mass and popular culture might be; we should interpret the desires for freedom, pleasure and happiness, however distorted or stereotypical, encrypted in cultural commodities, and try instead to critically awaken these desires and direct them towards emancipatory ends. Such, at least, was Benjamin's wager concerning the political potential of the new media technologies of photography and cinema, which dissolved the traditional work of art, divesting it of its unique "aura" and the artist of his/her privileged authority. On the one hand, mass culture is a cynical and destructive industry geared entirely towards profit and the manipulation of consumer desire at the expense of aesthetic and moral autonomy; but on the other, it also has encrypted critical potentials that can be deciphered and unleashed, communicative possibilities that run counter to the homogenizing tendencies of the culture industries.

Adorno's Hegel and negative dialectics

In response to this dire diagnosis, Adorno later developed an anti-totalizing "negative dialectics" that attempted to break free of the grip of "identity thinking". His philosophical aim was to do justice to the "non-identical" – the non-conceptualizable singularity of individuals in their multifarious aspects – a move that anticipates Derrida's deconstruction of metaphysics. At the same time, Adorno also presented a more nuanced reading of Hegel's thought (in his *Three Studies on Hegel*), which again resonates with deconstructivist approaches that find in Hegel both the epitome of identitarian metaphysics *and* the harbinger of a "post-metaphysical" thinking of difference.

Adorno's relation to Hegel is thus interesting and ambiguous. On the one hand, Hegel is the representative *par excellence* of identity thinking, reducing sensuous particularity to universality, non-identity to conceptual unity. As the great thinker of the philosophical "system", Hegel provides an exemplary conceptual model expressing the allegedly "totalitarian" drive of modern rationality and its manifestation in social domination. On the other hand, Hegel is also presented as a thinker whose "system" is shot through with moments of non-identity, sensuous particularity, metaphorical ambiguity and so on. In a virtuoso display of interpretation, Adorno's *Three Studies on Hegel* brings out the elements of poetic sensuousness, historical contingency, of conceptual and rhetorical ambiguity in Hegel's texts – in a word, the aspect of *non-identity* sequestered within Hegel's own system. Even Hegel's legendary obscurity is defended on philosophical grounds: it is an attempt to articulate the complexity of modern experience with a language that seeks to speculatively mimic its objects, refusing the Cartesian will to clarity of philosophical discourse modelled on mathematics and the exact sciences (Adorno 1993: 102 ff.). All the ambiguities and contingencies – the aspect of non-identity – inherent in our social experience must be acknowledged and reflected in the form of conceptual thought.

Adorno's negative dialectics, in brief, is an attempt to avoid some of the impasses afflicting any "totalizing critique" of modernity (a critique that, in construing reason as instrumental reason in the service of the domination of nature, leaves no space for any account of how emancipatory practice might be possible). It presents dialectics without *Aufhebung*, without the subordination of sensuous particularity to the unity of conceptual thought. How to do this philosophically? What Adorno is attempting can be illustrated more precisely by drawing a parallel with modernist art, for example cubism, which attempted, in pictorial terms, to present things in the multiplicity of all their sensuous facets (Brunkhorst 1999: 2–3). In this respect, non-identity thinking, like cubism, can be considered an *anti-representationalist* mode of thought: the open-ended, non-coercive presenting of the singular object in the plurality of its various aspects (a perspective he also describes as restoring the *primacy of the object* over the subject). Adorno thus turns to exemplars of non-identity thinking, for example, modernist writers, artists and composers (Beckett, Klee, Schoenberg) whose radically "negativistic", anti-representationalist artworks present an indirect symbol of freedom – a moment of emancipated non-identity – that is suppressed within the reified world of modernity.

The basic problem Adorno is responding to is how to find a different way of thinking the relationship between *concept and intuition*. If we remember Kant's dictum that concepts without intuitions are empty, while intuitions without concepts are blind, we can gain a sense of the problem that concerned Adorno. How to do justice to the moment of *non-identity* (roughly, what Kant called intuition), the ineffable singularity of things? Art is one way that non-identity can be preserved: aesthetic theories from Kant to Adorno have tried, in various ways, to give an account of this relationship in the experience of artistic works.

Yet Adorno maintains that even in aesthetics, conceptual discourse has dominated its object – namely art and its expression of non-identity – such that philosophy maintains its position of epistemic and metaphysical superiority over art.

Negative dialectics eschews conceptual subordination of the non-identical by remaining sensitive to the sensuous, subjective and contingent aspects of meaning that remain irreducibly linked with conceptual discourse. As J. M. Bernstein argues, Adorno's project can be regarded as an attempt to open up the suppressed forms of *material inference* that are essential to the constitution of meaning and discursive communication, but which rationalist conceptions of meaning tend to suppress in favour of formal relations of inference, such as we find in formal logic and conceptual analysis (2004: 39 ff.). Adorno's aim, on the contrary, was to find a way of doing philosophy that would invoke the dimension of non-identity by negative means: critically dissolving philosophical concepts by showing their dependence upon non-conceptual forms of meaning (metaphor, imagery, aphorism and so on). Only in this way, Adorno maintained, could a space of *freedom* be maintained – like that made possible by modernist art – that resisted the will to identity, systematicity and instrumental control so characteristic of modern thought, culture and society.

In many ways, Adorno's retreat into aesthetic theory and the difficult thought of negative dialectics represented a certain withdrawal from Marxist political philosophy and from political practice in the more concrete sense. His aesthetic critique of modernity – an aesthetic theory that would show how avant-garde art, in its refusal of conventions of representation, implicitly criticizes the unfree character of modern social experience – might be regarded as a sophisticated form of political pessimism, a symptom of Adorno's refusal to countenance the possibility of social transformation. Indeed, Adorno has been criticized for ending up in a negativistic, self-undermining impasse that avoids recognizing the positive institutional achievements of modernity that ought to be preserved in any rational form of critique (see Habermas 1987; Honneth 1995). At the same time, Adorno's aesthetic writings and discussions of music, art and literature present an aesthetic theory of modernism that would also serve as a critical philosophy of freedom responding to a cultural and social modernity under siege. The aesthetic critique of modernity – the way art can disclose forms of truth concerning our social experience – remains a powerful way of understanding our historical reality.

The impasses of Adorno's negative dialectics

Adorno's appropriation of Hegelian themes – his anti-Hegelian Hegelianism – was counterbalanced by his critique of Hegelian thought, which he claimed represented the highpoint of systematic identity thinking within Western philosophy. Adorno's response to this, however, raised many questions of its own. In conclusion, I want to discuss briefly some of the "aporias" (from the Greek, meaning "uncrossable path" or "impasse") of Adorno's dialectic of enlightenment and his negative dialectics, and to indicate how the next generation of Frankfurt school critical theorists, namely Jürgen Habermas and Axel Honneth, responded to Adorno by invoking either a communicative paradigm of reason (Habermas), or an intersubjectivist theory of recognition (Honneth).

The first difficulty has already been touched upon, namely the problem of engaging in a totalizing critique of instrumental reason, while appealing to philosophical–conceptual discourse in order to make this critique. This criticism can be summarized in a remark: surely not all conceptualization and discourse can be construed as a veiled form of domination! Adorno's critique of Hegelian dialectics, as suppressing the moment of non-identity intrinsic to conceptual thought, ignores crucial distinctions in what we might take reason to encompass. Chief among these is the failure to distinguish between the narrow subject–object framework of instrumental reason, and the complex intersubjectively mediated forms of linguistic–communicative and practical–moral reason. For all his radical criticisms of identity thinking, Adorno remained wedded to the subject–object framework of representation – albeit exploded from within in the name of liberating the object in its sensuous non-identity – that Hegel was among the first to seriously challenge.

Moreover, the aporetic character of negative dialectics suggests the need to move to a different conception of reason: one capable of sustaining non-identity, of preserving contingency, sensuousness and the openness to the future that Adorno claimed are becoming increasingly obliterated in modernity. As we shall see in Chapter 5, this move is made by the next generation of critical theorists, Habermas and Honneth. Habermas challenges Adorno's "totalizing" critique of reason: How does such a critique justify its own normative status if all forms of rational discourse are afflicted by reification and complicity with domination? The totalizing critique of reason undermines its own normative basis, since it relies on a form of normativity that is excluded by the theory itself. Habermas thus criticizes the impasses generated by Adorno's use of the subject–object paradigm of consciousness, which should therefore be superseded by an intersubjective conception of reason (what Habermas calls "communicative reason"). This "inter-subjectivist" turn also meant reappraising the role of Hegel within the history of modern philosophy: far from being an exemplar of the metaphysics of identity, Hegel was the first to develop such an *intersubjectivist* conception of reason.

This criticism is developed further by Habermas's heir, Axel Honneth. Drawing upon but also departing from Habermas, Honneth argued that Adorno's commitment to a conception of reason as instrumental reason in the service of self-preservation forecloses the realm of *the social* – of normatively oriented interactions between social agents – from his philosophy of history and social philosophy. Adorno's emphasis on the fundamental role of reason as oriented towards the domination of nature means that the role of the social as an *intersubjectively* mediated sphere of normatively guided interactions recedes to the background. Hence, for Honneth, the Habermasian communicative–theoretic turn needs to be supplemented by a neo-Hegelian account of intersubjectivity mediated by social psychology. For Honneth, this implies that we must return to the classic Hegelian theme of the "struggle for recognition" in order to develop an intersubjectivist theory of recognition with viable ethical, social and political dimensions.

Summary of key points

Adorno and Horkheimer's Dialectic of Enlightenment

- Adorno and Horkheimer's thesis is that both the social and cultural lifeworld of social and cultural experience and the psychic processes involved in individual subject-formation have become penetrated by processes of *reification*.
- Reason in modernity has been reduced to *instrumental rationality*, expressed in areas as diverse as modern science and technology, modern economy and bureaucracy, advertising and mass culture.
- Enlightenment reason, which was to liberate us from a mythic belief in blind forces of nature, transforms itself into a mythic belief in the reifying forces of instrumental reason in modern society.

Culture industry

- The industrialization of cultural production has resulted in the commodification of art, reducing it to entertainment, advertising or propaganda.
- The construction of consumer desires and manipulation of cultural forces serve the ends of cultural industries and enhance the techniques of social control.
- The pseudo-liberation promised by the culture industry is coupled with the end of autonomous subjectivity, its degeneration into reified *pseudo-individuality*.

Adorno's negative dialectics

- Adorno's anti-totalizing "negative dialectics" attempts to do justice to the "*non-identical*": the non-conceptualizable singularity of the individual in its multifarious aspects.
- Adorno's negative dialectics is one without *Aufhebung* – without the subordination of sensuous particularity to the unity of conceptual thought.
- Adorno invoked the dimension of non-identity by critically dissolving philosophical concepts and showing their dependence upon non-conceptual forms of meaning.

Criticisms of Adorno's negative dialectics

- How does such a critique of instrumental reason justify its own normative status if all forms of rational discourse are afflicted by reification?
- The totalizing critique of reason undermines its own normative basis, since it tacitly relies on a form of normativity that is excluded by the theory itself.
- Habermas and Honneth criticize Adorno's use of the subject–object paradigm of consciousness, which should be superseded by an intersubjectivist conception of reason.

five

Modernity, intersubjectivity and recognition: Habermas and Honneth

In Chapter 4 we examined Adorno's anti-Hegelian Hegelianism, his attempt to construct a negative dialectic that would rescue the dimension of non-identity threatened by the rule of instrumental rationality. This chapter continues the exploration of what I am calling "German Hegelianism", which engaged in a critique of Hegelian thought but also retained a sense of its relevance for the problem of modernity and the theory of intersubjectivity. In this chapter I explore the appropriation of Hegelian themes in the work of the next generation of Frankfurt school critical theorists, Jürgen Habermas and Axel Honneth. In particular, I shall focus on their approach to the *critique of modernity*, their Hegelian-inspired turn to a theory of *intersubjectivity*, and their renewed emphasis on the concept of *mutual recognition* as an essential feature of social identity. In doing so, I hope to show that Hegelian thought remains a source of philosophical inspiration for comprehending our experience of modernity and for renewing contemporary social and political philosophy.

One of the most striking differences between French and German Hegelianism is the emphasis given to the philosophical problem of modernity. As we shall see in Part III, French Hegelians frequently turned to Hegel's master/slave dialectic and his account of the unhappy or alienated consciousness; but there is rarely any mention of Hegel in relation to what Habermas has called the "philosophical discourse of modernity". Indeed, French Hegelianism placed far more emphasis on the problem of alienated subjectivity and with the new generation of the 1960s turned sharply against Hegelian conceptions of the subject. This difference between French and German Hegelianism has had important consequences for the debate over the historical fate of the modern "project of enlightenment". Indeed, much of the antagonism between recent French and German philosophy – more precisely between French poststructuralism and German critical theory – derives from fundamentally different assessments of the significance of Hegel's legacy, in particular the related problems of modernity and intersubjectivity.

Hegel as philosopher of modernity

Hegel's contributions to the philosophical *critique of modernity* have played a profound role in recent social philosophy. This is evident in debates over whether the enlightenment project of achieving rational freedom is still a viable, albeit unfinished, project; or whether we have entered a postmodern epoch that has left behind modernist conceptions of the subject, of knowledge, and of history. As Habermas points out, Hegel is one of the first thinkers to develop a distinctively philosophical concept of modernity. Admittedly, "modernity" is a concept with a wide range of meanings. Habermas defines it as having distinct *historical, social, cultural* and *political senses*. In its *historical* sense, "modernity" defines the epoch of Western history since 1500, marked by the discovery of the New World, the Reformation, the Enlightenment and the French Revolution. Drawing on Weber's work on modern rationalization, "modernity" has a *societal* sense referring to the development of market economies and bureaucratic state organization as relatively independent spheres operating according to criteria of efficiency and productivity. Again drawing on Weber, "modernity" has a *cultural meaning*, referring to processes of cultural rationalization defined by the development of autonomous "value spheres" of science, law/morality and art, each with their own forms of knowledge and practice. Finally, "modernity" has a *political meaning*, defined by a history of revolutionary changes followed by the development of relatively stable and self-reforming constitutional and democratic forms of government.

At the same time, however, "modernity" also indicates a historical condition in which there is a strong social and cultural recognition of the "right of subjectivity". This was Hegel's term to describe the modern condition in which *individual freedom as rational autonomy* is taken to be the highest principle of rational legitimation. Indeed, modernity means that there needs to be a *rational legitimation* of theoretical and moral norms (tradition is not enough); that social and cultural practices should be ways for individuals to express their autonomy (rather than being a constraint on it); and that political institutions gain legitimacy only by being the rational expression of collective decision-making processes (constitutional democracy is the distinctively modern form of politics). The rational autonomy of the individual is the fundamental principle of social and political institutions; the latter derive their legitimacy from their recognition and promotion of this autonomy, but also provide the conditions that enable such autonomy to develop in the first place.

"Modernity" thus refers to the project of creating and sustaining individual and collective forms of life capable of being grounded in, and legitimated by, the free exercise of rational autonomy. According to Habermas, Hegel was the first among modern philosophers to recognize that modernity had become a philosophical problem: he was the first to investigate modernity's need for a self-generated normativity detached from any received body of traditions, institutions or practices of the past (PDM: 16); the first to reflect explicitly upon modernity's need for "self-reassurance" (*Selbstvergewisserung*) regarding this self-generated normativity (*ibid.*). For modernity no longer borrows the criteria for its institutions and way of life from the past; rather, "it has to create its normativity out of itself" (PDM: 7). For Hegel, the task of philosophy is that "of grasping *its own* time – and for him that means the modern age – in thought" (PDM: 16). In this way, philosophy contributes to the self-understanding of modernity in its social, cultural and political aspects, while offering a critical perspective on its problems and deficiencies; it can even offer alternative visions of life more in keeping with modernity's claims to articulate rational freedom. Habermas clearly endorses this broadly "Hegelian" (but also Marxist) conception of modernity; but it is also a model that has been rejected by critics who dispute that philosophy should provide modernity with critical legitimation.

The modern age, moreover, is marked universally and legitimated "by a structure of self-relation that [Hegel] calls subjectivity" (PDM: 16). Subjectivity does not refer here to personal experience, feeling, beliefs and so on; rather, it is a structure of *self-relation* that can be applied at psychological, social, cultural and institutional levels. The four primary aspects of "subjectivity" in this Hegelian sense can be listed as follows:

1. *Individualism*, whereby the individual subject can pursue its own particular self-chosen ends.
2. *The right to criticism*, whereby whatever claims, norms or practices make a claim upon rational individuals should reveal themselves as entitled to recognition according to reasons.
3. *Autonomy of action*, whereby individuals are held responsible for their self-determined actions.
4. *Philosophical idealism*, whereby modern philosophy, with Kant, "grasps the self-conscious (or self-knowing) Idea" (PDM: 17).

From a historical point of view, the principle of subjectivity was established with the Reformation (which made the subject's own insight central to religious faith), the Enlightenment (which valorized the rational power of judgement of every human being) and the French Revolution (which defended the liberty, equality and dignity of every individual). Within the realm of culture, the principle of subjectivity finds expression in modern *science*, which "disenchants nature at the same time that it liberates the knowing subject"; in modern *morality*, whose concepts presuppose the power of individuals to exercise rational judgement and an ability to self-legislate; finally, subjectivity finds expression in modern art, particularly with Romanticism, which gives full voice to forms of subjective inwardness, irony, creative imagination and aesthetic experimentation (PDM: 17–18).

In sum, modernity is the condition in which "religious life, state, and society as well as science, morality, and art are transformed into just so many embodiments of the principle of subjectivity" (PDM: 18). From the abstract subjectivity of Descartes's *cogito ergo sum* to Kant's principle of pure self-consciousness, modern philosophy grasps this condition through the structure of subjectivity as a self-relation that is also a *self-reflection*: the self-relating, knowing subject "which bends back upon itself as object, in order to grasp itself as in a mirror image – literally in a 'speculative' way" (*ibid.*). Kant brings this conception of subjectivity to its most complete philosophical expression in his three critiques. Reason, the source of judgement for all validity claims, is divided up into moments or aspects (theoretical and practical reason) such that it now has only a *formal*, rather than substantive, unity. In accordance with the Kantian self-critique of reason, the practices of science, morality and art become institutionally differentiated as distinct spheres of activity and of knowing, each with its own criteria for the adjudication of validity claims (PDM: 19). Hegel thus grasps the

Kantian philosophy as reflecting the essential features of modernity as governed by the principle of subjectivity.

By criticizing the key philosophical oppositions marking the Kantian project – nature and spirit, sensibility and understanding, understanding and reason, theoretical and practical reason, finite and infinite, knowledge and faith – Hegel at the same time attempted to respond to the diremptions or divisions of modernity itself. As Habermas puts it, "The critique of subjective idealism is at the same time a critique of modernity; only in this way can the latter secure its concept and thereby assume its own stability" (PDM: 21). Hegel carries out this task, argues Habermas, but at the cost of exhausting the critical impulse that first motivated it. From the start, Hegel's desire to construct a philosophy of unification – from the earliest Romantic sketch of a new mythology of reason through the early theological writings to the *Phenomenology* and the mature *Encyclopaedia*-system – prompted him to embrace the reconciling power of reason in its expanded dialectical sense. The mature Hegel developed a conception of absolute knowledge that enabled him to go beyond "the products of the enlightenment – Romantic art, rational religion, and bourgeois society" – but in doing so, Habermas argues, Hegel abandoned the critical intuitions of his youthful period. To put the point bluntly: "Hegel has ultimately to deny to the self-understanding of modernity the possibility of a critique of modernity" (PDM: 22). In positing reason as capable of overcoming all oppositions, and finding reconciliation with the rationality of historical actuality, Hegel provides modernity with an excessive self-reassurance that effectively neutralizes his earlier critique.

Labour and interaction

Early in his career, Habermas turned to Hegel's pre-*Phenomenology* Jena texts in order to indicate the "path not taken" in modern thought: that of *communicative reason*. He thereby uncovered the traces of a theory of intersubjectivity in Hegel's account of labour and interaction, which became obliterated, Habermas argued, in the mature Hegel's reversion to a "philosophy of consciousness" and monological metaphysics of spirit. Habermas's essay, "Labour and Interaction: Remarks on Hegel's Jena *Philosophy of Mind*" (from the early 1960s) is fascinating in this respect. Here we find the seeds of Habermas's own project of a theory of communicative rationality, an alternative paradigm from the prevailing subject–object model of the "philosophy of conscious-ness". Habermas's key move in this essay is to focus on Hegel's discussion of *interaction*: the moment of *intersubjectivity* in Hegel's account of the constitution of self-consciousness, which shifts from a monological to a *dialogical* conception of the subject. Although we can find the beginnings of a theory of intersubjective recognition in Hegel's Jena texts, Habermas claims that the mature Hegel reverts to the subject–object paradigm that obliterates the dimension of *communicative action*. This line of criticism will reappear in Axel Honneth's neo-Hegelian theory of recognition.

Habermas commences his discussion by pointing out how Hegel presents us with a critique of Kant's account of the "I" as formal universality, and Fichte's conception of the "I" as self-positing activity. (We should note that Fichte is the first philosopher to introduce the theme of recognition – the summons or *Aufforderung* from the Other that calls me toward my free self-development – as a constitutive element of the formation of the "I".) The subject, for Hegel, is not only the formal universal, the empty "I" in general, but also this singular individual, the "I" as "me", so to speak. The subject links and unites the universal "I" (the "I" as any linguistic, rational subject) with the individualized "I" (the "I" as *this singular* individual). This identity between universal and singular is what provides the basis for Hegel's conception of the "I" as subject.

This social subject, however, is not only defined by the relationship between universal and singular. The subject as a social being comes to a sense of its own self-identity in the context of communicative inter-action with others. This is evident in the case of moral relationships between human subjects. The young Hegel uses the example of *love* as a form of reconciliation in which identity and difference are brought together without subordinating one partner to the other. In the Jena lectures, Hegel explains that love is a form of "knowing (*Erkennen*) which recognizes itself in the other" (TP: 147). Love as a movement achieves a reconciliation regarding a pre-existing conflict, but it does not yet articulate an account of how ego-identity is based upon relations of reciprocal recognition. Recognition, in Hegel's sense, is a *dialogical* relation between opposing subjects that is at once theoretical and practical; recognition is a movement that signifies both "a relation of logic *and* of the praxis of life" (*ibid.*). This is evident in the dialectic of the moral relationship, which Hegel develops in terms of the *struggle for recognition* (*ibid.*). In this dialectic, Habermas emphasizes how communication relations can be distorted by force, yet these distorted forms of communication nonetheless exercise practical force upon interacting subjects. The dialectical movement is from distorted communication to mutual recognition; the distorting force of miscommunication is negated such that it establishes "the noncompulsory character of dialogic recognition of oneself in the other" (TP: 148). Love is one such instance of a dialogical relation that overcomes distorted forms of communication.

At the same time, Hegel talks of crime as a form of distorted dialogical relationship in which an individual cuts himself off from the context of communal life and asserts his own particular interest against this communal whole. This dialectical movement is what Hegel calls the "causality of fate", the clearest example of which is the process of punishment striking the criminal who attacks the moral totality. The criminal act undermines the intersubjective conditions of shared communal life, namely non-compulsory communication and mutual satisfaction of interests, which sets in motion the process of punishment which the criminal experiences as a destiny striking back at him (TP: 148). The criminal is confronted with the power of deficient life and thus feels guilt; he suffers under the power of the repressed and lost life that he himself has provoked, and experiences the deficiency he has caused in his own life by repressing others (*ibid.*). This turning away from others, and the community more generally, is experienced as his own alienation from himself. This alienation can be overcome only when the criminal, longing for what he has lost, identifies himself with the alien power that he once attacked and thereby becomes reconciled with the social totality (*ibid.*). With this dialectic of crime and punishment, of reconciliation and forgiveness, the opposition and separation from the moral totality is overcome: "in the dialogic relationship of recognizing oneself in the other, they experience the common basis of their existence" (*ibid.*).

In Hegel's Jena lectures, this struggle for recognition takes place in the sphere of primitive property relations, where it occurs as a life-and-death struggle (TP: 149). Each protagonist engages in an "abstract" self-assertion (asserting its independence merely as a property-owner), but in this process each undergoes the same process of self-alienation that we observed above. In their struggle, each protagonist takes the other as an opponent and risks his life against the other; in doing so, however, each also cuts himself off from intersubjective dependence that sustains his own life. Destiny as the "causality of fate" avenges itself here too, not as the punishment of crime but rather as the destruction of the self-asserting individuals that try to sever themselves from the moral totality (*ibid.*). These subjects in mortal conflict are not reconciled with each other, in the sense of immediately recognizing themselves in the other, but they do attain a new basis of mutual recognition – an understanding that "the identity of the 'I' is possible solely by means of the identity of the other, who in turn depends on my recognition, and who recognizes me" (*ibid.*).

What emerges out of this experience is an acknowledgement of the mutual dependence of subjects attempting to satisfy their own interests. At a deeper level, such subjects learn that their subjectivity is dependent upon the unity between universal and singular. This Hegelian conception of the "I" as the identity of the universal and the singular, an identity grounded upon mutual recognition, is thus opposed to Kant's monological conception of the "I": "the abstract unity of pure consciousness relating solely to itself" (TP: 149–50). Indeed, Hegel will draw radical consequences from his analysis of the dialectical movement of mutual recognition, from his insight that this experience of this dialectic derives from the *practical*, rather than the theoretical, sphere.

The problems afflicting Kant's moral philosophy, in Habermas's reading of Hegel, stem from the neglect of the *intersubjective* and *communicative* dimensions of reason; Kant's monological conception of moral decision abstracts away from the intersubjective basis of moral interaction. For Hegel, to abstract from this communicative context means that the unity between universal and singular can never be achieved; the individual remains forever subordinated to the (abstract) universal. In Hegel's words: "As long as laws are the highest 'instance' . . . the individual must be sacrificed to the universal, i.e., it must be killed" (TP: 152). This is an important point because Hegel has frequently been accused, mostly by his existentialist critics, of forgetting the individual and subsuming the singular under the universal. Habermas shows that this stereotypical criticism of Hegel cannot be valid. On the contrary, Hegel is among the first to point to the interplay of universal and singular within the constitution of subjectivity, and to argue that subjectivity is fundamentally *intersubjectivity*, that is, grounded in mutual recognition. Hegel's innovation is to show that the constitution of the "I" is not a matter of the self-reflection of the solitary "I" but involves rather the communicative agreement of opposing subjects (*ibid.*).

What is decisive, moreover, is the *medium* in which the identity between universal and singular is formed. Hegel identifies three such media: *social interaction* (family), *language* and *labour*. Communicative action is thus introduced as the medium for the formative process of self-conscious spirit, even though Hegel does not fully develop all these as intersubjective media founded in mutual recognition. Habermas's criticism of Hegel will be that not only the interpersonal interactions within the family, but also *language* and *labour* have to be understood as intersubjective phenomena, grounded in rational communication.

Language: Hegel's account of language, at least in these Jena lectures, is not yet fully communicative or intersubjective. Rather, it is representational and instrumentalist; predicated, according to Habermas, on the image of the solitary individual who employs symbols in confronting nature and giving names to things. The pre-representational level of immediate perception or intuition is "still animalistic" in the sense of not yet being part of the intersubjective, symbolic realm. Indeed, Hegel's description of the pre-linguistic realm of images is suggestive of the Freudian unconscious. Hegel even speaks of "the nighttime production of the representational faculty of imagination, of the fluid and not yet organized realm of images" (TP: 153). For Hegel, it is only within language that the subject–object distinction begins to emerge, that consciousness and the being of nature begin to separate for consciousness: the pre-representational realm of images is translated into representational realm of names (*ibid.*). The birth of memory also happens thanks to the subject's entry into the symbolic realm of language, which allows it to make distinctions and at the same recognize what it has distinguished (*ibid.*). Naming and memory are the two sides of the symbolic power of representation.

Labour: The other essential category for the constitution of the "I" is labour, which Hegel describes as "that specific mode of satisfying drives that extinguishes existing spirit from nature" (*ibid.*). Just as language breaks the immediacy of perception, so too does labour break the immediacy of our desires, postponing immediate satisfaction and arresting the process of drive-satisfaction. And like the symbol, *the tool* is also something that has a general aspect as against the ephemeral moments of perception and desire. The experience of the worker is given permanence in the tool, which permits the repeated working over of our natural environment: "instruments retain the rules according to which the domination of natural processes can be repeated at will" (TP: 154). The human being, subjected to the causality of nature, makes itself into a thing through labour; the subject transmits the energies of human effort to the object that is laboured upon in accordance with the laws of nature by which the subject too is dominated (*ibid.*). The subject is able to deposit its subjectivity, its practical experience, into tools and techniques; it thus overcomes its subjection to nature, via tools, in order to let nature, so to speak, work for the subject (*ibid.*).

Tools or technical artefacts more generally thus provide a medium in which spirit attains existence. The labouring subject, having reified itself into an object, acquires as an unintended product of its labour the knowledge of technical rules that enable it to return back to itself from out its reification (TP: 155). Whereas language gave rise to the name-giving subject, labour gives birth to the cunning or artful consciousness (*ibid.*). The cunning consciousness controls nature by means of tools, by the exercise of instrumental rationality; it turns its subordination *by* nature into a subordination *of* nature. The speaking subject, on the contrary, is penetrated by symbolic representations that shape its perceiving consciousness; it remains dominated by the objectivity of language. By contrast, the cunning consciousness, in exercising instrumental rationality, is able to control nature and thus extends its subjective freedom over the power of objective spirit (*ibid.*). This technical control of nature allows the subject to regain the freedom that it alienated in reifying itself, since it is able to expand the possibilities for satisfying its various needs. The process of labour, which began as a curtailing of desire, ends in a socially mediated satisfaction of desire – "the satisfaction in commodities produced for consumption, and in the retroactively changed interpretation of the needs themselves" (*ibid.*).

Hegel thus identifies the *naming*, *cunning* and *recognizing* consciousnesses as three distinct dialectical patterns of the formation of subjectivity. The question is how these three self-formative processes are united: do they cohere with each other as related patterns of the formation of consciousness? Habermas argues that these three dialectical self-formative processes can be unified according to an *intersubjectivist* paradigm of *communicative action*. The transmission of cultural tradition depends upon language as communicative action, for only the intersubjective meanings drawn from a linguistic–cultural tradition enable speakers to reciprocally orient themselves through complementary expectations of behaviour (TP: 158). Instrumental action is also embedded in the context of communicative interaction. Social labour along with the solitary use of tools is dependent upon the use of symbols, for the moderation of animalistic drives presupposes a distanced attitude to identifiable objects that in turn depends upon linguistic consciousness (TP: 159). The question of the interrelation between labour and interaction, Habermas observes, is more interesting, if less obvious (*ibid.*). Norms of communicative interaction are independent of instrumental action; technical rules, on the other hand, are elaborated under conditions of linguistic communication but have nothing in common with rules of communicative interaction (*ibid.*). Instrumental action is governed by the causality of nature rather than the causality of destiny. For this reason, interaction cannot be reduced to labour, since communicative norms are at odds with the norms of instrumental action (*ibid.*).

For all that, Hegel does not reduce interaction to labour, nor elevate labour as a version of interaction (TP: 161). Instead, Hegel links labour and interaction "under the viewpoint of emancipation from the forces of external as well as internal nature" (*ibid.*). The importance of this idea for Adorno's critique of instrumental reason, directed towards the domination of nature in the interests of self-preservation, should be clear. In the end, Habermas argues that Hegel abandons this intersubjectivist account of the three dialectical patterns of consciousness (family, language, labour) in favour of a monological conception of spirit that comes to know itself and relate to itself historically. In doing so, Hegel gains a good deal in theoretical clarity, allowing him to construct a progressive dialectic of connected shapes of consciousness; but this gain involves the reversion to a philosophy of consciousness in which the subject–object identity takes precedence over communicative interaction. The philosophical task, Habermas argues, is thus to retrieve the intersubjectivist moment in Hegel's work, and thereby restore the model of communicative action to the centre of our understanding of subjectivity.

Honneth's neo-Hegelian theory of recognition

Habermas's thesis – that the seeds of an intersubjectivist theory of recognition are to be found in the young Hegel's Jena texts – provides the basis for Axel Honneth's appropriation of Hegelian thought in his own theory of recognition. Whereas Habermas argued for a theory of communicative action, Honneth presents the theory of *recognition* as a way of overcoming the deficiencies of the subject–object philosophy of consciousness. To put it briefly, Habermas's theory of communicative action has two key elements: it posits universal formal–pragmatic conditions of achieving mutual linguistic understanding; and it holds to a sharp distinction between the communicatively structured lifeworld of everyday practices, and the functionalist economic and bureaucratic systems that increasingly "colonize" the lifeworld. To this we should add the normative theory of *discourse ethics* that Habermas also develops: his communicative–theoretic version of the Kantian categorical imperative. Habermasian discourse ethics provides a formal procedure for ensuring the rational resolution of conflicts in validity claims, one that rests upon the universalist principle of recognizing the right of every subject to the unconstrained communication of their interests.

Honneth argues, however, that Habermas's theory of communicative action is prone to a Kantian-style formalism that abstracts from the forms of intersubjective recognition that make possible the self-identity of communicative agents and that structure the institutions and practices of social life. In this sense, Honneth repeats Hegel's criticism of Kant but directs it at his own teacher. For Honneth, Habermasian communicative rationality and its normative ideal of undistorted communication cannot really explain the experiences of suffering and moral injury that motivate subordinated subjects to demand justice or develop social movements. Rather, these experiences of social disrespect and suffering constitute forms of *misrecognition* that potentially disrupt or damage the forms of self-relation essential for the development of autonomous subjectivity. Hence the need to renew the Hegelian theory of intersubjectivity, now recast in empirical, non-metaphysical terms through the social psychology of G. H. Mead.

Honneth's reading of the Jena Hegel

According to Honneth's account in *The Struggle for Recognition*, modern social philosophy begins once ancient conceptions of the communal good life give way to the modern emphasis on the struggle for self-preservation. For Machiavelli and for Hobbes, the struggle for self-preservation provides the foundation for a rational conception of society and politics no longer bound to a conception of the human good or to the ethical life of the *polis*. The result is a political philosophy oriented towards controlling the fundamental struggle for self-preservation through a contractual model of rational self-interest and mutual self-restraint. In both cases, however, the political task of keeping social conflict in check is achieved either through the suspension of normative constraints on the sovereign (Machiavelli), or else by substituting authoritarian rule for the liberal content of the social contract (Hobbes) (SR: 9–10). Hegel's innovation is to appropriate the model of social struggle while removing it from the dehistoricized framework of moral naturalism on the one hand, and the formalist framework of Kantian morality on the other. Instead, drawing upon the Aristotelian conception of communal human flourishing, and Fichte's account of the summoning by the Other that consolidates our self-identity, Hegel recasts this originary struggle as a *struggle for recognition* of one's independence.

Honneth then explores the novel conception of intersubjective recognition that Hegel develops in some of his early works (such as the 1802 essay on natural law, and *System of Ethical Life* [*System der Sittlichkeit*], with its fascinating account of the dialectical relationship between crime, law and the context of ethical life). Hegel's radical insight was to challenge the *atomistic* assumptions of social contract theories of sociality and political legitimacy. Indeed, both Hobbesian and Kantian conceptions of natural law presuppose the primacy of the isolated individual, whether as fearful and self-interested or as moral and disinterested (SR: 11–12). The problem with such a model is that it cannot account for *sociality* and so must try to construct the social out of an aggregate of pre-given individuals. For Hegel, then, the task was to criticize these conceptions of natural law and to develop an inter-subjectivist approach to the problem of social and political freedom: how to reconcile subjective freedom and particularity with the univer-sality of the rational political community.

Hegel rejected the "social contract" model of modern philosophy. As is well known, the latter posits a hypothetical "state of nature" inhab-ited by isolated individuals who secure their survival by agreeing to a social contract that institutes social life under shared norms. In its place, Hegel drew on both the Aristotelian conception of the *polis* as an ethical totality, and his earlier Romantic ideal of the reconciled society as "an ethically integrated community of free citizens" (SR: 12–13). Rather than relying on the moral convictions of individuals or on formal laws enforced by the state, Hegel chose the concept of *Sitten* (mores, customs) to articulate the way shared norms that enable the exercise of social freedom have to be embedded within a communal way of life (SR: 14). In order to advance beyond the classical and Romantic conceptions of community as "ethical life", Hegel incorpor-ated the system of property and law along with the insights of modern political economy into his conceptualization of modern forms of social existence. This combination of ethical life with economic processes provided the basis of what became Hegel's famous account of the sphere of *civil society*, which is distinguished both from the domestic sphere of the family and the political institutions of the state. But how should we explicate that form of social organization "whose ethical cohesion would lie in a form of solidarity based on the recognition of the individual freedom of all citizens" (*ibid.*)? Hegel's model of different forms of *mutual recognition*, as developed in his Jena lectures, is an attempt to answer this question.

To this end, Hegel draws on Fichte's conception of *recognition* as the reciprocal interaction between individuals (their mutual self-limiting action) that grounds the space of legal relations. Hegel then applies this modified concept of recognition to different forms of social interaction and communicative forms of life (SR: 16). Social relations are now understood as normative relationships of practical intersubjectivity "in which the movement of recognition guarantees the complementary agreement and thus the necessary mutuality of opposed subjects" (*ibid.*). This means that within the context of mutual recognition, subjects are always learning or revealing further aspects of their self-identity; hence they seek further recognition of more complex forms of their individuality. The result is a movement of recognition that provides a basis for ethical relationships between subjects, but which also necessarily involves conflicts and negations that must be resolved in more complex forms of intersubjective recognition (SR: 17). Here Hegel argues that the Hobbesian violent struggle for self-preservation is, rather, a conflictual, yet ethical, relationship that is oriented towards the "intersubjective recognition of dimensions of human individuality" (*ibid.*). Here we have in skeletal form the core of Hegel's celebrated account (in the *Phenomenology*) of the dialectical experience of consciousness as intersubjective spirit. With his reinterpretation of Hobbes's model as a struggle for recognition, Honneth contends, Hegel introduces a novel conception of social struggle in which "the practical conflict between subjects can be understood as an ethical moment in a movement occurring within a collective social life" (*ibid.*).

Love, sociality and the struggle for recognition

The most important insight that Honneth draws from Hegel concerns the fundamental role of mutual recognition in our becoming autonomous social and moral subjects. Hegel correctly identifies, according to Honneth, the three primary forms of intersubjective relationship: (1) experiencing *love* or intimacy within familial and interpersonal contexts; (2) having *rights* as a morally responsible agent within legal and moral contexts; and (3) attaining a sense of *solidarity* or belonging within the social community. To be sure, the mature Hegel moved away from this conception, developing a system of different forms of spirit grounded, according to Honneth (following Habermas), in the subject–object model of the philosophy of consciousness. Yet during his Jena period, Hegel emphasized these forms of primary recognition without integrating them into a coherent theory, which is what Honneth will attempt to do. His wager is that the foundations for a theory of recognition, updated through social psychology, are already present in the work of the young Hegel.

Hegel conceived of love as an interpersonal relationship of mutual recognition in which the "natural" individuality or uncultivated self is confirmed (rather than one's social role or contribution to the community). Even sexual relationships involve the reciprocity of knowing oneself in the other; in sexual relations, both subjects can recognize themselves in their partner, since each one desires to be desired by the other. In Hegel's view, sexuality thus represents "the first form of the unification of opposing subjects" (SR: 37). This Hegelian idea of desire as recognition – desire as the desire of the other's desire – will be developed further by Kojève, Lacan, and French psychoanalytic theory (see Butler 1988). This reciprocal knowing-oneself-in-the-other, however, can become a relationship of love only if the relationship becomes one of shared intimacy or intersubjective acknowledgement. This process of mutual recognition in turn presupposes that one has had the experience of being loved as a child, of being an utterly dependent being reliant on the love of a care-giver for meeting its basic needs.

For Honneth, Hegel's thesis can be generalized: the conditions ensuring the successful development of a subject's personal and social identity presuppose, in principle, "certain types of recognition from other subjects" (SR: 37). This goes beyond the common claim, also found in theories of socialization, that the formation of a subject's identity is supposed to depend upon the experience of intersubjective recognition. Rather, Hegel's deeper point is that an individual can only experience him- or herself as a certain type of person if he or she recognizes others too as being such and such a type of person (*ibid.*). If I fail to recognize my partner as, say, honest, then his or her reactions cannot give me the sense that I am recognized as honest either; this is because I deny him or her precisely the characteristic (honesty) that I desire the other, by his or her reactions, to attribute to me (SR: 38). In this sense, there is an obligatory reciprocity built into relations of intersubjective recognition.

Honneth thus draws the conclusion, which Hegel does not, that the experience of being loved "constitutes a necessary precondition for participation in the public life of a community" (*ibid.*). Love constitutes one of the emotional conditions of successful ego-development: it is only by feeling that one's particular needs and desires are recognized and affirmed that one can develop the basic sense of trust or self-confidence that gives one the capacity to participate, along with others, in what Habermas calls "political will formation" (*ibid.*). The idea is that recognition provides the means by which individuals are capable of becoming autonomous social agents and responsible political subjects. Love provides a hint, an anticipation, of ethical life; it constitutes the primary experiential context in which human beings acquire the capacity to engage in more complex forms of mutual recognition that make possible the unification of opposing or conflicting subjects.

Nonetheless, as Honneth points out, Hegel still has to clarify the distinction between love relationships and social bonds: the interpersonal bond of love cannot be equated with the intersubjective bonds constituting the social–ethical community. Although familial relations involve interpersonal relations of mutual recognition, these relations are clearly not at the same level as intersubjectively guaranteed rights within the normative framework of society (SR: 40). The field of love, of interpersonal relations within the family or between particular individuals, proves inadequate for the comprehension of the *universal intersubjective norms* that introduce the concept of the legal person (*ibid.*). Without this experience of *generalized* norms of interaction, spirit cannot conceive of itself as a person with legal rights (*ibid.*).

For this reason, Hegel turns again to the theme of a "struggle for recognition", now construed as a critique of the Hobbesian account of a "state of nature" as an original condition of "war of all against all" (*ibid.*). Indeed, according to Honneth, Hegel displaces the state of nature into a form of *primitive sociality*, where one family totality is pitted against another totality; the plurality of different families with their respective property generates a condition of emergent social relations of competition (SR: 40–41). Now, as is well known, social contract theories do not claim to present an empirically verifiable or historical instantiated condition with their fiction of the "state of nature". Rather they present a thought-experiment that aims to show how rational agents might be prompted to agree to abide by social and moral norms in order to secure their own self-preservation and enhance their welfare. Nonetheless, Hegel's central objection to the Hobbesian account of the "war of all against all" is that it struggles to explain how individuals arrive at an idea of intersubjective "rights and duties" in a quasi-social situation defined by relations of mutual competition (SR: 41). In standard accounts within the natural law tradition, the act of making the contract is "posited either as a demand of prudence (Hobbes) or as a postulate of morality (Kant, Fichte)" (*ibid.*). The transition to the social contract is thus presented as an intellectual, rational decision; a *theoretical* act that somehow enters into the pre-rational situation of the "state of nature"(*ibid.*).

By contrast, Hegel attempts to show that the constitution of the social contract – hence of legal relations – emerges as a *practical* (rather than theoretical) event; an empirical necessity "that necessarily follows from the initial social situation of the state of nature itself" (*ibid.*). The only way that we can account for how subjects can agree to resolve conflicts through law, as defined in the social contract, is to presuppose that such subjects are willing to reciprocally restrict their own spheres of liberty. And this in turn is possible because they are social beings engaged in intersubjective relations "that always already guarantee a minimal normative consensus in advance" – an *intersubjective normativity* that underlies even relations of social competition (SR: 42).

Hegel's critical point is that human subjects must have *already recognized each other* in order to be able even to enter the violent conflict that brings about the formation of the social contract. In Hegel's words, human beings as social beings are fundamentally defined by relations of recognition: "as recognizing, man is himself this movement, and this movement itself is what supersedes his natural state: he is recognition" (Hegel, *Jena Philosophy of Spirit*: 111, quoted in SR: 42). Human beings are always already mutually recognized; that is what makes possible the kind of rational interaction described in the fiction of the formation of the social contract. What Hobbes describes as the struggle for self-preservation that generates a condition of hostile competition, Hegel recasts as an account in which "the unilateral seizure of possessions are interpreted not as 'struggles for self-assertion' but as 'struggles for recognition'" (SR: 43).

The idea that intersubjective relations of recognition underlie social conflict provides the core of Honneth's theory of recognition as a way of conceptually analysing the "moral grammar" of such conflicts. Indeed, Hegel outlines the elements of an intersubjectivist account of the construction of the social world as "an ethical learning process" that leads, through various forms of the struggle for recognition, "to ever more demanding relationships of recognition" (SR: 62). Although Hegel's early work has the beginnings of an intersubjectivist theory of the social, Honneth claims that Hegel failed to take this logical turn to a conception of ethical life based on the theory of recognition. Instead, Hegel turns back emphatically towards the philosophy of consciousness, with a correlated turn in his political philosophy from an intersubjectivist model of the political to one based upon the self-relation of spirit. In the *Phenomenology of Spirit*, for example, the struggle for recognition is no longer the "moral force that drove the process of Spirit's socialization" but is confined, rather, to the function of the formation of self-consciousness through the master/slave dialectic (SR: 62). For Honneth, this reversion to the philosophy of consciousness marks the end of Hegel's intersubjectivist theory of recognition, blocking the development of a model of the "struggle for recognition" (SR: 63). Honneth will therefore develop those elements of Hegel's Jena lectures that are neglected in Hegel's mature political philosophy: the intersubjectivist concept of human identity; the distinction of various media of recognition; and the idea of a historically productive role for moral struggle (*ibid.*).

Ethics and politics of recognition

Honneth takes up these themes in the rest of *The Struggle for Recognition*, developing a post-metaphysical version of the Hegelian theory of recognition, which provides a theoretical framework for analysing the "moral grammar" of social conflicts. Drawing on the social psychology of George Herbert Mead (1863–1931), Honneth argues that the young Hegel, as we have seen, correctly identified the three crucial forms of self-relation that are constituted through intersubjective relations of mutual recognition. Within the sphere of *familial relations*, it is *love* that enables a basic sense of self-familiarity, trust or *self-confidence* to flourish; within the sphere of *rights* and *law*, recognition as a fully fledged participant in social and political institutions endows individuals, subjects and groups with a sense of social *self-esteem*; and within the sphere of *work and social interaction*, the recognition of an individual's worth and value to the community contributes to the development of a sense of *social solidarity*, of belonging within and being valued by a community of peers. Taken together, these forms of interpersonal and social recognition create the conditions necessary for the development of positive forms of practical self-relation, and thus make it possible for social agents to exercise their autonomous freedom within a social and political community.

These three spheres of mutual recognition (love, rights and social solidarity) with their corresponding forms of practical self-relation (basic self-confidence, moral self-respect and social self-esteem) provide a matrix in which one can account for the way in which failures of recognition in any of these spheres can generate disturbances in different aspects of the subject's basic personality structures. In this way, failures within any of these three spheres of recognition – misrecognition as social disrespect in the spheres of familial relations, legal rights and social contribution – constitute a form of *moral injury* motivating various kinds of social struggle. Drawing on empirical studies of social movements, Honneth points out that these struggles are generally defined by a core of moral normativity. They are not primarily about the allocation of resources or the defence of moral principles, but are motivated rather by a sense of moral indignation, the sense that one has been denied what is one's due, whether that is respect, honour, dignity or justice. Indeed, social struggles typically arise in situations that are experienced as *intolerable* by subjects who experience themselves as socially excluded, as subordinated, marginalized or stigmatized.

Misrecognition within the sphere of the family – the lack of affective bonding and loving contact with a primary carer, for example – can profoundly disrupt a person's sense of bodily and affective self-confidence, the expectation that one's basic needs and desires are valid and will be met by an other. Misrecognition in the sphere of moral and legal rights (as in the exclusion of individuals of a certain race or gender from full political participation) can disrupt the sense that one is acknowledged as an autonomous moral subject and social agent, and hence undermine one's (or one's community's) capacity to participate in public deliberation or political decision-making processes. Misrecognition in the sphere of social community – for example the devaluation of one's culture, way of life, sexuality, work and so on – can undermine the form of self-relation that Honneth describes as *social self-esteem* (which is not the same as personal self-esteem!). This experience of misrecognition corrodes a subject's or group's sense of self-identity and social agency by devaluing their individual contribution to the social community.

All these distinct forms of misrecognition are forms of disrespect that constitute different kinds of moral injury, or at least distinct forms of social disadvantage that ought in some way to be corrected. Subjects who experience such forms of misrecognition can react in a negative, even pathological, manner (which might involve different forms of psychic disturbance or social dysfunction); or, if circumstances are propitious, they can respond with a demand for recognition, organizing social movements demanding to have their claims to social inclusion and equal participation acknowledged. Honneth's theory of recognition thus attempts to find a way of explaining the origin and legitimacy of social movements that understand themselves as "struggles for recognition".

Hegel's original idea regarding the role of mutual recognition in the development of social identity has thus found a fruitful elaboration in both Habermas's and Honneth's work. From the theory of modernity to the ethics of recognition, Habermas and Honneth have productively developed Hegel's conception of the intersubjective conditions of the constitution of social agency. In this respect, they succeed in renewing the critical theory of modernity, and overcome some of the impasses facing Adorno's negative dialectics. Habermas's interest in Hegelian intersubjectivity and Honneth's more explicit appropriation of the Hegelian theme of recognition have proven very productive for theorizing intersubjectivity and developing a normative account of modernity. But does this critical theory approach deal adequately with the dimensions of singularity, finitude, negativity and difference that define the experience of modern subjectivity? Is Hegelian inter-subjectivity an adequate response to the claims of radical difference? To answer these questions we must turn to the rich tradition of French Hegelianism that has decisively shaped much twentieth-century French philosophy. Only then can we understand how these competing strains of Hegelianism – the contrast between the German emphasis on modernity and intersubjectivity, and the French focus on singularity and difference – constitute a conceptual matrix generating much contemporary "Continental" philosophy.

Summary of key points

Hegel as philosopher of modernity

- "Modernity" describes a historical condition in which there is a recognition of the *"right of subjectivity"*: *individual freedom as rational autonomy* is taken as the highest principle of rational legitimation.
- Hegel was the first, Habermas claims, to investigate the philosophical problem of modernity's need for a self-generated normativity detached from any received body of traditions, institutions or practices of the past.
- Hegel's critique of the dichotomies defining modern philosophy is also a critique of the dichotomies of modernity; for Habermas, Hegel's attempt to unify the divided character of reason blunts the force of his earlier critique of modernity.

Labour and interaction

- Habermas focuses on Hegel's discussion of *interaction*: the moment of *intersubjectivity* in Hegel's account of self-consciousness, which shifts from a monological to a *dialogical* conception of the subject.
- Hegel examines the identity between universal and singular in three distinct media: social interaction (family), language and labour. Communicative action is thus introduced as the medium for the formative process of self-conscious spirit.
- Habermas argues that Hegel later abandons this intersubjectivist account of the three dialectical patterns of consciousness (family, language, labour) in favour of a monological conception of spirit that comes to know itself historically.

Honneth's theory of recognition

- Habermas's thesis – that the seeds of an intersubjectivist theory of recognition are to be found in the young Hegel's Jena texts – provides the basis for Honneth's appropriation of Hegelian thought in his own theory of *recognition*.
- Hegel reinterprets Hobbes's model as a struggle for recognition, introducing a conception of social struggle in which "the practical conflict between subjects can be understood as an ethical moment . . . within a collective social life".
- Hegel identifies three primary forms of intersubjective relationship: *love* within familial contexts; having *rights* as a morally responsible agent within legal and moral contexts; and attaining a sense of *solidarity* with the social community.
- Failures within any of these three spheres of recognition – misrecognition in the spheres of familial relations, legal rights and social contribution – constitute a form of *moral injury* motivating various kinds of social struggle.

part III

French Hegelianism

six

French Hegelianism and its discontents:
Wahl, Hyppolite, Kojève

The importance of Hegelian themes and the critique of Hegelianism for modern French philosophy can hardly be overestimated. Having discussed the way German Hegelianism drew on Hegel to theorize modernity, intersubjectivity and recognition, I now turn to the rich tradition of French Hegelianism, which foregrounded the unhappy consciousness, the master/slave dialectic, and transformed Hegelian dialectics. In this chapter, I shall explore the work of some of the most significant French Hegelians, commencing with Jean Wahl (1888–1974) and Alexandre Koyré (1892–1964), who set the agenda for the more famous work of Jean Hyppolite and Alexandre Kojève, whose work in turn shaped the following generation of thinkers, including Sartre, de Beauvoir, Bataille, Lacan, Merleau-Ponty, even Deleuze and Derrida. The Hegelian theme of the alienated or "unhappy consciousness" proved decisive for these thinkers, since it was a figure that could express equally well the existential alienation of the human subject, or the historical and social alienation of the individual under modern capitalism. To this we must add Hegel's account of a struggle for recognition and the famous master/slave dialectic, both of which inspired a good deal of existentialist as well as Hegelian-Marxist thought. As I shall argue, it is the highly original interpretations of these key Hegelian themes that gave French Hegelianism its distinctive character as combining existentialist and Marxist motifs. Indeed, French Hegelianism can be understood, I suggest, as a sustained meditation on the fate of the alienated subject in modernity, a fate to be overcome either by an existentialist embracing of finitude or else a Marxist transformation of society.

A French Hegel

According to a well-known story, Hegel was virtually unknown in France until the extraordinary lecture course given by Russian émigré Alexandre Kojève at the Ecole Pratique des Hautes Etudes from 1933 to 1939, attended by such future luminaries as Georges Bataille, Maurice Merleau-Ponty, Jacques Lacan, even surrealist André Breton. Kojève's idiosyncratic, even violent reading of Hegel – combining Heideggerian and Marxist motifs – ignited the passion of a generation for Hegelian-Marxist thought, thus setting the stage for the flourishing of French Hegelianism and anti-Hegelianism from existentialism to poststructuralism (see Butler 1988; Descombes 1980; Roth 1988). While there is a degree of truth to the legend, the story of Hegelianism and its legacy in France is more complex than this picture suggests (see Baugh 2003). Standard accounts of French Hegelianism tend to jump directly to Kojève's dramatic lecture courses on Hegel in the 1930s (Descombes 1990; Butler 1988). As Baugh argues, however, this overlooks two key figures in the story of the French Hegelianism: Jean Wahl and Alexandre Koyré. In what follows I shall discuss the unhappy consciousness and its adventures from Wahl to Hyppolite, before turning to Kojève's celebrated account of the struggle for recognition and Hegel's master/slave dialectic.

Wahl's unhappy consciousness

As Bruce Baugh points out, Wahl's influential book from 1929, *Le malheur de la conscience dans la philosophie de Hegel*, was in many respects the primary stimulus for the twentieth-century renaissance of French Hegelianism. It introduced a theme that was to prove very significant for a number of philosophers emerging in the 1930s: the existential plight of the alienated or unhappy consciousness. Reacting against the earlier epistemological reading of Hegel centred on the *Encyclopaedia*, Wahl emphasized the theological–existential dimensions of Hegel's early theological writings and the *Phenomenology of Spirit*. From this point of view, the figure of the unhappy consciousness represented a fundamental existential condition of human beings as divided, self-alienated subjects. In this respect, Wahl presented a "pan-tragicist" view that focused primarily on the phenomenology, arguing that speculative logic could not overcome the tragic self-division that afflicts not only consciousness but also the Hegelian Concept (Baugh 2003: 19 ff.). Wahl thus developed an influential existentialist critique that Hegel's speculative conceptual system was unable to do justice to the singularity of individual existence: Hegel subsumed the individual under the unity of the universal and thereby eliminated the accidental, the contingent, and sensuous intuition. The mature Hegel was a philosopher striving after a unity that would reconcile all differences and oppositions; but this attempt to overcome all oppositions through a concrete universal would end up obliterating individuality.

Here we recognize one of the fundamental themes of twentieth-century French philosophy: the tension between *reason and its other*. From Wahl to Derrida and Deleuze, the concern was that an expanded Hegelian conception of reason would lead to a *domination of otherness*, a *reduction of the other to the same* (see Descombes 1980). This critique of Hegelian thought, emerging already with Wahl, thus links reason with repression. According to this critique, as Baugh vividly observes, "a reason that seeks to be all-inclusive falsifies reality by suppressing or repressing its 'other', much as a police state achieves a certain homogeneity by repressing dissidence" (2003: 12). Variations on this existentialist-inspired critique, which equates Hegel's striving for philosophical "totality" with the slide towards political "totalitarianism", would become a mainstay of the critical response to Hegelianism, including poststructuralist critiques.

Wahl is the first of the French readers of Hegel to give such a central role to the unhappy consciousness: a figure of alienated subjectivity that strives to overcome the pain of its self-contradictoriness. Philosophy itself, for Wahl, begins with the experience of alienation, of division and separation, and aims at achieving a unity in thought that reconciles all such oppositions, what Hegel elsewhere calls the "concrete universal". Hegel's Concept is a translation of this desire for organic unity in which particularity and universality are reconciled in speculative thought. Consciousness itself, Wahl maintains, is defined by this ever-present self-division and incessant striving for unity. Moreover, the experience of consciousness, as shown in the *Phenomenology*, is at bottom the experience of *negativity*: the power to negate each and any of its own determinations (I can always deny or withdraw from or alter any one of my attributions, qualities, roles). At the same time, however, consciousness also has the experience of how its attempts to achieve unity are constantly undermined (as Hegel depicts in the case of religious consciousness). Consciousness thus experiences the pain of its own disunity and self-division, its own void or negativity, which is expressed in the religious and Romantic intuition that life intrinsically lacks wholeness. The truth of Hegelian dialectics is therefore not the abstract unity of a purely conceptual reconciliation, but the restlessness of consciousness in its self-undermining search for unity with itself (whenever it tries to identify itself with one of its attributes, it finds itself confronted by its opposite).

In his later work, Wahl extends his criticism of Hegel's speculative solution to the problem of the unhappy consciousness (namely reconciliation through philosophical reason); for this "reconciliation" confuses a synthesis in thought with the real existential unity of the self (Baugh 2003: 33 ff.). Wahl's Kierkegaardian-inspired critique leads to his positing of an "existential empiricism", a philosophical pluralism that regards beings as contingent, relational, and independent of the constructs of abstract thought (*ibid.*: 37–8). This is evident in Wahl's short study of Anglo-American empiricism, *Les Philosophies pluralistes d'Angleterre et d'Amérique* (1920) – an important reference for Deleuze – in which he expounds a view of empiricism as affirming contingency and plurality, where individuals are no longer understood as internally related parts of a non-relational Absolute, but rather as singular individuals independent of the relations linking them. Such a view entails radical pluralism, along with philosophical realism; it affirms difference and individuality and thus acts as "a democratic, polytheistic, and anarchistic remedy for absolutism of all kinds" (Wahl 1920: 69–70; quoted in Baugh 2003: 38). Wahl's importance in this respect is to have introduced a number of themes that reappear in the 1960s with the French philosophy of difference: the Deleuzean concern with difference rooted in a transcendental empiricism, Levinas's positing of an absolutely transcendent Other as the ground of subjectivity, and the Derridian themes of *déchirement* (splitting), dispersal and dissemination (*ibid.*: 33–4).

Koyré and Hegelian time

Alexandre Koyré accepts much of this existentialist critique of Hegel, but rejects Wahl's Romantic emphasis on the young Hegel of alienation over the mature Hegel of the speculative system. Without the latter, Koyré observes, there is not much to distinguish Wahl's Hegel from

Romantic thinkers such as Friedrich Hölderlin and Novalis. Contra Wahl's emphasis on alienated subjectivity, Koyré questions whether we can take the unhappy consciousness to be the proper ground of Hegelian philosophy. Whereas Wahl took the Hegelian Concept to be an idealized expression of the self-dividing nature of consciousness, Koyré argued that the forms of self-division that Wahl identifies with the unhappy consciousness are to be found within the Hegelian Concept itself: "the unhappiness of human consciousness and the unhappiness of man is the sign, the symbol, of a rupture, an imbalance, an unhappiness at the very heart of Being" (quoted in Baugh 2003: 24). In a manner recalling Heidegger, Koyré claimed that the restlessness of the unhappy consciousness is rooted in the restlessness of being and the structure of human temporality. As Heidegger had analysed in *Being and Time*, in such temporality the future determines both the endurance of the past and the constitution of the present (*ibid.*: 24).

The impact of Husserlian phenomenology and Heidegger's analysis of human temporality becomes unmistakable here: human temporality – the temporality of *Dasein* or being-there – is always "ahead of itself" in the sense of being oriented by a projecting into the future in light of inherited meanings that disclose present possibilities for action. Koyré thus repeats a Hegelian phrase that will have a long career in French thought: that the human being is a being "who is what he is not and is not who he is" (cf. Hegel's *Encyclopaedia*, §258). Indeed, Koyré defines the "human reality" as "a being which is what it is not and is not what it is", a definition subsequently taken over by Kojève and then made famous by Sartre in *Being and Nothingness*. The phrase signifies that the human being is not a being defined by a fixed essence (we are not this or that identity) but rather one that is always acting, becoming, and hence transforming what he or she is (we are always becoming what we are). We are open temporal projects rather than fixed identities, in continuous becoming rather than static being, an idea that has returned in poststructuralist critiques of identity and subjectivity.

For Koyré, this phenomenological account of human temporality sheds light on the Hegelian understanding of time and spirit. Koyré's emphasis on human temporality is carried over to his account of Hegel's philosophy of history. Hegelian time is the human time of historical experience, of self-realization through historical action: a time of progressive self-development in which human beings consciously transform their world. Historical time is defined by continuous *self-transcendence*, an attempt to overcome present limitations for the sake of future possibilities to be realized through action. The fact that human reality is always self-transcending means that history can never come to an end: such a condition would mean extinguishing our human capacity for self-transcendence, condemning us to remain within the alienation of the Hegelian unhappy consciousness, without any hope of transcendence.

Hyppolite's Hegel: humanism, tragedy and being

Jean Hyppolite is undoubtedly one of the most important figures in the dissemination of Hegelian philosophy in France. Hyppolite's French translation of the *Phenomenology of Spirit* appeared between 1939 and 1941, while his magisterial commentary on the text (appearing in 1946) immediately had a profound impact on the French reception of Hegel. In presenting a counterpoint to Kojève's emphasis on the master/slave dialectic, Hyppolite attempted to steer a course between Wahl's existential reading of the unhappy consciousness and Koyré's affirmation of the future possibilities of historical transformation. Following the publication of Heidegger's famous "Letter on Humanism" (1947), however, Hyppolite adopted a more Heideggerian-inspired approach to language and Being. This is evident in his 1952 work *Logic and Existence*, which abandons the "humanist" Hegel of the *Phenomenology* and reinscribes Hegelian logic, now grasped as a "logic of sense", within a Heideggerian philosophy of language. In this section, I briefly discuss Hyppolite's emphasis on the centrality of the unhappy consciousness, his emphasis on the tragic but also affirmative dimension of history, and his shift from Hegelian humanism, centred on the power of the human subject to transform itself, to a more Heideggerian approach to the history of Being. These elements of Hyppolite's Hegelianism will help us understand the later questioning of Hegel carried out by Derrida, Foucault and Deleuze.

Hegelian humanism: between existentialism and Marxism

Hyppolite follows Wahl in making the unhappy consciousness the "fundamental theme" of Hegel's phenomenology (GS: 190). For Hyppolite, reading Hegel was a "revelation", his interest being sparked by Wahl's *Le Malheur de la conscience dans la philosophie Hegel* (1929), and Koyré's seminal essay, "Hegel à Iena" (1934). Hyppolite contributes a historicist and humanist approach to the *Phenomenology* tempered by an accent on finitude, negativity and the restlessness of Being. Hyppolite retains the Marxist emphasis on the power of human beings to rationally transform their social and historical reality, but in keeping with the "existentialist" reading of Hegel, he also acknowledges the finite character of human action and tragic dimensions of historical experience. Hyppolite's influential reading could be described as a "heroic Hegelianism", affirming the ultimate realizability of our historical freedom, tempered by a "pan-tragedism" that acknowledges the insurmountable nature of loss, pain, suffering, that inevitably accompanies the historical realization of freedom (Roth 1988: 19–45).

For Hyppolite and many others of his generation, existentialism presented itself as a powerful response to contemporary historical conditions, above all the apparent historical failure of the ideas of progress and community (*ibid.*: 32). The Hegelian emphasis on the rationality of history as a march of progress seemed less convincing after the horrors of Nazism. The Hegelian integration of the individual into the rational political community also presented difficulties in light of contemporary historical experiences. Rather, the resistance of the individual, who faces up to his or her groundless finitude, and yet affirms the necessity for action in their particular historical situation, struck a chord with many postwar French thinkers. The whole question of history and its meaning was crucial for Hyppolite and his contemporaries.

Linked with this, the question of *political action* and *engagement* also loomed large in the context of postwar Europe. *Marxism* thus presented itself as the other major philosophical and political influence on French intellectual life, an influence also heightened by the role of communists in the French resistance and subsequent prestige of the PCF (*Parti communiste français*) in postwar France. The Russian Revolution, which inspired hope but also uncertainty as to its historical and political results, along with the theme of *alienation* – mediated via Hegel and Marx's 1844 *Philosophic and Economic Manuscripts* – both pointed towards Marxism as the philosophical discourse most capable of confronting the contemporary historical and political situation. To understand contemporary political and historical reality required an engagement with both Hegel and Marx as the essential philosophers of history and politics respectively.

Hyppolite also turned towards Marxism and the Hegel–Marx relationship, publishing studies on Hegel and Marx after the war (see Hyppolite 1969). He argued that Marx had appropriated key philosophical elements of Hegel but had also showed the limitations of Hegelian idealism and the need to negate philosophy through political action. Hegelian Marxism thus seemed to provide a way of reintegrating the individual with the community, and of giving a direction and purpose to history, without succumbing to the twin temptations of *metaphysical totalization* (subsuming the individual under the universal) and *idealist mystification* (justifying historical catastrophe in the name of rational progress). At the same time, however, Hyppolite maintained an ambivalent stance towards Marxism, never fully endorsing Marx's "materialist" critique of Hegelian idealism, and remaining critical of Marxism's version of historical progress, which eliminated the "existential tragedy of history". By contrast, Hegelian dialectics, Hyppolite argued, "always maintains the tension of opposition within the heart of mediation, whereas the real dialectic of Marx works for the complete suppression of this tension" (quoted in Roth 1988: 35). Marxism suppresses the tragic dimensions of history in order to effect a political overcoming of the irreducible contradictions of historical experience.

Unlike Kojève, who forged an independent philosophical position combining Hegelian, Marxist and Heideggerian themes, Hyppolite preferred to remain in the role of commentator, explicating the text and highlighting its difficulties and impasses. At the same time Hegel remained, for Hyppolite, the authoritative philosopher through which existentialism and Marxism could be critically evaluated. This of course raised the question of how authoritatively we should take Hegel's own account of alienation, history and politics – a question that Hyppolite was criticized for not confronting directly. Nonetheless, Hyppolite's complex movement between Hegel and Marx again shows us the importance of Marxism and existentialism in shaping French Hegelianism, which in Hyppolite's case was later modified by Heidegger's history of Being as a way of overcoming the limitations of Hegelian historicism.

Unhappy consciousness revisited

As mentioned above, Hyppolite follows Wahl in taking the unhappy consciousness to be not only the fundamental theme of the *Phenomenology*, but a figure for alienated consciousness as such in its historical experience. By this Hyppolite means the way consciousness always strives for unity in its experience, for a *beyond* in which it will finally be whole, but at the same time always remaining conscious of its own division, separation, and disunity within experience. "This feeling of disparity within the self, or of the impossibility of the self coinciding with itself in reflection, is indeed the basis of subjectivity" (GS: 191). To be a subject is to be conscious of this disunity and restlessness at the heart of subjectivity, while also being conscious of the desire to overcome this restlessness and attain "the repose of unity" (GS: 195). The unhappy consciousness, for Hyppolite, thus connects Hegel's *pantragedism* (the irreducible pain, loss and disunity at the heart of subjectivity) with his *pan-logicism* (the way this pain and loss is translated conceptually into *contradiction*, which is what drives Hegel's dialectics in regard to work and struggle). Indeed, the unhappy consciousness is the very experience of contradiction, which is explicitly conceptualized in Hegel's logic; contradiction, in turn, is what drives historical development towards its end, achieving the true universality of reason. In this universality, the unhappy consciousness is integrated as a particular individual into the historical whole, and the historical whole is comprehended philosophically by the individual. Such would be the Hegelian remedy to the alienated condition of the unhappy consciousness.

Hyppolite tempers this account of history and reason, however, by an existentialist emphasis on the restlessness and dissatisfaction of self-consciousness. Subjectivity is fissured by negativity, loss, by elements that resist rational integration; and this negativity of subjectivity means that Being remains *non-totalizable* – resisting closure and completion within a comprehensible totality – even for Hegel's speculative logic. History cannot simply be the triumphant march of reason because the subject of history remains the unhappy consciousness whose alienation is an *existential*, rather than merely historical, condition. The realization of freedom is also the experience of alienation, without any guarantee that it will be overcome through historical progress, philosophical wisdom or political revolution. Hyppolite thus created a "hybrid" reading – combining existentialist and Marxist elements – that resisted the subordination of difference, negativity and division to the dialectical unity of reason. As Roth remarks, "Hyppolite meant the emphasis on the unhappy consciousness to keep the Hegelian dialectics open, to undermine the totalizing aspects of Hegelian systematization" (1988: 39). In this respect, Hyppolite's Hegel proved congenial to the existentialist emphasis on individual alienation and demand for freedom, as well as to the Marxist emphasis on conflict and division (contradiction) as generating historical and political struggle. It also laid the ground for Hyppolite's students to rebel against Hegelian humanism, while also remaining indebted to Hyppolite's treatment of the Hegelian themes of negativity, alienation and history.

Hyppolite's humanist reading of the *Phenomenology* and tragic approach to history began to change during the late 1940s and early 1950s. In all probability, this was due to the impact of Heidegger's critique of philosophical humanism. It is no exaggeration to say that Heidegger's 1947 "Letter on Humanism" – in which he criticizes Sartre and deconstructs the concept of humanism underpinning existential-ist, Hegelian and Marxist movements – marked the end of Hegel's ascendancy in France. Hyppolite's shift from Hegelian humanism to what Roth calls "Heideggerian Hope" (1988: 66–80) is thus emblematic of the shift from Hegelianism and Hegelian Marxism to Heideggerian and Nietzschean (but also structuralist) perspectives during the 1960s.

Hyppolite treats the relationship between the *Phenomenology* and the *Logic* – or the passage from the temporal to the eternal – as Hegelianism's "most obscure dialectical synthesis" (LE: 188). Given the predominance of the anthropological and humanist reading of Hegel, Hyppolite questioned the assumptions in such a reading regard-ing the relationship between anthropology and ontology. What is the proper relationship between these in Hegel's philosophy? Hyppolite's response was to argue for a "correspondence" between phenomeno-logy and logic: logic appears once the phenomenological journey – the dialectical experience of human history – has been traversed; the phe-nomenology, on the other hand, presupposes logical categories that give it its structure and intelligibility, driving us on to the perspective of absolute knowing.

Following Heidegger, for Hyppolite it is *language* that provides the medium for disclosing and mediating phenomenological and ontolo-gical truth. The reductive anthropological reading of Hegel cannot be correct, since it cannot account for speculative logic and the ontologi-cal disclosure of truth through language and conceptuality. By the same token, for Hyppolite self-consciousness cannot simply be reduced to the self-consciousness of individuals; rather, it is "Being's self-consciousness across human reality" (LE: 179). Adopting Heidegger, who described language as the "house of Being", Hyppolite argues that the nothingness of Being – expressed in the Hegelian idea of freedom that realizes itself in history – means that human beings do not domin-ate Being or history. Rather, "man is the house [*le demeure*] of the Universal, of the logos of Being", and only thereby "becomes capable of truth" (LE: 187). The human subject could not, therefore, be elevated to a metaphysical absolute, but must disclose the truth of Being in language, historical action and philosophical thought. In this way, Hyppolite sought a mediating path between the phenomenological emphasis on history and the human subject, and the speculative–logical emphasis on ontology and truth.

Why the Heideggerian turn against Hegelian humanism? The first reason, which is historical, concerns the doubts that were raised about rationality of history given the experiences of Nazism and World War II. The second reason is more conceptual, having to do with the problem of *historicism*: the question of whether one can identify suprahistorical criteria for evaluating historical phenomena. If all moral and political phenomena are historical, how do we distinguish better from worse forms of morality, society or politics? Either we revert to a radical historicism without suprahistorical criteria, which then threatens to degenerate into historical relativism; or we advert to some suprahistorical standard that would be able to account for historical change without abandoning normative criteria for transhistorical judgement. Such suprahistorical criteria, however, are subject to a good deal of sceptical doubt in modernity. How then to legitimate historicism without pernicious relativism or metaphysical mystification?

For Hyppolite, Heidegger's history of Being pointed the way forward. Hegelian historicism remained restricted to a story about beings (human beings) rather than the history of Being itself. It thereby reduces to philosophical anthropology or philosophy of culture, which, however rich, "does not overcome humanism – the interpretation of Being by man" (Roth 1988: 70). Humanism, in positing the human subject as the measure of Being, risked elevating the subject to the level of Being, or else reducing Being to the experience of the subject, both of which obliterated the truth of Being as such. As Roth points out, Hyppolite thus turned to the Heideggerian history of Being in order to overcome the perceived flaws of humanism (relativism or reductionism). Humanity is no longer the hero of history but rather the mouthpiece of Being. The Heideggerian shift in language and perspective – from the activist humanist subject to the decentred post-humanist being – transforms the role of human beings and the very meaning of historical experience in Hegelian thought: "Our roles have changed from heroes to prophets, from political actors to shepherds" (*ibid.*).

For Hyppolite it is thus Heideggerianism that becomes the authoritative philosophical discourse that would supplement Hegelian thought. While Hyppolite's recourse to Heidegger provides a salve to the problems of historicism, it is at the cost of positing a metaphysical narrative of Being remote from the concerns of desire, recognition and struggle that dominated the earlier humanist approaches to the *Phenomenology*. From Hyppolite's Heideggerian perspective, history becomes a repetition of the Same – a revealing of the poem of Being – rather than opening up possibilities for progress, regress, or even the "end of history". Hyppolite's retreat from history and politics thus stands in stark contrast with Kojève's anthropological–Marxist reading, which was also influenced by Heidegger. In contrast with Hyppolite's embrace of the history of Being, Kojève celebrated the necessity of historical conflict arising from the struggle for recognition, and affirmed the "end of history" as a way out of the impasse of historical relativism and metaphysical absolutism.

The struggle for recognition and the end of history: Kojève

Russian émigré Alexandre Kojève is perhaps the most famous of the French Hegelians, primarily because of his celebrated lecture courses on the *Phenomenology of Spirit* held between 1933 and 1939. These lectures – published in 1947 by surrealist Raymond Queneau – have taken on a legendary status in many accounts of Hegelianism in French philosophy (Descombes 1980; Butler 1988). Although Kojève's provocative theses on the struggle for recognition have proven decisive for postwar French thought, Kojève also follows in the footsteps of Koyré's anthropological approach to Hegel with its emphasis on time and history (Roth 1988: 95–7). Hegel's innovation, for both Kojève and Koyré, was to emphasize the centrality of history by way of a paradigm of human time as organized by our orientation towards the *future*. Hegelian philosophy is the comprehension of human time as defined by a future-oriented negation of the present, which is to say by self-conscious, goal-directed, rational action. For all their agreement on the primacy of the future, Kojève sharply rejected Koyré's optimistic reading of Hegel's philosophy of history, replacing it with a much darker vision of the violent conflict attending the struggle for recognition that drives history towards its end – a condition of mutual recognition and ironic freedom in which the basic possibilities for transforming our historical world have been exhausted.

Kojève's highly original reading of Hegel should be tackled with a degree of caution. As Roth observes: "[i]f Koyré's reading of Hegel is original, Kojève's is violent; if the former sheds light on difficult texts, the latter explodes them" (1988: 96). Kojève's "explosion" of Hegel's texts is generated by his idiosyncratic combination of Marxist and Heideggerian themes, which together gave his reading of Hegel's master/slave dialectic both revolutionary and existential dimensions. Kojève even remarks that he adopted the mask of Hegel interpreter all the better to develop "a work of propaganda designed to jolt the spirit" (Letter to Tran Duc Thao, 7 October 1948; quoted in Roth 1988: 97). This Hegelian "propaganda" was to profoundly affect the following generation of French thinkers, who turned to Hegel and Marx in order to confront twentieth-century history and politics.

Human desire as the desire for recognition

In his lectures Kojève presents a strong, even violent interpretation of Hegel's *Phenomenology* as a "phenomenological *anthropology*" (IRH: 39); Hegel's philosophy more generally is construed as a radically atheistic expression of modern humanism. The novelty of Kojève's approach was to generalize Hegel's account of the *struggle for recognition* across human history, combining it with the Marxist thesis about the centrality of *class struggle* in historical development. This Hegelian-Marxist philosophy of history was supplemented further by the Heideggerian existential themes of temporality, mortality and the finitude of *Dasein*. Indeed, Kojève argued that it was our experience of freely confronting death in order to satisfy our desire for recognition that is the hallmark of being a free human subject. The result was a potent philosophy in which the *desire for recognition* – paradigmatically portrayed in the dialectical relationship between master and slave – becomes the fundamental source of human action and progressive historical development. Adapting Hegel, Kojève contended that Western history has now reached its end by overcoming the opposition between master and slave. History has begun to realize the institutional forms of mutual recognition that make historical action – in the emphatic sense of war, conflict and social struggle – all but redundant. We have arrived at the "end of history": a condition of post-historical freedom where the institutional conditions of mutual recognition, and hence freedom, have in principle been achieved. This condition of universal equality and "classless" homogeneity, however, leaves post-historical human beings without reasons to engage in the conflictual struggle for recognition that generates historical action in the proper sense.

To understand Kojève's Hegelian "end of history" thesis, we must begin with his anthropological account of human beings, which, rightly or wrongly, is attributed to Hegel. Unlike Hegel, Kojève insisted on a *sharp dualism* between nature and spirit: the transformation of human history through action is opposed to the non-historical cycles of nature (an opposition we shall find again in Sartre). This dualism is most striking in Kojève's account of *human* (as distinct from merely animal) *desire*. Human desire differs from animal desire, first, in being directed not towards an object as such, but rather towards *another desire*. Human sexual desire, for example, is not merely the effect of biological instinct, nor mere lust for someone's body, but a complex relationship of desire for another's desire. What I desire in desiring another is for that person to desire me as well; I desire to be *recognized* by my beloved, and thus find his or her desire for me desirable. Human desire differs from animal desire, secondly, in frequently being directed towards objects that have absolutely no "biological" value; such objects become desirable only once they are mediated by another human desire. The object of my human desire – be it a commodity, a value or ideal, a symbol or flag – is desirable precisely because others also desire the object in question. Kojève thus calls human desire "anthropogenetic desire": it is desire that produces us as free individuals, consciously acting and transforming ourselves within an intersubjective social and historical world.

The human desire for recognition is contrasted with the animal desire for *self-preservation* (a scenario vividly depicted in Hobbes's *Leviathan*, which describes the "natural condition" or "state of nature" as a brutal "war of all against all"). Human desire, to prove itself as human desire, must therefore renounce its animal desire for self-preservation in favour of the desire for another human desire. In Hegel's account of the origin of self-consciousness, according to Kojève, this will take the form of a struggle between desiring individuals, each of whom risks his animal desire for self-preservation in order to prove his human desire for recognition. All human desire that generates self-consciousness, Kojève argued, is a "function of the desire for 'recognition'" (IRH: 7). Self-consciousness is constituted through the *desire for recognition*; and this desire is expressed through action, a process of continuous transcending of our given conditions of historical existence.

Masters and slaves

Hegel analyses the character of human desire, according to Kojève, in his phenomenological analysis of the master/slave dialectic as a struggle for recognition between desiring subjects. We should recall here the importance of Hegel's master/slave dialectic for subsequent generations of French philosophy. In Kojève's hands it becomes the defining feature of human anthropological and historical experience in general. According to Kojève, the origin of self-consciousness lies in a struggle to the death for recognition, which he sharpens into a struggle for "pure prestige". In this struggle both protagonists seek to impose their own desire for recognition on the other; each is willing to sacrifice his natural desire for self-preservation in order to achieve the social recognition of his own value or prestige by another: "Man appears therefore (or creates himself) for the first time in the (given) natural World as a combatant in the first bloody Struggle for pure prestige" (Kojève 1947, in Keenan 2004: 62). Indeed, what defines us as human beings is the possibility of *consciously confronting and freely risking death* in the name of a desire for recognition: "a being cannot live humanly except on condition of 'realising' his death: becoming conscious of it, 'bearing' it, being capable of facing it voluntarily. To be a man – is, for Hegel, to be able to know how to die" (Kojève 1947, in Keenan 2004: 62).

To be sure, this emphasis on the experience of finitude, and of freely confronting death, is certainly present in Hegel's account of the life-and-death struggle and master/slave dialectic. But it clearly owes much to Heidegger's reflections on how *Dasein* becomes singularized through the anxious encounter with death, and thereby free for resolute decision and authentic historical action. Kojève heightens the significance of death and the experience of finitude via these Heideggerian motifs, thereby intensifying the "existential" dimensions of the Hegelian struggle for recognition. We should note, however, that Heidegger never discusses anything like a life-and-death struggle for pure prestige; on the contrary, the Heideggerian confrontation with death is supposed to disclose our authentic character as finite temporalizing beings, rather than satisfying our anthropogenetic desire for recognition by another subject. We should note, moreover, that "prestige" is a social, intersubjectively mediated concept, which is therefore inappropriate for the life-and-death struggle between "proto-subjects" of desire.

Be that as it may, as Hegel makes clear, this struggle cannot simply end in death, which of course would cancel the recognition desired by both protagonists, for human desire presupposes and depends upon the continuance of our natural life and animal desire. Hence the only viable outcome is that one of the protagonists surrender his desire to the other: "He must give up his desire and satisfy the desire of the other: he must 'recognise' the other without being 'recognised' by him" (IRH:

8). He must recognize the other as *master*, and consequently recognize himself as the master's *slave*. The outcome is an unequal, one-sided relation of recognition: "For although the Master treats the Other as Slave, he does not behave as a Slave himself; and although the Slave treats the Other as Master, he does not behave as Master himself. The Slave does not risk his life, and the Master is idle" (IRH: 19). The slave remains tethered to his animal desire for self-preservation, while the master, who has risked death, ceases to work and enjoys the fruits of the slave's labour.

Kojève faithfully interprets the experience of mastery, which is described as resulting in an "existential impasse" (*ibid.*). It is an impasse not only because the master finds that he is dependent on the labour of the slave, but because the master merely gains the recognition of a dependent, "thing-like" consciousness, which means that he fails to satisfy his desire for recognition. Indeed, the more he seeks to enslave the other in order to prove his mastery, the more this thwarts his desire for recognition from an independent subject. "The Master fought and risked his life for a recognition without value for him. For he can be satisfied only by recognition from one whom he recognizes as worthy of recognizing him" (*ibid.*). The master can never be satisfied; his desire for recognition will always be thwarted. The satisfied man, on the other hand, will be the one who has overcome slavery; the emancipated slave is genuinely free, having dialectically overcome the opposition between mastery and slavery, and forcibly attained the equality of recognition that was initially denied him. The truth of the "autonomous Consciousness", in short, is "the *slavish Consciousness*" (IRH: 20).

While Kojève's account of the experience of the master is more or less faithful to Hegel's exposition, his account of the experience of the slave assumes a decidedly *Marxist* character. Indeed, the emancipation of the slave becomes the motor of historical development and eventually the source of the revolutionary transformation of society. "If idle Mastery is an impasse, laborious Slavery, in contrast, is the source of all human, social, historical progress. History is the history of the working Slave" (*ibid.*). Kojève's reading of the Hegelian master/slave relationship thus recapitulates Marx's thesis on class struggle as the motivating force in history. Human history becomes the history of the *struggle for recognition between masters and slaves*, a movement that reaches its end once this opposition is dialectically superseded. At this point, true equality through mutual recognition is achieved in what Kojève calls the "universal and homogeneous" political state ("universal" in the sense of upholding the principle of equality for all, and "homogeneous" in the sense of eliminating cultural, religious, ethnic and other particularities in favour of equal citizenship). We have arrived at Kojève's Hegelian-Marxist version of the *end of history*, the end of historical struggle as such, a history conceptually comprehended in Hegelian philosophy.

To be sure, Kojève does not pretend that Hegel actually argues for the slave's revolutionary overcoming of the master. Rather, for Kojève the Marxist theory of revolutionary conflict is *implied* by Hegel's analysis of the struggle for recognition that generates the master/slave relationship. In this respect, Kojève's political thesis is a radical one: the slave recognizes the master but the master does not recognize the slave, so all that is needed for overcoming mastery and slavery – that is, for the achievement of equal recognition – is for the slave to revolt against the master. "In order that mutual and reciprocal recognition, which alone can fully and definitively realise and satisfy man, be established, it suffices for the Slave to impose himself on the Master and be recognised by him" (IRH: 21). It goes without saying that this demand for recognition takes the form of a bloody revolution rather than rational discussion.

Two problems with Kojève's Hegel

Although Kojève's Heideggerian-Marxist account of the struggle for recognition has been enormously fruitful, there are two critical points to make concerning Kojève's account of the origin of self-consciousness.

First, Kojève presents the master/slave relationship as an *anthropological–historical thesis* about human historical development, which culminates in the achievement of equal recognition at the end of history. For Hegel, however, the master/slave relationship describes the origin of intersubjective self-consciousness through a philosophical fiction in which "proto-subjects" of desire enter into a life-and-death struggle to assert their independence. This experience of the origin of sociability in relations of domination and subjection, however, cannot be taken as an *historical* thesis, for it appears at the most rudimentary level of self-consciousness – of proto-subjects immersed in nature – rather than at the developed level of reason or spirit. The master/slave relationship is not yet a properly historical standpoint in Hegel (although it marks the emergence of historical awareness). For Kojève, by contrast, the master/slave relationship is the basis of Western history: the key to understanding the conflictual struggle between classes that will culminate in a revolutionary overthrow of the masters by emancipated slaves.

The second problem concerns the *circularity* of the relation between self-consciousness and the desire for recognition. On the one hand, Kojève makes the desire for recognition the *aim* of the struggle; the protagonists risk their lives in order to enjoy pure prestige. But Kojève then takes the desire for recognition to explain the *emergence* of self-consciousness, the way the protagonists become self-conscious in the first place. Self-consciousness emerges out of the struggle for recognition between desiring individuals; but these desiring individuals could only struggle for recognition if they were already self-conscious to begin with (conscious of oneself in relation to another self-conscious being). Recognition *produces* self-consciousness and yet is also the *aim* of the struggle between self-conscious beings. This circularity makes Kojève's account susceptible to the further criticism that it conflates Hegel's description of a *deficient* form of the struggle for recognition (mastery and servitude) with the *paradigmatic* way that self-consciousness is constituted (through intersubjective recognition).

The end of history?

Kojève's reading of Hegel's master/slave dialectic concludes with the famous claim that we have entered the "end of history": a condition of achieved mutual recognition in what he called "the universal and homogeneous political state" (initially socialist states but later on also liberal democratic ones). This thesis at first seems rather bizarre. With the experiences of World War II still fresh in people's minds, could Kojève seriously have claimed that history was at an end? It is true that these tumultuous events marked a profound shift in Western historical and political experience. Yet for Kojève, they only confirmed his Hegelian thesis that we have entered a post-historical condition in which the basic possibilities for political and historical action have been exhausted. Although wars, conflicts and struggles would doubtless continue, there would be no further development beyond the principle of achieved equality of recognition in the universal and homogeneous state. If history is driven by the struggle for recognition, once we reach the goal of historical progress – satisfaction of our desire for mutual recognition – the motivation for historical transformation ceases. For Kojève, this means a condition in which "man", in the emphatic sense of the subject of history, "dies" or disappears. With the "definitive annihilation of Man properly so-called or of the free and historical Individual", what disappears is human action as the negation and transformation of our given historical circumstances (IRH: 159).

In practical terms, Kojève adds, this means "the disappearance of wars and bloody revolutions" (*ibid.*), along with the emergence of a new reconciliation with nature.

On the other hand, the end of history also implies the disappearance of philosophy: since human historical action ceases, so too does the need for philosophy as the self-comprehension of our historical experience. In Kojève's eyes, Hegelian philosophy is the definitive expression of philosophical wisdom, the completed form of historical self-comprehension that accounts for the end of history and hence the end of philosophy, which is the comprehension of our own historical time in thought. Post-historical culture nonetheless preserves forms of cultural life that remain after the end of historical struggles: "art, love, play, etc., etc.; in short, everything that makes Man *happy*" (IRH: 159). As in Marx's utopian vision, the "realm of necessity" (of work, conflict and struggle) will be supplanted by a "realm of freedom" (of art, play, criticism) "in which men (mutually recognizing one another without reservation) no longer fight, and work as little as possible" (*ibid.*).

Kojève later criticized this rather romanticized account and turned instead to an increasingly ironic conception of post-historical man, who has now entered a condition of material abundance coupled with a re-animalized "happiness". Given the disappearance of historical man, art, love, play and so on must also become purely "natural" again in the sense of being merely personal appetitive pursuits. Postmodern subjects, whom Kojève calls "the post-historical animals of the species *Homo sapiens*", will live amidst material abundance and complete security in the new consumer society; but this security, affluence and private play will not be tantamount to *happiness* (whether taken in the emphatic Greek sense of the good life or in the modern sense of personal fulfilment). On the contrary, they "will be *content* as a result of their artistic, erotic, and playful behaviour, inasmuch as, by definition, they will be contented with it" (IRH: 159). Cultural aestheticism, mass consumerism and personal hedonism will be our banal forms of post-historical satisfaction.

For Kojève, this trivial contentment with consumer pleasures and private satisfactions is the ironic outcome of post-historical freedom, which embraces both the dissolution of historical subjects and the re-animalization of human beings. We not only lose the need for philosophy but the desire to pursue discursive understanding (Hegelian wisdom) concerning our relationship to the world: meaningful rational discourse (*logos*) in the strong sense also disappears (IRH: 160).

This post-historical condition of animalization and idle chatter, Kojève maintained, was already an emerging reality in the postwar world. Indeed, his observations of life in America, China and the Soviet Union lead him to conclude that the post-historical condition dawning around the globe was not leading to a quasi-communist classless society, but rather to the universal ascendancy of the consumerist–democratic "American way of life". The United States would thus prefigure "the 'eternal present' future of all of humanity" (IRH: 161). It is for us to decide whether Kojève's prediction has proven correct, and if so, whether this should be a cause for celebration or for despair.

Kojève's legacy

Kojève's account of human desire as the desire for recognition, along with his famous reading of the master/slave dialectic, inspired many thinkers such as Jean-Paul Sartre, Simone de Beauvoir, Georges Bataille, Frantz Fanon and Jacques Lacan. Indeed, Kojève's idiosyncratic Heideggerian-Marxist reading has continued to cast a long shadow over the French reception of Hegel. Bataille, for example, based his reading on Kojève's "Heideggerian" approach to the significance of death in Hegel's philosophy; psychoanalyst Jacques Lacan drew upon Kojève in developing his own theory of desire and subjectivity; the theme of the "end of man" was explicitly taken up by Foucault and Derrida in the 1960s. Indeed, much of the poststructuralist critique of Hegelianism amounts to a retrospective attack on Kojève's Hegel (mediated via Hyppolite's Heideggerian approach). Kojève ironic post-historical Hegelianism, moreover, anticipates postmodernist critiques of modernity.

Kojève also had a profound impact upon American intellectual and political life, primarily through debates with adversary Leo Strauss (see Strauss and Kojève 2000). The latter introduced Kojève's work to his political science students at the University of Chicago, which included such important American intellectuals as Allan Bloom and Francis Fukuyama. The latter recently came to prominence by arguing, in *The End of History and the Last Man*, that the global spread of neo-liberalism since the fall of communism in 1989–91 represented the "end of history" as propounded by Kojève. Fukuyama's defence of neo-liberalism as the historical realization of freedom, however, has been criticized for turning Kojève's "end of history" into an ideological affirmation of the prevailing economic, cultural and political order now being imposed increasingly across the globe.

This raises a question that occupied Kojève and Strauss in their most vigorous debates: the relationship between philosophy and politics. Kojève, who worked in the French Ministry of Foreign Affairs as an architect of the Common Market, saw his philosophical work as propaganda that would bring about the state of affairs that it described. Fukuyama, who served as a political advisor for neo-conservative American presidents such as Ronald Reagan, seems to have intended his thesis on liberal democracy as the end of history to be an intervention in contemporary politics. This continuing debate over the "end of history" clearly affirms the social and political relevance of Kojève's Hegel. It also shows that the history of Hegelianism is very far from being at an end.

Summary of key points

Wahl and Koyré on the unhappy consciousness and time

- Wahl is the first French reader of Hegel to give a central role to the unhappy consciousness. Consciousness itself is defined by self-division, the experience of negativity and an incessant striving for unity that is constantly undermined.
- Wahl's Kierkegaardian critique of Hegel (that the singularity of existence is subsumed under conceptual universality) leads to his "existential empiricism", a pluralism of beings as contingent, relational, and independent of abstract thought.
- Koyré questions whether we can take the unhappy consciousness to be the proper ground of Hegelian philosophy; he argued that the forms of self-division within the unhappy consciousness are to be found within the Hegelian Concept.
- Koyré defines the "human reality" as "a being which is what it is not and is not what it is", a Hegelian definition taken over by Kojève and famously by Sartre.
- Hegelian time is the human time of historical experience, of self-realization through historical action that consciously transforms our world.

Hyppolite's reading of Hegel

- Hyppolite makes the unhappy consciousness central to Hegel's phenomenology, retaining the Marxist emphasis on the rational transformation of social reality, but also acknowledging the finite character of human action and tragic dimensions of historical experience.

- Hyppolite thus created a "hybrid" reading of Hegel – combining existentialist and Marxist elements – that resisted the subordination of difference, negativity and division into the dialectical unity of reason.

- The later Hyppolite turned to the Heideggerian history of Being in order to overcome the flaws of Hegelian humanism (relativism and reductionism). Humanity is no longer the hero of history but rather the mouthpiece of Being.

- From Hyppolite's Heideggerian perspective, history becomes a repetition of the Same – a revealing of the poem of Being – rather than opening up possibilities for progress, regress, or even the "end of history".

Kojève's reading of Hegel

- Kojève combined Hegel's *struggle for recognition*, generalized across human history, with Marx's *class struggle* as the driver of historical development.

- This Hegelian-Marxist philosophy of history was supplemented by the Heideggerian existential themes of temporality, mortality and finitude.

- Western history – driven by the struggle for recognition – has reached its end by overcoming the opposition between master and slave. We have thus entered the "end of history": a condition of post-historical freedom where mutual recognition has been institutionally achieved.

- Such a condition of universal equality and "classless" homogeneity leaves post-historical human beings without reasons to engage in the conflictual struggle for recognition that generates historical action in the proper sense.

seven

Between existentialism and Marxism:
Sartre, de Beauvoir, Merleau-Ponty

One of the most intriguing aspects of French postwar Hegelianism is the way various thinkers critically transformed important Hegelian themes. There are of course many examples one could mention here, such as Jacques Lacan's psychoanalytic theory of the desiring subject. In what follows, however, I shall focus on three important moments in twentieth-century French philosophy: Sartre's critique of Hegel's account of the relation to the Other, de Beauvoir's appropriation of Hegelian themes in her ethics of ambiguity, and Merleau-Ponty's appraisal of the relationship between Hegel and existentialism, along with his attempt to transform Hegelian dialectics into a pluralistic "hyperdialectic". The basic problem at issue for Sartre and de Beauvoir, I suggest, is to comprehend the relationship between individualism and intersubjectivity: how to reconcile the existentialist emphasis on the individual with the Hegelian emphasis on intersubjectivity. For Merleau-Ponty, by contrast, there is a distinctive Hegelian existentialism that Jean Hyppolite has revealed for contemporary thought; the point is not to rehearse the standard existentialist criticisms of Hegel (subsuming the individual under the universality of the Concept), but rather to rethink dialectic such that it no longer obliterates contingency, singularity and plurality. In this respect, Merleau-Ponty's interesting appropriation of Hegelian thought sets the stage, as I discuss in Chapter 8, for the complex engagement with Hegelian dialectics by poststructuralist philosophers of difference (Deleuze and Derrida).

Sartre's existential critique of Hegel

Jean-Paul Sartre is among the most famous philosophers of the twentieth century. For many, he and his partner Simone de Beauvoir epitomized French intellectual life in the postwar period. While Sartre's thought was given powerful expression in his 1938 novel *Nausea*, his most famous philosophical work was *Being and Nothingness: An Essay on Phenomenological Ontology*, published in 1943. *Being and Nothingness* is clearly indebted to Heidegger (whom Sartre had studied while in a German prison camp) and to Husserlian phenomenology; but it also involved a critical appropriation of certain Hegelian themes – notably the master/slave dialectic and the unhappy consciousness – that Sartre had adopted from the French Hegelianism of the 1930s. There is controversy over the precise source of Sartre's Hegelianism, with many commentators claiming that Sartre learned his Hegel from Kojève (Butler 1988; Poster 1975); Kojève, however, pointed out that Sartre never attended his lecture course on Hegel (unlike Lacan and Merleau-Ponty). Nonetheless, it is hard to understand the emphasis Sartre gives to Hegel's master/slave dialectic without thinking of Kojève's Heideggerian-Marxist reading of Hegel.

Whatever the case, the master/slave dialectic and unhappy consciousness are clearly crucial to Sartre's existential phenomenology, which includes an explicit critique of Hegel's *Phenomenology* and its failure to account for the existence of the Other. What we find in Sartre's work more generally are moments of tension between his existentialist commitment to the freedom of the individual, and his acknowledgement of the existential situation of human beings caught between the inert materiality of the world and the openness of human action (what Sartre and de Beauvoir called *immanence* and *transcendence*). This is more clearly expressed in Sartre's later work, which attempted to synthesize the existentialist emphasis on the freedom of the individual with the need to acknowledge the universal in the political sphere. This tension between his earlier existentialist project and later commitment to collective politics led Sartre – along with numerous other French political philosophers in the 1950s – to attempt a synthesis of existentialism and Marxism, a project culminating in Sartre's two-volume *Critique of Dialectical Reason*. This attempted synthesis prompted a debate with his colleague Maurice Merleau-Ponty, who gave an alternative critical perspective on the relationship between Hegelianism, existentialism and Marxism.

Sartre's overall project, to put it roughly, involved a number of elements: a critical rejection of idealist phenomenology (Hegel) coupled with a selective appropriation of transcendental phenomenology (Husserl) and existential–ontological phenomenology (Heidegger). Indeed, Sartre describes his project as a "phenomenological ontology" that is clearly indebted to Husserl and Heidegger while also being critical of both these versions of phenomenology. What distinguishes Sartre's approach in this respect is his return to the primacy of the Cartesian *cogito*, which is given a novel phenomenological interpretation as "pre-reflexive" *cogito* or "non-thetic" consciousness. This Cartesian "egological" approach to phenomenology is then given an existentialist cast via an atheistic reading of Kierkegaard's emphasis on the primacy of individual decision. The result is an ontology comprising two fundamental categories – the "in-itself" (basically, inert matter) and the "for-itself" (free consciousness), with the category of "for-others" appearing along the way – that metaphysics has traditionally attempted to synthesize in various ways (as the "in-and-for-itself" or God). It is these ontological, categorial relationships between the "in-itself" and the "for-itself" that Sartre analyses phenomenologically (hence the title "Being and Nothingness"). Human freedom, for Sartre, must be understood as the ungrounded possibility for action by a conscious subject who is always "decentred" in relation to its environment – that is, capable of taking different attitudes and actions towards (or "negating") its current circumstances and indeed its own existence – coupled with the inescapable necessity to choose, decide and act. Hence, Sartre contends, we must take responsibility for our freedom to act, which is an ontological condition of our existence, and do so in ways that avoid reducing ourselves to the sum of our physical, material and social circumstances. As we shall see, while Sartre articulates the relationship between individual freedom and the conditions of exercising this freedom (what Sartre, following Heidegger, called facticity and situation), his ontological account can be questioned as to whether it can also adequately explain the ways in which our situation can thwart the exercise of our freedom. This is the problem at the heart of the criticism levelled by de Beauvoir and Merleau-Ponty, namely that Sartre fails to account properly for the experience and effects of *oppression*: the alienated internalization of disempowerment – arising directly from an existential *and* social situation – that prompts subjects to accept subordination and abandon their freedom.

Sartre's critique of Hegel in *Being and Nothingness* appears in a chapter entitled "The Existence of Others", the first chapter in Part III dealing with the phenomenon of "Being-for-Others". From the perspective of action and of the Cartesian *cogito*, Sartre has described what he calls "human reality" (our active and temporal existence in the world) according to the Hegelian category of "being-for-itself" (BN: 221). Contra Descartes, in Sartre's account of human reality (a dubious translation of Heidegger's *Dasein*), we do not actually exist as isolated knowing subjects confronting a world of objects. Rather, human reality includes experiences in which we encounter *other consciousnesses* that are part of, yet irreducibly distinct from, one's subjective experience of the world.

This is what Sartre calls the *problem of the Other*: what is the *being* of these other free, conscious human beings? What is the *ontological relationship* between my consciousness and theirs? Sartre's approach to this problem is not epistemological but *existential* – a problem of lived existence and individual experience – and *ontological*, a problem of the *being* of Self and Other in their constitutive relationships. The epistemologist, Sartre contends, ought to consider the phenomenon of *shame*: how could such an emotion be possible without presupposing the existence of Others before whom the significance of one's actions – indeed one's being – is revealed? "I am ashamed of myself as I *appear* to the Other . . . I recognise that I *am* as the Other sees me. . . . Nobody can be vulgar all alone!" (BN: 222). Sartre draws the conclusion that my consciousness, as a *being-for-itself*, necessarily refers to the being of Others for its significance. The existential and ontological problems to be investigated are therefore those of "the existence of the Other", and "the relation of my *being* to the being of the Other" (BN: 223).

The real ontological problem here, for Sartre, is to consider the *existence* of the Other, "the self which *is not* myself": what is the *being* of the Other defined as "the one who is not me and the one who I am not" (BN: 230)? And what is *my being* in so far as I am revealed before Others for whom I am an Other in turn? These formulations suggest, for Sartre, the importance of *negation* in the relationship between Self and Other: "a negation which posits the original distinction between the Other and myself as being such that it determines me by means of the Other and determines the Other by means of me" (BN: 232). Fortunately there are at least three philosophers who have taken seriously the problem of the Other as constituted by such a negative relation. Husserl, Hegel and Heidegger each attempt, in different ways, "to seize at the very heart of consciousness a fundamental, transcending connection with the Other which would be constitutive of each consciousness in its very upsurge" (BN: 233). Despite this, all three thinkers, according to Sartre, nonetheless privilege *knowledge* as the way our fundamental relation with the Other is realized; thus they fail to properly address the *being* or *existence* of the Other and its negative relationship to my conscious existence.

Hegel on the Other: epistemological and ontological optimism

Sartre's critique begins with an exposition of what he takes to be Hegel's account of the relation with the Other, drawing heavily from the sections in the *Phenomenology* on the life-and-death struggle and the experience of mastery and slavery (BN: 235–8). We should note that Sartre's reading of Hegel is hampered by the use of very limited sources, quoting mostly from a narrow selection of texts (*Morceaux choisis de Hegel*) translated by Lefebvre and Guterman in 1939 (see Baugh 2003: 98; Williams 1992: 292, 303). Be that as it may, Hegel's achievement, according to Sartre, was to take the existence of the Other to be constitutive of "the very existence of my self as self-consciousness" (BN: 235). My self-consciousness is constituted through my relation with the Other: the formulation "'I' am 'I'" (deriving from Fichte) expresses my self-knowledge and self-identity, which are both achieved through the mediation of the Other who recognizes the objectivity and validity of my own self-consciousness. How does this occur?

According to Sartre, my self-consciousness is defined, in the first instance, by the *exclusion* of the Other. This Other, however, is also the mediator enabling me to define my self-identity through the process of *recognition*, which begins, as Hegel (in Kojèvian style) maintained, via a violent life-and-death struggle. As we have seen, the Other is initially presented to me as an object "immersed in the being of life" (BN: 236); I too appear as such an object to the Other, which means that each of us seeks to assert our individuality, refusing the status of being merely an object for the Other (thus anticipating Sartre's analysis of the unavoidably conflictual nature of human relations). Sartre acknowledges that Hegel's account of the relation of mutual exclusion between subjects thus rejects the isolated Cartesian *cogito* (the famous "I think therefore I am") as the starting point of philosophy. Indeed, for Hegel, the *cogito* is made possible, rather, by the existence of the Other: "the road of interiority passes through the Other" (*ibid.*). My self-consciousness is made possible by the fact that I experience myself in relation to Others as *being-for-the-Other*. However, although I appear to the Other as a body-object and the Other appears as a body-object to me, I nonetheless demand recognition of my free subjectivity from the Other who does precisely the same. We therefore both risk our lives in a struggle for recognition of our independent subjecthood. The well-known conclusion is the submission of one protagonist, who becomes *the slave*, and the dominance of the other protagonist, who by risking his life becomes *the master*.

According to Sartre, Hegel's master/slave dialectic, which proved so important for Marx, showed the way the conflictual relation between Self and Other is constitutive of self-consciousness. As Sartre concludes, Hegel's "brilliant intuition is to make me depend on the Other in *my being*" (BN: 237). What Hegel calls self-consciousness, in Sartre's terminology, is a "being-for-itself which is for-itself only through another"; it involves an active consciousness of oneself that is conditioned through one's ontological relationship with Others for whom one is also an Other (*ibid.*). The Other thereby "penetrates me to the heart": to doubt the Other would be to doubt the very condition of my being self-conscious. Hegel's account of the indubitability of the Other for my self-consciousness thus goes far beyond what Descartes accomplished with the indubitability of the *cogito ergo sum* (*ibid.*). Hegel effectively vanquishes solipsism – which still dogged Husserl's account of the Other – by making my "being-for-others" a necessary condition for my "being-for-myself" (BN: 238).

After praising Hegel's breakthrough (which marks "an advance upon Husserl"), Sartre then presents his major criticism (BN: 238–40), namely that Hegel reduces the *ontological* problem of the Other to an *epistemological* problem concerning our knowledge of the Other. We could call this Hegel's *epistemological reductionism* concerning the being of the Other. This general criticism prepares the way for Sartre's two key objections.

The first is what he calls Hegel's "epistemological optimism" (BN: 240–43), the view that Hegel construes the relationship with the Other as a *knowledge relation*. Indeed, Sartre takes Hegel to claim that the relationship between self-certain subjects is one where each attempts to turn the Other into an object that can be known and thus mastered. By turning the Other into an object of knowledge for me, Hegel reduces the being of the Other to my knowledge of him or her as an object.

The second is Hegel's "ontological optimism" concerning the existence of the Other (BN: 243–4), the view that Hegel adopts the *standpoint of the Absolute* in accounting for the experience of self-consciousness. The result of this assumption of the standpoint of the Absolute is to thereby subsume the plurality of individual subjects into the unity of the rational whole.

These criticisms should be familiar by now, particularly the second charge, which is a repetition of the existentialist complaint that Hegel's system fails to do justice to the ineffable singularity of the individual in his or her unique existence. Sartre draws here again on a classic objection to be found in Kierkegaard: that Hegel has excluded his own consciousness and individual existence from his phenomenological exposition; moreover, that Hegel has presupposed the standpoint of the Absolute, forgotten his own finitude, and thus assumed the "mind of God", with the lamentable result that the irreducible plurality of consciousnesses is subsumed within an "inter-monad totality" (BN: 244).

The implication of Sartre's criticism is to argue for a return to the Cartesian *cogito*, now modified into a *pre-reflective cogito* or *non-thetic* consciousness. The being of my individual consciousness is not reducible to knowledge; hence it is impossible that I can transcend my individual being towards a reciprocal recognition – taken as a relation of *knowing* oneself through the Other – in which my being and that of Others are rendered equivalent (*ibid.*). Hegel's aim, Sartre contends, is an epistemological and ontological illusion, namely to show that reciprocal recognition, and hence an overcoming of alienation, are possible through a philosophical comprehension of our historicity. The ontological separation between the plurality of consciousnesses, however, is an existential scandal that cannot be dialectically overcome either in thought or action. Rather, Sartre contends, "the sole point of departure" for a genuine grasp of the problem of the Other must be "the interiority of the cogito" (*ibid.*).

Sartre's critique, however, tends to misinterpret crucial aspects of Hegel's account of self-consciousness and recognition. The relationship between self-conscious subjects outlined in the *Phenomenology* is not a knowledge relationship but a description of the dialectical relationship between independent and dependent consciousnesses; the master/slave relationship is a *deficient* realization of the freedom of self-consciousness, rather than an account of what defines human subjectivity *per se*. Moreover, what Hegel calls the "unhappy consciousness" is not an ontological condition of human consciousness *per se* but rather a recurring historical configuration of alienated subjectivity that strives to overcome its alienation through developing a more comprehensive understanding of rational freedom.

Sartre, by contrast, argues that there is an ontological separation between subjects which renders mutual recognition impossible. The ontological separation between the Other and me is not a social and historical condition of alienation (as for Hegel) but an ontological and therefore insuperable condition of human reality. Moreover, the attempt by each subject to render the Other as an object in order to assert one's freedom results in human relations being inescapably *conflictual*. Because we never escape the desire to turn the Other into an object, while demanding that the Other recognize me as subject, we are doomed to a perpetual struggle for recognition that can end only in "bad faith" (the various ruses by which I deny my freedom or transcendence and define myself as an object bound by given circumstances). What Sartre takes to be an ontological characteristic of human beings, Hegel presents as an inadequate historical realization of intersubjective freedom that can be overcome in principle. This is a point that Sartre came to acknowledge in his later attempts to synthesize existentialism with Marxism, notably in his unfinished tome, the *Critique of Dialectical Reason* (1960).

De Beauvoir's critique of Sartre: freedom and oppression

Simone de Beauvoir (1908–86) – pioneer feminist philosopher, novelist, activist, and Sartre's lifelong partner – identified an important difficulty within Sartre's existentialism: that Sartre's version of the problem of the Other tended to underplay the effects of the experience of *oppression*. This was a criticism also later made by Merleau-Ponty. Without the possibility of mutual recognition between subjects, which Sartre denied on ontological grounds, the possibility of developing an ethics that would extend beyond the parameters of personal authenticity seemed rather doubtful. Although she remained indebted to Sartre's existentialist account of freedom, and to Sartre's criticisms of Hegelian thought, de Beauvoir developed an alternative existentialist model of ethics that would supplement Sartre's thought in important ways. Indeed, it was her experience of the unequal character of gender relations – but also her concern with class politics and colonial struggles – that persuaded de Beauvoir to develop an existentialist account of freedom, subjectivity and ethics that would do justice to the experience of oppression.

Although at the very end of *Being and Nothingness* Sartre gestured towards the possibility of an existentialist ethics, and emphasized (in "Existentialism is a Humanism") the ethics of authenticity implicit in his philosophy of radical freedom, he nonetheless confronted difficulties in producing such an ethics based upon his dualist existential ontology. In the end, he was unable to fulfil his promise to devote a future work to ethics (BN: 628) apart from (the posthumously published) *Notebooks for an Ethics* (*Cahiers pour une morale*). In his postwar writings, however, Sartre significantly modified some of the more strident claims of *Being and Nothingness*, arguing for the possibility of ethical forms of mutual recognition and claiming that the ideal of authenticity requires "the existence of a society where each is recognized by all" (quoted in Baugh 2003: 102).

All the same, Sartre's more familiar existentialist ideal of *authenticity* – of embracing our freedom and contingency, affirming the necessity of choice and of being responsible for our actions – could not satisfactorily explain why some subjects, within particular situations, seemed unable to exercise their freedom or exist authentically in the existentialist sense. Although Sartre does not deny the possibility of psychological, social or political forms of oppression, these remain without fundamental ontological significance for our existence. Indeed, these experiences point to the fact that at some level (which may be pre-reflective or inaccessible to psychological reflection), the individual has already chosen to assume this particular form of psychosocial stigma, or alternatively, already chosen to reject it. Like Sartre's famous examples of the woman being courted, the earnest café waiter, or the homosexual in the closet (BN: 55–67), individuals who declined to assert their freedom to act within their given circumstances could only be described, from an ontological point of view, as living in "bad faith" – taking themselves for inert objects defined by their facticity rather than free subjects with an inalienable power of transcendence.

This typically existentialist emphasis on complete freedom and responsibility of the individual, however, left little room for any developed account of the effects of the experience of oppression in psychological, social and political terms. Indeed, Sartre underplays the way that certain situations of inequality, disadvantage or discrimination can undermine – psychologically, socially and politically – the subject's capacity to exercise his or her freedom effectively. Instead, Sartre develops an ontological–phenomenological analysis of the strategies and ruses of bad faith through which we evade our existential freedom and responsibility by reverting to our facticity or circumstantial object-status. Yet this self-objectification – a process involving the internalization of a negative self-image, which results in the diminution of our capacity for transcendence – is also what structures the experience of *oppression* for many dominated subjects and groups, a situation that is also extremely difficult to transform. Instead of describing women, sexual minorities or the working class as living in bad faith, de Beauvoir turned to an analysis of the mechanisms of oppression that would liberate dominated subjects from their passive position as objects of manipulation and help to foster their own creative self-definition.

Woman as the other

The most interesting example of de Beauvoir's use of Hegelian themes is her celebrated account of the unequal character of gender relations presented in *The Second Sex*. In this work, de Beauvoir develops a modified version of Sartrean existentialist analysis – using the dualist categories of consciousness or the *for-itself* in contrast with inert being or the *in-itself* – that is applied to understanding the relationship between the sexes and the particular lived situation of women. As de Beauvoir points out, according to a still-pervasive model, men have traditionally been associated with consciousness and rationality, while women have been associated with the body, that is to say with nature, the emotions and the "irrational". Men are defined by their status as conscious subjects whereas women are defined by their status as objects; their subjectivity thus remains inadequately recognized, expressed in ways and according to terms imposed or defined by men rather than women.

Now this situation of women under conditions of patriarchy (the historical and social rule of men over women), de Beauvoir argues, can be understood in terms modelled on the Hegelian master/slave dialectic: men have occupied the role of master, seemingly independent of nature and of the body, while women have been forced to assume the role of slaves, tethered to nature and the body, without recognition of their equal status or their possibilities for self-definition. This condition is then "naturalized" through forms of ideology that present the unequal relation between the sexes as preordained by nature, biology, religion, philosophy, or even justified by personal choice. The result is that women are relegated to the status of "second sex" in regard to men, whose gender covers both the particular condition of being male and the generic condition of being human (hence the sexist usage of the word "Man" to designate both males and human beings in general).

In the "Introduction" to *The Second Sex*, de Beauvoir explicitly defines the condition of women – drawing on literary, anthropological, philosophical and biological examples – according to the asymmetrical relation between the Self and the Other: "He is the Subject, he is the Absolute – she is the Other" (SS: 16). This distinction between the categories of "Self" and "Other" is evident in so-called primitive cultures, ancient mythologies, as well as in psychological and social relations between individuals and groups, which gain their very identity by defining themselves in opposition to an Other (SS: 17). This is evident, for example, in the hostility towards outsiders expressed by members of a village, the xenophobia of native-born citizens towards "foreigners", as well as the more explicit prejudices against Others expressed by anti-Semites, racists, white colonists and the ruling classes (*ibid.*). All these instances support the anthropologist Claude Levi-Strauss's contention that human cultures are marked by the construal of biological relations as a series of oppositions between Self and Other, an opposition that is expressed in hierarchical and conflictual relations. This pattern of group self-definition by excluding and stigmatizing the Other, de Beauvoir argues, challenges the romantic claim that human social relations are inherently harmonious, a fellowship "based upon solidarity and friendliness" (*ibid.*).

On the contrary, these phenomena of hostility and conflict support Hegel's (or Kojève's) contention that "we find in consciousness itself a fundamental hostility towards every consciousness; the subject can be posed only in being opposed – he sets himself up as the essential, as opposed to the other, the inessential, the object" (*ibid.*). We should note in passing that de Beauvoir deploys "the other" here in a second sense: that of the *other subject* in a conflictual struggle for recognition, as distinct from the "absolute" sense of the Other as a *fundamental category* of human thought and experience. As we have seen, the subject positioned as "the Other" sets up a reciprocal claim in turn, positing the dominating subject as "the Other" and itself as "the One". The result is the now-familiar struggle for recognition culminating in a non-reciprocal relationship between *the master* (the one who has prevailed as subject or as the Other) and *the slave* (the one who has been relegated to the status of the Other by the master).

In reality, various social rituals and cultural practices exist (wars, festivals, trading, treaties, contests) that tend to relativize the relation between Self and Other (SS: 17). De Beauvoir's question is why this reciprocity has not been recognized in the case of relations between the sexes (*ibid.*). Why have women submissively accepted their male-designated status as the Other? Unlike a racial, ethnic or religious minority, women roughly equal men in numbers in any given society; unlike the proletariat, women have not come into existence as a historical or political class. Indeed, women's biological and anatomical differences from men may be one reason why the difference between the sexes has tended to assume an "absolute" rather than a "relative" character. Moreover, the fact of dependence between men and women – biologically, socially, sexually and personally – has historically tended to prevent women from recognizing themselves as belonging to a common group with a shared identity or common goals (SS: 18–19).

The sexual and social bonds between men and women have thus contributed to the maintenance of her position as the Other; gender relations involve a fixed and hierarchical relationship, which de Beauvoir argues can be understood as a version of the Hegelian master/slave dialectic (SS: 20). Indeed, aspects of the master/slave relationship "apply much better to the relation of man to woman", in particular the description of the slave as a dependent consciousness that remains tethered to (biological) life and reliant upon the recognition bestowed upon her by men; women also aspire to recognition of their value but this is as yet a value defined by and achieved by men (SS: 90). What women demand, then, is recognition of their status as free subjects: to overcome their positioning as the Other by no longer subordinating their human existence to life or "animality" (SS: 97).

Women participate in this unequal relation – living in "bad faith" by accepting the role of the Other – because they derive certain benefits from it, not least that of succumbing to the "temptation to forego liberty and become a thing" (SS: 21). De Beauvoir thus ameliorates Sartre's insistence on absolute responsibility by arguing that freedom always presupposes a lived or *existential situation* that may diminish a subject's freedom to act. In the case of women, there may be a variety of reasons why she may submit to the rule of men, accept her status as the Other, including lack of definite resources, the power of the bond that ties her to men, and the psychological benefits of assuming her role as the Other (*ibid.*). From de Beauvoir's perspective (that of existentialist ethics), the situation of women is such that they can either affirm their freedom through a "continual reaching out towards other liberties"; or they can relapse into the immanence and stagnation of the in-itself, "the brutish life of subjection to given conditions" (SS: 29). Submitting to the role of the Other is a "moral fault" if the subject consents to it; if forced to submit, it is oppression and frustration (SS: 29). Such is the situation of women, who find themselves living in a world where they are compelled to assume the status of the Other, forced into the position of passive object for the sovereign male subject, yet still retain the aspiration of every subject to be recognized as free (*ibid.*).

The Second Sex is devoted to examining the motivations, mechanisms and effects of women's positioning as the Other. De Beauvoir's aim, however, is positive; she suggests that women might change their situation by transforming the meaning of gender roles, overcoming their status as the Other in order to become self-defining subjects. As many feminist critics have pointed out, however, there are tensions in de Beauvoir's analysis between her commitment to Sartrean premises – such as the primacy of individual freedom, and centrality of "bad faith" in the behaviour of women – and her feminist account of how oppression functions within a shared social situation. Unlike Sartre, de Beauvoir argues that conflictual relations *can* be overcome through mutual recognition, and that women must take responsibility for their oppression while at the same time liberating themselves from it. Indeed, many of the difficulties in de Beauvoir's account derive from the Sartrean and Kojèveian framework she adopts, which combines – in an unstable fashion – the existentialist emphasis on the ontological separation of the individual with the primacy of the intersubjective recognition between subjects.

The ethics of ambiguity

In this respect, de Beauvoir presents a more nuanced account of "existentialist ethics" in her 1948 text, *The Ethics of Ambiguity*. In the latter, Beauvoir developed a version of Sartrean existentialism that sought to provide an explicit account of oppression while also underlining individual freedom and responsibility. *The Ethics of Ambiguity* acknowledged the fundamental dualities constitutive of human existence (individual and social, life and death, nature and freedom, subject and object, and so on), while also avoiding the subtle strategies of bad faith that deny these ambiguities and construe our existence as immutable. In keeping with Sartre, de Beauvoir argued that freedom as transcendence is the capacity of self-defining subjects to transform their own individual existential situation. De Beauvoir thus supplemented Sartre's analysis by arguing that this freedom must also be understood (a) as *situated*, as dependent upon, indeed limited by, the concrete lived situation of individuals; and (b) individual freedom requires that we also will the *freedom of other subjects* – a view that Sartre also advocated in his famous 1945 lecture, "Existentialism is a Humanism" (published in 1946). My freedom requires that I am recognized by other free subjects, upon whose freedom my own freedom depends, and hence that those subjects who are oppressed must be liberated as well.

What is most interesting for us is that while de Beauvoir acknowledges the ontological separation between subjects, she rejects Sartre's implication that this separation forecloses the possibility of mutual recognition. De Beauvoir questions whether the *a priori* ontological separation of individuals makes the quest for a universalist ethics an idealist abstraction: "An ethics of ambiguity will be one which will refuse to deny *a priori* that separate existents can, at the same time, be bound to each other, that their individual freedoms can forge laws valid for all" (EA: 18). Thus while de Beauvoir underlines the primacy of the individual as against the abstract universal ("humanity"), she also argues that such a freedom of the individual is empty without a universalist dimension. In attempting to mediate between the primacy of the individual and the demand of universality, de Beauvoir's position comes very close to a Hegelian perspective that runs counter to the professed anti-Hegelianism of her existentialist ethics. As Kimberly Hutchings points out, this is one of the numerous points where de Beauvoir's existentialist framework comes into conflict with some of the Hegelian conceptual dualities (derived from Sartre and Kojève) that she employs within that framework (Hutchings 2003: 57 ff.). How is the existentialist ethics of individual freedom consistent with the demand that one also will the freedom of others? De Beauvoir's response, that my individual freedom is conditional upon others recognizing me as free and vice versa, clearly echoes Sartre's claims in his lecture "Existentialism is a Humanism". At the same time, this emphasis on individual freedom being conditional upon the freedom of others raises certain challenges. How to reconcile existentialist individualism with a commitment to the primacy of intersubjectivity, the interdependence of free subjects upon each other, given Sartre's claim that the ontological separation between subjects can never be bridged?

Instead of tackling this important issue directly, de Beauvoir repeats the now familiar French existentialist criticisms (introduced by Wahl) of Hegel's alleged forgetting of the existence of the individual. According to de Beauvoir, Hegel subordinates the particularity of the individual subject to an all-encompassing totality (EA: 17), and maintains that "the individual is only an abstract moment in the History of absolute mind [spirit]" (EA: 104–5). It should be said, however, that this is a criticism already made *by Hegel* in his *Logic*, which analyses the deficiencies of the analytic understanding and its use of the categories of abstract identity and formal universality: the way these categories reduce each individual identity to a substitutable unit within an undifferentiated whole. The existentialist criticism directed against Hegel is already Hegelian!

Be that as it may, de Beauvoir goes on to develop an existentialist critique of the Hegelian concept of totality and its alleged subordination of the individual to universal (whether of reason or of history). Hegel's emphasis on the universal is thus said to be a denial of "the concrete thickness of the here and now" in favour of the abstract universality of thought (EA: 121–2). Here again we recognize the standard existentialist criticism that Hegel reduces being to thought, and thereby subordinates the freedom of the individual to that of the universal state or reason in history. De Beauvoir even accuses Hegelianism of being a ruse that assumes the standpoint of Absolute in order to find solace in our existential impotence; far from being a philosophy of freedom, Hegelianism is, rather, a deathly refuge from ambiguities of life (EA: 158–9).

De Beauvoir's own attempt to mediate between individualism and intersubjectivity does not clearly account for why my individual freedom necessarily depends upon the freedom of others. Philosophers who make this claim (such as Kant, Fichte and Hegel) do so either by invoking a principle of universality (for example, Kant's universality of reason) or one of constitutive interdependence (intersubjective recognition as a condition of individual self-consciousness, as for Hegel). At times, de Beauvoir deploys a consequentialist form of reasoning that willing the freedom of others will enable me better to realize my own projects. At other times, she makes the Hegelian claim that mutual recognition of others as free is a condition of my own freedom as a subject (since my self-identity is dependent upon the recognition of others, whom I must also recognize as free). De Beauvoir appears to draw on this (Hegelian) assumption of universal interdependence while also maintaining the Sartrean position of an ontological separation between individuals. These two assumptions, however, are inconsistent unless an account can be given of how individuals are ontologically separate yet universally interdependent. This inconsistency undermines de Beauvoir's project of an existentialist ethics with universalistic dimensions. This difficulty in reconciling ontological individualism with a commitment to intersubjectivity perhaps also explains the challenges both Sartre and de Beauvoir experienced in attempting to marry existentialism and Marxism. Despite this, de Beauvoir's feminist ethics of ambiguity, as Hutchings argues, could be rethought from a Hegelian perspective in order to foreground intersubjective recognition as a way of mediating between the particularity, universality and individuality of gendered subjects (2003: 56–79). Overcoming de Beauvoir's adherence to the existentialist reading of

Hegel might thus open up a way for a "feminist rethinking" of her ethics of ambiguity.

Merleau-Ponty: from Hegel's existentialism to hyperdialectic

A contemporary of Sartre and de Beauvoir, Maurice Merleau-Ponty (1908–61) is another major postwar philosopher whose thought intersected with Hegelianism in complex ways. Merleau-Ponty is perhaps best known for his version of existential phenomenology, articulated in his major work, *The Phenomenology of Perception* (1945), which analysed phenomenologically the complexity of embodied perception and developed original accounts of corporeal intersubjectivity, temporality and freedom. Throughout his career, Merleau-Ponty also wrote extensively on political philosophy, particularly Marxism, as well as commenting on broader cultural, aesthetic, literary and political events. Along with Sartre and de Beauvoir, Merleau-Ponty was a co-founder of the famous journal *Les Temps Modernes*, dedicated to exploring the relationship between philosophy, culture and politics in the traumatic aftermath of World War II. These historical and political experiences sharpened Merleau-Ponty's conviction that we had to reconsider the naive Hegelian and Marxist optimism that reason would inevitably be realized in history. This is especially evident in *Adventures of the Dialectic*, which includes an important essay on "Western" Marxism (particularly the Hegelian Marxism of Lukács), and a long critique of Sartre's rather uncritical embrace of communism, which remained wedded to a Leninist "oppositional" form of Marxism (Merleau-Ponty 1973).

Like Sartre, Merleau-Ponty maintained an ambivalent relationship with Hegel. He emphasized the importance of retrieving and renewing Hegel's thought, drawing on elements of Hegelian dialectics while also critically transforming it in his original version of phenomenology. Hegel's attempt to explore the relationship between reason and unreason, his emphasis on the historicity of spirit, and his attempt to uncover an immanent logic of experience, all left their mark on Merleau-Ponty's work. An example would be Merleau-Ponty's rejection of the Hegelian Absolute in favour of a historical and finite conception of experience that would be articulated in an "ontology of sense". In his later work, Merleau-Ponty was working on a distinctively post-Hegelian project that he at one point called "hyperdialectic": dialectic without final synthesis or definitive supersession. Hyperdialectic was one way of describing Merleau-Ponty's unfinished attempt to capture the multiform, pluralistic, chiasmatic relationship between the visible and the invisible that opens up our embodied, sensuous experience of the world (Merleau-Ponty 1968: 94–5). In this respect, the importance of Merleau-Ponty's work for the poststructuralist philosophers of difference (Deleuze, Foucault, Derrida) is only now being fully appreciated (see Lawlor 2003).

Far more than many contemporaries, Merleau-Ponty highlighted the profound debt that modern thought owed to Hegel. He even claimed, in rather hyperbolic fashion, that Hegel remains the source of everything important in modern thought!

> All the great philosophical ideas of the past century – the philosophies of Marx and Nietzsche, phenomenology, German existentialism, and psychoanalysis – had their beginnings in Hegel; it was he who started the attempt to explore the irrational and integrate it into an expanded reason which remains the task of our century. (SNS: 63)

This quotation comes from his 1948 essay, "Hegel and Existentialism", published in *Sense and Non-Sense*, a review of Hyppolite's just-published commentary on the *Phenomenology of Spirit*. Merleau-Ponty uses the occasion, however, to reflect on the significance of Hegelian thought, as opened up by Hyppolite, for the various currents of postwar French philosophy. For it is Hegel, Merleau-Ponty remarks, who attempted to encompass, through an expanded conception of reason, the singularity of the individual and the universality of thought, a philosophical project particularly significant in the wake of the experiences of twentieth-century history (SNS: 63). All of modern thought is post-Hegelian; hence interpreting Hegel – as Hyppolite has done – means "taking a stand on all the philosophical, political, and religious problems of our century" (SNS: 64). Merleau-Ponty thus takes issue with both existentialist and Marxist repudiations of Hegel, arguing that Hegel can be reclaimed as an existentialist thinker.

The standard existentialist criticism (deriving from Kierkegaard) is that Hegel forgets individual existence in constructing his speculative system of thought. History is regarded as the articulation of reason, where events are taken to express logical relations between ideas; the individual experience of life is integrated into the universality of thought. As Kierkegaard remarks, Hegel leaves us only with a "palace of ideas", where the contradictions of existence are reconciled at the level of thought. Drawing on Hyppolite, Merleau-Ponty suggests that although this existentialist criticism might be directed at Hegel's later works (the *Encyclopaedia* and *Logic*), it cannot be maintained against Hegel's *Phenomenology*, which presents rather a philosophy of immanent historical experience or of finite human existence. Hegelian phenomenology is an attempt to comprehend the history of experience, of consciousness becoming reason and spirit, which includes "customs, economic structures, and legal institutions as well as works of philosophy" (SNS: 64). Against existentialist critics, Merleau-Ponty argues that there is a *Hegelian existentialism* that Hyppolite brings to light, an attempt "to reveal the immanent logic of human experience in all its sectors" (SNS: 65). Compared with Kant, Hegel's concept of experience is expanded considerably, encompassing moral, aesthetic and religious phenomena, as well as scientific knowledge and philosophical thought. Hegel's thought is existentialist, moreover, in describing the experience of consciousness as a life that is self-responsible and defined by *perpetual unrest*; it moves from self-certainty though radical scepticism, learns from its experience that it has only a partial grasp of truth, until it arrives at self-comprehension within historical time (SNS: 65–6). This restless experience is alienated or unhappy, sundered from the innocence of natural life, because it is conscious of death and mortality as much as of reason and freedom.

Having presented this account of Hegel's existentialism (courtesy of Hyppolite), Merleau-Ponty engages in an interesting reflection on Hegel's master/slave dialectic. He emphasizes the importance of the experience of *mortality* that constitutes our humanity, and the implicit mutuality that underlies the conflict between self-certain subjects striving to assert their independence. It is difficult not to take these "existentialist" remarks as an implicit criticism of Sartre's appropriation of this famous Hegelian figure, which is supposed to show the inevitably conflictual nature of self-conscious freedom. (In fact Merleau-Ponty makes this criticism against Sartre more explicitly in the *Phenomenology of Perception* (2002: 414), and at greater length in his later text, *The Visible and the Invisible* (1968: 77–83).) Following Sartre, Merleau-Ponty comments on the conflictual relationship between subjects that strive to turn each other into objects: I become an object under the gaze of the other, just as he becomes merely an object in the world under my own gaze; each consciousness thus seeks the death of the other "which it feels dispossesses it of its constitutive nothingness" (SNS: 68). But this conflict – explored in Sartre's famous chapter on "The Look" in *Being and Nothingness* – presupposes that each subject retains a level of subjectivity (how else could I feel threatened by the other?); moreover, it presupposes that each protagonist has already recognized the other as a subject, albeit one that threatens its own selfhood. Conflict between subjects presupposes mutual recognition: "We cannot be aware of the conflict unless we are aware of our reciprocal relationship and our common humanity. We do not deny each other except by mutual recognition of our consciousnesses" (SNS: 68). Conflict between subjects does not show the impossibility of mutual recognition; rather, mutual recognition is what makes possible intersubjective conflict.

Merleau-Ponty makes this Hegelian point against Sartre's contention that the ontological separation between individual subjects necessarily renders mutual recognition impossible. Sartre's ontology is too one-sided, or as Merleau-Ponty says in "The Battle over Existentialism" (a critical essay on *Being and Nothingness*), it is "too exclusively antithetic" (SNS: 72): in-itself and for-itself are opposed; freedom as transcendence is antithetical to the immanence of the in-itself; the for-itself clashes with the "objectifying" experience of the look, when I realize that I am reduced to an object for-others, and so on. Instead, Merleau-Ponty argues, myself and the other remain mutually intertwined: "I discover myself in the other . . . because I am from the start this mixture of life and death, solitude and communication, which is heading toward its resolution" (SNS: 68). Indeed, in his own phenomenology of embodied perception, Merleau-Ponty will consistently emphasize the *ambiguity* of human existence, the complex intertwining of freedom and facticity, self and other, body and world, the visible and the invisible.

Where Hegel ceases being existentialist, Merleau-Ponty suggests, is when he moves from the experience of death and struggle to the experience of history, overcoming history's contradictions not just through thought but through the "living relationship" among human beings (SNS: 69). Whereas Heidegger claimed that we exist for the sake of death, our awareness of mortality remaining essential to thought and action, for Hegel death is transmuted into "a higher form of life", namely the transition from individual to historical existence. Here too one can discern a subtle criticism of Sartre's "truncated dialectic", for which there is no remedy for the conflict between consciousness as a subject for-itself and consciousness as an object for-others (*ibid.*). Sartre's lack of a genuine account of the *historicity* of consciousness, moreover, is contrasted with Heidegger's insistence on the historicity of

Dasein; the latter is not only a being-toward-death but a being-with others that is an essential part of existing historically within a shared world or clearing of Being. Indeed, what Heidegger lacks, Merleau-Ponty points out, is not historicity but rather an affirmation of *the individual*. Heidegger omits to analyse the Hegelian conception of a *struggle for recognition* between free subjects or "opposing freedoms", that oppositional becoming within historical experience "without which coexistence sinks into anonymity and everyday banality" (SNS: 69).

Interestingly, this echoes to some extent Sartre's criticism of Heidegger's *Mitsein* or being-with (BN: 244–50), which he argues fails to properly individuate individuals from the communal being-with, which for Heidegger is closer to an anonymous "crew" than the inherent conflictuality that Sartre posits. Drawing on its complex Hegelian inheritance, Merleau-Ponty concludes by venturing a more complete definition of existentialism, one that eloquently articulates themes belonging to his own existential phenomenology. Against the familiar existentialist emphasis on awareness of death, conflict and solitude, he affirms an understanding of existence that is defined by the shared universality of being human, even within conflict, a reason that is immanent in unreason, and a freedom that acknowledges limits, yet is profoundly affirmed by our perceptual experience of bodily existence and action in their most intimate and everyday manifestations (SNS: 70).

Merleau-Ponty continued his criticism of Sartre, more explicitly, in his late unfinished work, *The Visible and the Invisible* (he died at the relatively young age of 53 before completing this enigmatic final manuscript). In an extended engagement with Sartre's analysis of the relationship between Being and Nothingness, Merleau-Ponty turns his attention to the difficulties presented by the Hegelian dialectics taken up in Sartre's existentialist Marxism. As Merleau-Ponty remarks, dialectic is the attempt to articulate philosophically the conceptual relations between categories; to show the relatedness of opposing terms, the negative movement of thought from one determination through to its opposite, and their synthesis within a more complex configuration of conceptual meaning. Dialectic thus underscores the role of *negation* in the constitution of positivity (the new emerges out of the negation or superseding of the old). In Hegel's dialectics, the movement of thought-determinations proceeds via a determinate negation that both cancels and preserves; this is the famous movement of *Aufhebung* or supersession that "synthesizes" opposing terms into a more complex conceptual unity.

Much as Adorno does with his negative dialectics, however, Merleau-Ponty questions whether Hegel's dialectical supersession does justice to the plurality of our experience of corporeal being. Indeed, Merleau-Ponty rejects as an abstraction the reduction of being to thought, the integration of sensible multiplicity into conceptual totality. Such is the movement characteristic of "bad dialectics": the philosophical attempt to impose a theoretical framework of explication on the complex intertwining of both perceptual and historical experience. On the contrary, Merleau-Ponty contends, the only good dialectics is one that self-critically surpasses itself, one that refuses the theoretical closure of bad dialectic – the rigid movement of thesis, antithesis and synthesis – in favour of an open-ended, pluralistic and ambiguous "hyperdialectic".

> What we call hyperdialectic is a thought that on the contrary is capable of reaching truth because it envisages without restriction the plurality of the relationships and what has been called ambiguity.   (Merleau-Ponty 1968: 94)

Hyperdialectic refuses the abstractions of traditional dialectic; it is dialectic without totalizing synthesis, without a supersession that results in a new positive or new position (*ibid*.: 95). It is a dialectic that acknowledges the inherent instability of all thought, one that embraces only concrete, partial and hybrid surpassings that reassemble without ordering opposing terms – such as Sartre's being for-itself and being in-itself – into any fixed hierarchy or conceptual opposition. Rather, hyperdialectic is an attempt to move beyond these metaphysical oppositions in order to think what Merleau-Ponty calls "wild Being": the "being of the sensible" in its multiplicity and ambiguity, irreducible to conceptual or discursive articulation. The point here, Merleau-Ponty argues, is not to abandon dialectical thought; rather, it is to deploy dialectic as a way of thinking the complex intertwining or "chiasm" between perception and being that opens up our embodied experience of self and world – a project Merleau-Ponty was pursuing at the end of his life.

This critique of dogmatic or metaphysical dialectic, moreover, has strong ethical and political dimensions. The dogmatic imposition of a conceptual framework emphasizing unity and totality over plurality and divergence readily translates into a politics of domination, even terror. Such is the philosophical background to Merleau-Ponty's critique of Sartre's Marxism. The latter falls victim to the illusion that historical experience can be renewed according to an oppositional dialectics of history, one that posits the party as subject, reducing workers to objects, and that culminates in a revolutionary transformation of society which risks legitimating violence against whatever remains irreducible to such a dialectics (see Merleau-Ponty 1973: 95 ff.).

One is struck here by the resonances between Adorno's negative dialectics and Merleau-Ponty's hyperdialectic, both of which affirm a pluralist dialectic without totalizing synthesis in order to do justice to the singularity of nature and embodied being (see Coole 2000). Merleau-Ponty's criticism of the dogmatic use of Hegelian dialectics, whether in existentialism or Marxism, also prefigures the critique of totalizing dialectics in the next generation of French thinkers, who turned sharply against the existentialist and Hegelian-Marxist projects of their teachers. Inspired by Merleau-Ponty, Derrida and Deleuze sought in different ways to subvert conventional Hegelian dialectical thinking in order to rethink it as a philosophy of difference (see Reynolds 2004). It is not surprising, then, that the next major episode in the adventure of French Hegelianism was what we might call its dialectical reversal: the poststructuralist challenge to Hegelianism.

Summary of points

Sartre's critique of Hegel

- According to Sartre, Hegel's master/slave dialectic shows how the conflictual relation between Self and Other is constitutive of self-consciousness.
- Sartre claims that Hegel reduces the *ontological* problem of the Other to an *epistemological* issue concerning our knowledge of the Other. Sartre makes two related criticisms on this point:

  - Hegel's "epistemological optimism" (BN: 240–43): Hegel construes the relationship with the Other as a *knowledge relation*, where each self-certain subject turns the Other into an object that can be known and mastered.
  - Hegel's "ontological optimism" (BN: 243–4): Hegel adopts the *standpoint of the Absolute* in accounting for the experience of self-consciousness, thereby subsuming the plurality of individual subjects into the unity of the whole.

- Sartre argues that there is an ontological separation between subjects which renders mutual recognition impossible; each subject attempts to render the other as an object, which results in human relations being inescapably *conflictual*.

De Beauvoir's Second Sex and Ethics of Ambiguity

- Simone de Beauvoir argued that Sartre's version of the problem of the Other tended to underplay the experience of *oppression*.
- Gender relations under conditions of patriarchy can be understood via the Hegelian master/slave dialectic.
- De Beauvoir further defines gender relations in terms of the asymmetrical relation between the Self and the Other: "He is the Subject, he is the Absolute – she is the Other" (SS: 16).
- De Beauvoir acknowledges the ontological separation between subjects, but she rejects the implication that this forecloses mutual recognition.
- De Beauvoir claims that my individual freedom is conditional upon others recognizing me as free; this challenges the Sartrean existentialist framework central to her ethics of ambiguity.

Merleau-Ponty: Hegel's existentialism and hyperdialectics

- Merleau-Ponty rejects the standard existentialist criticisms of Hegel, arguing that there is a *Hegelian existentialism* that attempts "to reveal the immanent logic of human experience in all its sectors".
- In Hegel's master/slave dialectic, Merleau-Ponty emphasizes the implicit mutuality that underlies the conflict between self-certain subjects.
- Against Sartre's account, Merleau-Ponty argues that the conflict between subjects does not show the impossibility of mutual recognition; rather, mutual recognition is what makes possible intersubjective conflict.
- As does Adorno with his negative dialectics, Merleau-Ponty questions whether the Hegelian dialectics does justice to the plurality of our experience of corporeal being.
- Against traditional dialectics, Merleau-Ponty posits a "hyper-dialectics" that remains open-ended and ambiguous: a dialectics that reassembles differing terms without ordering them into any fixed hierarchy or conceptual opposition.

eight

Deconstructing Hegelianism: Deleuze, Derrida and the question of difference

The major postwar movements of French philosophy (existentialism, phenomenology and Hegelian Marxism) regarded Hegel as one of the key thinkers of the modern age. By the 1960s, however, Hegel's dialectics was the philosophical project most in need of deconstruction and transformation. This chapter thus focuses on two major poststructuralist thinkers: Gilles Deleuze (1925–95) and his critical encounter with, and conceptual transformation of, Hegelian dialectics; and Jacques Derrida (1930–2004) and his Heideggerian-inspired deconstruction of metaphysics, for which Hegelian dialectics is both an essential reference point and primary target. At issue here is the problem of constructing a genuinely post-Hegelian philosophy, a project that presents us with at least three alternatives: (a) can Hegelian dialectics be overcome via Nietzschean anti-dialectics? (b) should Hegelian dialectics be transformed, rather, into an experimental thinking of non-conceptual difference? or (c) should the Hegelian system be submitted to a deconstruction of its limits, confronting it with a radical difference that exceeds its dialectical unity? I shall suggest that Deleuze initially explores the first path (a) before turning to the second (b); Derrida pursues the third path (c), which submits Hegelian dialectics to a radical "displacement" that unravels its metaphysical claims to totality, unity and closure.

In this respect, Deleuze and Derrida both engage in related confrontations with Hegelian thought; but they do not reject or repudiate Hegelian dialectics so much as transform it such that it opens up a different way of thinking – a *thinking of difference* as such. As we saw with Adorno and Merleau-Ponty, the problem with Hegelian dialectics is that it subsumes difference understood as opposition into a higher conceptual unity. For Deleuze, it is unable to think pure difference or "becoming" as a process involving a multiplicity of contingent, overlapping forces. For Derrida, it remains caught within the closure of metaphysics – the attempt to subordinate difference to identity, to incorporate radical negativity into the *logos* of reason. In conclusion, I suggest that the Deleuzean and Derridian encounters with Hegel open up the possibility of rethinking Hegelian dialectics; they also raise the question of the future of Hegelianism.

Hegel and poststructuralism

In the Preface to *Difference and Repetition*, Deleuze makes a remark that encapsulates the "anti-Hegelian" animus of much French philosophy of the 1960s. Deleuze mentions Heidegger's thinking of the ontological difference, the structuralist project, modernist novels, the power of repetition in psychoanalysis, linguistics, modern art and so on. "All these signs", Deleuze continues, "may be attributed to a generalised anti-Hegelianism: difference and repetition have taken the place of the identical and the negative, of identity and contradiction" (DR: xix). Deleuze also identifies the critical issues in his confrontation with Hegelian dialectics: the need for a critique of the philosophy of representation that privileges identity and the negative, including the Hegelian construal of difference as contradiction; and consequently, the need to move beyond Hegel's dialectics in order to elaborate a genuine thinking of pure difference or "difference in itself".

This project of thinking radical difference involves a complex movement, even a complex dialectics; for to assume an "oppositional" stance towards Hegel is to risk remaining tethered to his metaphysical system even in the attempt to overcome it. As Derrida argues, the attempt to be simply anti-Hegelian falls prey to Hegelian dialectics, since dialectical thinking functions by appropriating what opposes it, integrating into a more complex unity. Poststructuralist feminist philosopher Judith Butler made a similar point, particularly against Deleuze, in her illuminating study of French Hegelianism and its legacy (1988). As we shall see, this is also the thrust of Derrida's deconstructive reading of Emmanuel Levinas (1906–95), whom Derrida criticized for attempting to oppose Hegelian discourse – the discourse of metaphysics itself – in the name of a transcendence beyond all conceptual mediation. As Derrida remarks:

> Levinas is very close to Hegel, much closer than he admits, and at the very moment when he is apparently opposed to Hegel in the most radical fashion. This is the situation he must share with all anti-Hegelian thinkers, and whose final significance calls for much thought. (WD: 99)

Given the power of Hegelian dialectics, which readily subsumes that which opposes it, Derrida adopts an oblique strategy, deconstructing Hegelian dialectics at the limit of its system of conceptuality in order to reveal its structuring elements. For Hegelianism both exemplifies the privileging of identity and opens up the possibility of a thinking of radical difference. Such are the stakes for Deleuze and Derrida in their confrontation with Hegelian dialectics, a confrontation that still marks the conceptual horizon of much contemporary European philosophy.

Deleuze: from anti-dialectics to dialectics of difference

Deleuze's 1962 work, *Nietzsche and Philosophy*, is one of the seminal texts of French poststructuralism, influencing thinkers such as Foucault, Derrida and Lyotard. The French rediscovery of Nietzsche during the 1960s can be understood as an expression of acute dissatisfaction with the amalgam of Hegelian-inspired dialectics, phenomenology and Hegelian Marxism that dominated the postwar philosophical landscape. It also represented the beginnings of an attempt to transform Hegelian dialectics into a thinking no longer oriented towards unity, totality and finality. There are many statements in *Nietzsche and Philosophy* that vividly dramatize the conflict between Hegel and Nietzsche: one risks failing to understand Nietzsche's philosophy at all, Deleuze claims, unless one grasps "against whom" it is directed (Hegelianism). Far from being dialectical, Nietzschean pluralism is the dialectic's "most ferocious enemy, its only profound enemy" (NP: 8). Indeed, "there is no possible compromise between Hegel and Nietzsche", Deleuze affirms; Nietzscheanism comprises, rather, "an absolute anti-dialectics", one that seeks to expose "all the mystifications that find a final refuge in the dialectic" (NP: 195). Nietzschean genealogy or total critique is an attempt to overcome modern nihilism, which finds its most pernicious philosophical expression in dialectics:

> The dialectic is the natural ideology of *ressentiment* and bad conscience. It is thought in the perspective of nihilism and from the standpoint of reactive forces. It is a fundamentally Christian way of thinking, from one end to the other; powerless to create new ways of thinking and feeling.   (NP: 148)

Deleuze's core objection to Hegelian dialectics is that it subordinates difference and plurality and so is incapable of thinking individuation, becoming and the arrival of "the new". As we shall see, however, by the late 1960s, in *Difference and Repetition*, Deleuze modified his stance considerably, even positioning his own thought within the history of dialectical thought, including Hegel's (see DR: 179, 268). The point is not to oppose Hegelian dialectics or adopt an "anti-dialectical" stance, but rather to transform it into a genuine thinking of difference, a thinking that Deleuze even describes at various points as "dialectics", or what we might call a dialectical thinking of difference as multiplicity. This project is already under way to some extent in *Nietzsche and Philosophy*, which is marred by its stridently "anti-dialectical" rhetoric; but it is more explicitly and productively developed in Deleuze's 1968 masterpiece, *Difference and Repetition*. In this respect, both Deleuze and Derrida (much like Merleau-Ponty and Adorno) are concerned to rethink Hegelian dialectics: unchaining it from conceptual necessity and metaphysical closure, and thereby opening it up to contingency, singularity and multiplicity.

Active and reactive forces

Deleuze begins his Nietzschean reversal of Hegelianism by proposing a pluralist ontology of bodies as expressions of differential relations of force. Spinoza's challenge points the way: "we do not even know what a body *can do*" (NP: 39). Indeed, all bodies, for Deleuze, are composed of a plurality of relations of "dominant and dominated forces" (NP: 40). In this dynamic ontology, there are only individuals or bodies expressing certain degrees of power: "every relationship of forces constitutes a body – whether it is chemical, biological, social or political" (*ibid.*). All phenomena are thus interpreted as expressions of differential relations of force, while bodies are understood without recourse to the centrality of consciousness and subjectivity (the subject–object relation) defining the philosophy of representation (NP: 39, 62).

More specifically, Deleuze takes Nietzschean forces to be defined by the *relationship* of force to force; they are consequently reducible to two originary qualities: in any body, the superior or dominant forces are defined as *active*, the inferior or dominated forces as *reactive*. Reactive forces are those of conservation and adaptation, securing "mechanical and utilitarian accommodations, the *regulations* which express all the power of inferior and dominated forces" (NP: 41). Active forces, by contrast, are creative, dominating, expansive: they escape consciousness, go "to the limit of what they can do", and are defined by plastic powers of transformation. Consciousness, then, for Deleuze, is the expression of reactive forces of adaptation, which remain dominated by the unconscious active forces of the body (*ibid.*). The philosophy of consciousness operating within the paradigm of subjectivity (everything from Kantian and Hegelian idealism to phenomenology) thus remains wholly within the domain of reactive forces; as such it remains powerless to think the active forces of life itself.

The "triumph" of reactive forces

So far I have given a basic sketch of Deleuze's Nietzschean analytic of force relations, which is aimed primarily at Hegelian dialectics. Among other things, Deleuze goes on to propose a *Nietzschean* version of the famous Hegelian master/slave dialectic so beloved of postwar French philosophy. So what motivates Deleuze's challenge to Hegelianism? It is a critique that is simultaneously metaphysical, ethical and political. The problem with dialectics, for Deleuze, is that it remains a *restricted* form of critique that preserves established values, that dialectically supersedes its other by negating and preserving it, and thereby expresses "reactive forces" of conservation and preservation. Nietzsche's genealogical philosophy, by contrast, undertakes an aggressive, *total critique* by enquiring into the *origin* of values themselves, the *element* from which their value is derived. This means, according to Deleuze, that we must interpret the qualitative forces expressed in any given phenomenon (active or reactive) in order to thereby reach the *differential and genetic element* of these forces – what Nietzsche called the "will to power" with its primordial qualities of *affirmation* and *negation* (NP: 530–4). Deleuze's Nietzschean genealogical critique, as Descombes remarks, thus embarks upon a "quest for a 'differential' criterion", one that would allow us to distinguish that which originates with the reactive forces and negative will of the slave from that which originates with the active forces and affirmative will of the master (NP: 159).

Now this differential criterion between active and reactive forces is primordially found in the quantitative difference between forces, as expressed in their respective qualities as active (dominant) or reactive (dominated). But this is only at the level of what we might call their metaphysical "origin", where active and reactive forces coexist in relations of tension. As Nietzsche points out, it is not the active, but rather the *weak* and *reactive forces* that dominate in social and historical actuality. All of history, morality and law are expressions of reactive forces that have come to dominate *de facto*. The problem now becomes that of accounting for this *de facto* triumph of reactive forces despite the *de jure* superiority of active forces. Deleuze's answer is that reactive forces triumph by *decomposing* active forces: they "*separate active force from what it can do*", such that the latter becomes reactive (NP: 57). As Deleuze explains, this decomposition of active forces is achieved by instituting an ideological fiction, a "mystification or falsification" (*ibid.*) that restricts the aggressive expansion of active forces, rendering them docile and submissive (for example, the reactive values of Christian morality).

Deleuze thereby inverts the Hegelian phenomenological narrative, portraying the historical development of self-conscious subjectivity as the expression of reactive forces culminating in the *nihilism* of modernity (the condition in which the highest values devalue themselves). The historical triumph of reactive forces is thus traced through successive stages, from *negative* nihilism (Christianity, the depreciation of life in the name of higher values), *reactive* nihilism (enlightenment culture, the depreciation of these higher values), through to *passive* nihilism (modernity, the dissolution of all values and will). The figures or "types" representing these stages of nihilism are embodied by the priest, the dialectician and Nietzsche's "last man" – the passive nihilist who no longer values or wills anything but material comfort or "happiness".

So how can nihilism be overcome? Deleuze's proposal is that it can be vanquished through the *self-destruction* of reactive forces: *complete* nihilism overcomes itself through the *transvaluation* of all values; the "active destruction" of the negative and its transmutation into the affirmative – a proposal that bears an uncanny resemblance to the Hegelian thesis of a "negation of the negation". Deleuze performs this complex move by sundering the will to power into *immanent* and *transcendent* dimensions: there is the will to power as we can *know it* (reactive forces that culminate in nihilism), and there is the will to power as we can *think* it (active forces or creative becoming) (NP: 172–3). The critical standpoint Deleuze adopts here is that of "life" understood as will to power (NP: 94): active force expresses *affirmation* of life, an affirmative will to power; reactive force expresses a *negation* of life, a negative will to power. With the concept of "life", Deleuze now has the criterion that distinguishes active from reactive force: life as will to power grounds Nietzschean "total critique" as against the nihilism (life-negation) of Hegelian dialectical critique.

Here we must take care to distinguish *genuine* affirmation of life from *pseudo*-affirmation, Nietzschean affirmation from the apologias of reactive force. In a similar vein, Nietzsche's Zarathustra mocked the pseudo-affirmation of the ass, the one who blithely says "yes" to the reactive forces of the status quo. For Deleuze, this is none other than the Hegelian dialectician! Once again we encounter the existentialist and Marxist criticism that Hegelianism promotes reconciliation with actuality as acquiescence with the status quo: the Hegelian dialectician is the one who conflates "affirmation with the truthfulness of truth or the positivity of the real" (NP: 183). But Deleuze's critique of Hegelian dialectics does not stop with the existentialist call to return to the singularity of existence, or the Marxist demand for a revolutionary transformation of society. Nietzschean critique (and Deleuzean thought) strives for the transvaluation of all values: a creation of concepts and invention of new possibilities of life. Against Hegelian dialectics, which overcomes alienation via the comprehension of our historical experience, Nietzschean genealogy overcomes nihilism by harnessing the active forces of the body and unconscious in order to invent new concepts and modes of existence.

Deleuze's ingenious attempt to confront Hegelian dialectics with an anti-dialectical interpretation of Nietzsche raises a couple of critical questions:

1. *What is the status of the concept "force" in Deleuze's account of active and reactive forces?* Deleuze argues for a "typology of forces" that can be applied to a multiplicity of phenomena, from natural organisms, physical bodies, moral concepts, to social and cultural practices. What sense can we make of such a generalized concept of "force"? Are the forces operating at a physical–biological level of the same order as those operating in language, morality or cultural meaning? If the same concept of force is operating across the differing ontological levels, how can we analyse these

phenomena through a general concept of "force" without losing sight of their distinctive differences?

2. *How are we to understand the difference between active and reactive forces if it is not always (or even ever) the case that active forces dominate over reactive forces?* Deleuze's Nietzschean response is that we can postulate such active forces of life-affirmation as the condition of the (dialectical) development of reactive forces of consciousness, morality and history. Drawing on a Kantian (but also Heideggerian) distinction, Deleuze argues that we cannot *know* such forces but we can nonetheless *think* them philosophically as that which makes possible our experience. What Deleuze in effect proposes is a model of active forces (articulating difference and singularity) as the "transcendental condition" of our experience of reactive forces (constituting unity and sameness). In *Nietzsche and Philosophy*, however, Deleuze does not provide any real arguments for accepting the postulation of such unknowable active forces. This will be the project undertaken in *Difference and Repetition*, which abandons the Nietzschean-inspired rhetoric of "anti-dialectics" in favour of a transformation of Hegelian dialectics into a paradoxical dialectic of multiplicities.

Deleuze: from contradiction to non-conceptual difference

Deleuze's critique of Hegelian dialectics in *Nietzsche and Philosophy* becomes more interesting in *Difference and Repetition*, which attempts to transform the distorted image of dialectical thought that has held sway from Plato to Hegel. The basic problem with Hegelian dialectics, Deleuze claims, is that it remains a teleologically oriented process that subsumes singularity under universality, sensibility under conceptuality. It is the most formidable attempt to subsume difference into representational identity thinking by pushing it to the level of contradiction, and integrating dialectical contradictions into ever more encompassing forms of synthesis. Hegelian dialectics thus subordinates difference to identity, yoking it to the "fourfold root" of representation: *resemblance* in perception, *analogy* in judgement, *opposition* of predicates, *identity* of the concept, which together comprise the unity of the knowing subject (DR: 262 ff.). What is needed, then, is not a rejection but rather a *rethinking* of dialectic within a philosophy of "difference in itself". Deleuze thus attempts to transfigure Hegelian dialectics into a dialectic oriented towards difference, one that does justice to the interplay of multiple overlapping forces constituting individuals in processes of becoming.

Deleuze's project in *Difference and Repetition* is to overturn the "philosophy of representation" that privileges identity over difference, unity over multiplicity, generality over singularity. In order to appreciate the shift in Deleuze's approach to dialectics, it is helpful to compare this mature project with his early critical review (1954) of Hyppolite's Hegelian study, *Logic and Existence* (the English translation of *Logic and Existence* includes Deleuze's review as an appendix). Drawing on his former teacher's work, Deleuze takes from Hyppolite the concept of a "Logic of Sense", and agrees in part with Hyppolite's "Heideggerian" approach to Hegelian logic as a logic of sense. Philosophy can only be an ontology, in fact an ontology of sense, where sense is what unifies the ontological difference between Being and beings. We should note, however, that in his later work, *The Logic of Sense* (from 1969), Deleuze will argue that it is *non-sense* that presents the indeterminate chaotic background against which sense is articulated and can work its significatory effects in thought and language.

On the other hand, Deleuze argues that Hyppolite is thoroughly *Hegelian* in claiming that sense means the identity of being and difference, where difference is taken up to the level of contradiction (LE: 195). Hyppolite remains wedded to the Hegelian conception of difference, now construed as opposition and contradiction, where the latter remains a form of *conceptual difference* that obliterates *non-conceptual* difference. Here Deleuze offers his own critical conjecture, which he will explicitly develop in *Difference and Repetition*:

> can we not construct an ontology of difference which would not have to go up to contradiction, because contradiction would be less than difference and not more? Is contradiction itself only the phenomenal and anthropological aspect of difference?
>
> (*ibid.*)

Hyppolite's Hegelian response would be that such an ontology of pure difference remains stuck within the logic of reflection (the correlated interplay between opposing concepts of identity and difference, of opposition and contradiction). Deleuze questions, however, whether this Hegelian account of Being pushed up to the level of contradiction is the same as Being expressing itself as pure difference. In fact Hyppolite's more "Heideggerian" discussion of language (and allusions to forgetting, remembering, to the loss of sense) provide the basis, Deleuze suggests, for "a theory of expression where difference is expression itself, and contradiction its merely phenomenal aspect" (*ibid.*). Such a theory of difference as expression will be explicitly developed in other works of Deleuze, notably in his large study, *Spinoza: Expressionism in Philosophy* (from 1968).

Against difference as opposition or contradiction, "difference in itself" is non-conceptual difference or the "being of the sensible". In *Difference and Repetition*, Deleuze argues for a new metaphysics of difference that would genuinely "reverse Platonism", the original paradigm of the philosophy of representation that subordinates non-conceptual difference to conceptual difference. Such a philosophy is also motivated by the experience of modernity after "the death of God", a Nietzschean sensibility symptomatic of a "generalized anti-Hegelianism" that eschews universality, identity and the sovereign subject in favour of singularity, becoming and an affirmative concept of difference. In Deleuze's words:

> modern thought is born of the failure of representation, of the loss of identities, and the discovery of all the forces that act under the representation of the identical. . . . All identities are only simulated, produced as an optical "effect" by the more profound game of difference and repetition. We propose to think difference in itself independently of the forms of representation which reduce it to the Same, and the relation of different to different independently of those forms which make it pass through the negative. (DR: xix)

This remark is virtually a crystallization of the poststructuralist philosophy of difference. The world of representation, defined by the primacy of identity and the unity of the subject, has begun to dissolve; modern thought and art all articulate the experience of the loss of identity, the disruption of representation, and the impersonal forces of repetition (everything from the Freudian unconscious, repetition in modern art and literature, to the fetishistic world of commodities). The Nietzschean "death of God" prompted the resurrection of the figure of "man" in modern (existentialist and Hegelian-Marxist) humanism; but the "man" of modern humanism is now withering away. All these cultural signs indicate a paradigm shift, Deleuze contends, from the "Hegelian" model of identity and negativity to the anti-representationalist model of difference and repetition.

For our purposes, however, the most relevant aspect of Deleuze's fascinating project is his criticism of the Hegelian conception of difference as opposition and contradiction. Deleuze's criticism can be put very succinctly, since it repeats and develops the claim made in his critique of Hyppolite's reading of Hegel. According to Deleuze, Hegel follows Aristotle in conceptualizing the absolute maximum degree of difference as *contradiction*; but Hegel does not go on to subsume contradiction into an overarching category, such as Aristotle's "equivocal being" (DR: 44–5; Williams 2003: 71). Rather, Hegelian difference taken as contradiction drives onwards to ever-greater conceptual syntheses – difference is pushed to its limit, that is, to the infinitely large. This movement of difference as contradiction is what Deleuze calls "*orgiastic* representation": the discovery of negativity, of "tumult, restlessness and passion", at the limits of the order of representation (DR: 42). Hegel's thought of contradiction takes this order of representation to its extreme limit; contradiction is the movement of negativity, "the intoxication and restlessness of the infinitely large" (DR: 45).

Hegel's "orgiastic" representation of difference as contradiction, however, does not break free of the philosophy representation, for it still subordinates difference to conceptual difference (difference sublated as a moment within the unity of the concept). Rather than Hegel's orgiastic path, which "pushes" difference all the way to contradiction, Deleuze insists that contradiction must be "pulled" back to the level of non-conceptual plurality – to what Hegel demoted as mere sensation and intuition. Instead of conceptual difference inscribed within the concept (as with Hegel), Deleuze argues for a conception of "difference in itself"; for *non-conceptual difference*, which brings us to the difficult thought of a "concept" of difference that is no longer yoked to the framework of representational (subject–object) thinking. Here again there are striking resonances with Adorno's negative dialectics and Merleau-Ponty's hyperdialectic. Like these approaches, the Deleuzean philosophy of difference aims at overcoming the philosophy of representation (roughly equivalent to what Heidegger called "metaphysics"). The question is how to rethink dialectics as a dialectics of difference.

A Deleuzean dialectics?

A number of recent commentators have taken issue with the standard view of Deleuze as an enemy of dialectical thought. Daniel Smith, for example, suggests that "Deleuze is certainly not anti-dialectical, since he

explicitly places himself within a long tradition of dialectical thought"
(2000: 128). Catherine Malabou, moreover, questions Deleuze's professed anti-Hegelianism, arguing that both Hegel and Deleuze are
engaged in the task of "fluidifying" thought and hence that their philosophies can be construed as a paradoxical "block of becoming called
Hegel–Deleuze" (1996: 136). In this section, I shall explore the question of Deleuze and dialectics, suggesting that there is a paradoxical
"Deleuzean dialectics" that strives to think dialectics without any
all-encompassing synthesis. Deleuzean dialectics is oriented, rather,
towards pure difference, heterogeneous multiplicities; it is a thinking
that strives to liberate non-conceptual difference from the strictures of
representation.

It is true that Deleuze has frequently presented his philosophy as
anti-dialectical (in *Nietzsche and Philosophy*, for example). He has also
at times dismissed dialectics as unphilosophical, reducing "philosophy
to interminable discussion" (Deleuze and Guattari 1994: 79). For
example, in *What is Philosophy?*, co-authored with Felix Guattari,
Hegel is criticized for generating a conceptual system out of the dialectical conflict of rival opinions (*ibid.*: 80). Despite the genius of Hegel
and other dialecticians, Nietzsche's critique still holds true: dialectics
reduces concepts to propositions and opinions and thus destroys
the possibility of creating new concepts (*ibid.*: 80, 147). Despite this
popular view (encouraged by Deleuze and Guattari's polemical
remarks), Deleuze actually has a more ambiguous relationship with
Hegelian dialectics, attempting a transformation of dialectics rather
than demanding its outright rejection.

In *Difference and Repetition*, for example, Deleuze explicitly remarks
that his project of an anti-representationalist philosophy of difference
should be understood as a response to "the long history of the distortion of the dialectic" (DR: 268). Indeed, dialectics from Plato to Hegel,
Deleuze argues, is marred by two major difficulties:

1. The construal of difference as negativity and its "maximalization" as opposition and contradiction, what Deleuze describes as
   the substitution of the Hegelian "labour of the negative for the
   play of difference and the differential" (DR: 268).
2. The attempt to reduce the form of the philosophical question
   to the propositional form ("S is P"), a form that is taken to
   exhaust the possibilities of the question in general.

Such a "distortion" of the dialectic, thanks to the privileging of
negativity and of the propositional form, does not of course imply its

repudiation. The challenge, rather, is to rethink dialectics in terms of *problems* rather than propositions (creative responses to the singularity of events and ideas); and to reverse the subordination of difference to identity, negativity and contradiction in order to liberate thought from the yoke of representation.

There are, moreover, closely connected ontological and moral dimensions to Deleuze's criticism of traditional dialectical thought. First, there is an ontological claim, since Deleuze rejects the "being of the negative" that he insists drives the Hegelian dialectics. The emphasis on the negative in traditional dialectics reduces difference to non-being. This renders it amenable to the conceptual reduction of difference to opposition and contradiction, and hence its subordination to the identity of the concept (where contradictions are resolved in a "higher" conceptual unity). What we require, rather, is to think the *being of the problematic*, that is, the being of *problems and questions*: a paradoxical form of being (which Deleuze writes as "(non)-being" in order to distinguish it from traditional notions of non-being) that expresses difference *positively* and hence cannot be reduced to simple negativity. The reduction of the being of problems and questions to negativity results in the subordination of affirmation to negation. Dialectical affirmation can only ever be a derivative result of negation, as in Hegel's famous "negation of the negation"; in other words, the new can only ever be the negation of what already is; repetition is a repetition of the same rather than a production of difference. Differences are subsumed within the ideal unity of conceptuality, which negates what is deficient in empirical reality (contingency, singularity, diversity, indeterminacy), yet integrates these aspects of difference into the higher unity of reason.

This ontological claim is tied to a further criticism of the *moral presuppositions* and practical implications of the dialectic, its valorizing of the negative and reduction of difference to contradiction. Deleuze suggests that the relation of negative dependence on what already exists engenders the "conservative" spirit of dialectical negation; thought is directed towards comprehending what is or has been, towards negating rather than affirming differences, and is thereby lead away from its primary task: "that of determining problems and realizing in them our power of creation and decision" (DR: 268). History, Deleuze argues, does not progess by the dialectical movement of "negation of the nega-tion", but rather "by deciding problems and affirming differences" (*ibid.*). Contradiction will not liberate the oppressed; rather, it can be used by the powerful to defend their interests by deciding what the important problems are (the "contradiction" between profit and wages being decided in favour of capital, for example) (*ibid.*). Here we do arrive at a fundamental difference between Deleuze and Hegel. Whereas for Hegel philosophy always arrives "when a form of life has grown old", and can only retrospectively comprehend our historical experience, for Deleuze philosophy is provoked by the encounter with difference and by the creative response to problems and ideas generated by this encounter. It is not concerned with the reconciliation with actuality but rather with the invention of concepts and forms of existence to come.

In what sense, then, might we talk of a Deleuzean dialectics? Deleuze offers a conception of dialectics that restores its role in the thinking of problems and the response to questions. The mistake of traditional dialectics, Deleuze contends, is to reduce or obscure problems by tracing them from presupposed propositions (the "mind–body problem" as derived from the proposition that "consciousness is distinct from the world"). For Deleuze, propositions ("the mind is the brain") are always only responses to underlying problems ("what makes possible our embodied experience?"), which themselves are engendered by our experience of difference and singularity that remains resistant to received concepts and moral opinions ("what does this sensation mean?", "how could things be different?"). A Deleuzean problem is a way of arranging a multiplicity of elements into an articulated idea; ideas are multiplicities, ways of composing and thinking differences in their complex relations (DR: 182). The idea of "society", for example, is a way of articulating the problem of how a multiplicity of individuals can coexist within a shared form of life, and there will be many empirical ways in which a society can exist, some more life-affirming than others (see DR: 186).

Deleuzean dialectics is a way of thinking oriented towards difference that responds to problems with a creation of concepts or invention of different modes of existence (society as a collective assemblage of bodies capable of collective action and individual expression; no longer the individual versus the state but rhizomatic networks that bypass established economic, legal and political apparatuses – Internet activist communities). The aim is both critical and creative: a critique of established concepts, thought and values that privilege identity over difference, unity over multiplicity, universality over individuation; and a creation of concepts that foster experimentation with new forms of experience and different possibilities of existence. Deleuzean dialectics thus remains directed towards expressing the multiplicity of overlapping forces that compose a tendency towards individuation or becoming; but it also retains an experimental ethical aspect, namely the creation of new possibilities of thought and experience. One might ask at this point how we are to think non-conceptual difference in a "concept" of difference. Clearly, for Deleuze, we need a new concept of the "concept" or else an oblique strategy to think difference in itself. Art is certainly one way that such a thought of non-conceptual difference might be expressed (and Deleuze's work abounds with references to relevant artists and writers); but it is not clear whether philosophy should mimic art in this respect, or whether there is a genuinely philosophical way of articulating pure difference without repeating fundamental elements of representationalist discourse (such as Hegelianism). In this regard, Derrida's deconstruction of metaphysics presents a significant alternative to Deleuze's philosophy of difference. As we have seen, Deleuze develops a "metaphysics of difference" that does not reject metaphysics as such; rather, the long history of distorted dialectic must be transformed into a dialectic of multiplicities. Derrida's question, however, becomes pertinent here: can one engage in such a project without falling prey to systemic closure of metaphysics? Derrida will explicitly challenge Deleuze's "empiricist" assumption that one can "overcome" the abstraction of philosophical conceptuality, inventing new concepts in order to overcome inherited metaphysical systems (such as Hegelianism). Whereas Deleuze attempts to think non-conceptual difference without the negative, Derrida will propose thinking difference as non-totalizable negativity, as a radical differing/deferring he calls *différance*.

Derrida's "Hegelian" deconstruction of Levinas

Jacques Derrida is among the most controversial of the generation of French philosophers that came to prominence in the late 1960s. Derrida's deconstruction of the texts of key figures in the history of Western metaphysics – including Plato, Kant, Hegel, Husserl, Heidegger and Levinas – has had a profound impact on contemporary European philosophy as well as in many disciplines in the humanities and social sciences. For our purposes, I shall be focusing on Derrida's complex and ambivalent attitude to Hegel and the legacy of Hegelianism. In contrast with Deleuze's occasionally anti-Hegelian rhetoric, Derrida maintains a more consistently ambivalent attitude, combining proximity to Hegel with distance, an appropriation of

Hegelian arguments with a powerful deconstruction of the Hegelian system. On the one hand, Hegel embodies, for Derrida, one of the most comprehensive versions of the "metaphysics of presence" (the basic interpretation of being as presence); on the other, Hegel also provides a conceptual framework that can be drawn upon for the task of deconstructing the metaphysical tradition. As Derrida puts it, "Hegel *summed up* the entire history of the logos" (1976: 24) but also offers a meditation on writing, a rehabilitation of thought "as the *memory productive* of signs" (*ibid.*: 26). More than simply being a metaphysician of identity, "Hegel is *also* the thinker of irreducible difference"; this ambivalence makes Hegel simultaneously "the last philosopher of the book and the first thinker of writing" (*ibid.*). Hegel thus not only completes the modern metaphysics of the subject, he also opens up the horizon for a deconstructive engagement with this tradition. Derrida is thus very much a "post-Hegelian" thinker.

Evidence of Derrida's affiliation with Hegelian thought can be found in his long essay on the thought of Emmanuel Levinas, "Violence and Metaphysics" (first published in 1964). In this work, Derrida engages in a deconstructive reading of Levinas's own confrontation with the violence of traditional philosophy, which Levinas calls "ontology" or a theory of beings in general. For Levinas, the traditional philosophical privileging of ontology should be overturned in favour of an originary ethics that begins with the primacy of the relationship with "the Other" (*l'autrui* – the personal other, the you), where "the Other" refers to the "radically other" or "alterity" that is manifested in the presence and uniqueness of the singular human being. Indeed, it is in the immediacy of the face-to-face encounter with the Other – where "the face" refers to that which escapes my comprehension and to which I am absolutely responsible – that philosophy finds its true foundation and ultimate vocation. Derrida will engage in a deconstructive critique of Levinas's claims concerning the violence of metaphysics and the primacy of the face-to-face encounter. Interestingly, this deconstruction draws upon Hegelian arguments concerning the mediating role of language, and the inescapability of deploying metaphysical concepts – even the "deconstructed" categories of the *Other* and the *other* (*l'autre* – the other or otherness as a general category) – in any attempt at overturning metaphysics. Derrida's deconstructive reading of Levinas thus adopts a surprisingly Hegelian perspective.

Derrida begins by describing Levinas's anti-Hegelianism as an instance of the "existentialist protest" against Hegel's metaphysics, which is supposed to exemplify the violent reduction of alterity to conceptuality, of the other to the same (WD: 110–11). Against Hegel's conception of the rational or "good" infinite, Levinas's ethical thought embraces a version of the Hegelian "bad" infinite: an endless movement of transcendence towards the infinitely other, which never returns to the conceptual closure of the same. Levinas's anti-Hegelianism, moreover, is driven by an ethical impetus: to reject the Hegelian account of an originary violent struggle for recognition and to show instead the primacy of the ethical relation to the Other as a non-objectifying, non-negating relationship with alterity (radical otherness). For Levinas, the relationship with the Other is originarily a non-violent relationship with alterity, and only secondarily an attempt to negate, objectify, or identify, and thus dominate, the Other (as for Hegel, according to Kojève, whose reading still marks Derrida's approach).

As Derrida rightly points out, however, Levinas's claim that we can have a relationship with alterity without negativity would have struck Hegel as "absolutely mad" (WD: 119). Derrida's critique here follows the Hegelian criticism of the Romantic philosophy of immediacy, namely that immediacy is always already a mediated experience, one made possible by language and conceptuality. Immediate intuition, or the immediate encounter with the Other, is conceptually mediated; the concepts of the Other and the Same are mutually dependent, so the attempt to separate and prioritize one over the other is inherently questionable. Moreover, from a phenomenological point of view, I could not experience the otherness of the Other if I did not already recognize that I am also an Other from the Other's point of view, and further, that my identity as a subject depends upon my realizing that I am such an Other for another subject. This is the reflective movement that Hegel famously called "recognition" or *Anerkennung*. Derrida, for his part, makes it clear that the meaning of the Other for me is that of *an Ego* that I know is related to me as *its* Other. Levinas's account of the movement of transcendence toward the other, Derrida argues, "would have no meaning if it did not bear within it, as one of its essential meanings, that in my ipseity [selfhood] I know myself to be other for the other" (WD: 126). In other words, there can be no radical separation between Same and Other, since the very meaning of "the Other" necessarily implies reference to the Other *for me*, that is, to the Ego as the Same. As Hegel argued in the *Phenomenology*, the relationship between Self and Other is a relation of *reflection*: I am *recognized* by the Other for whom I am *recognized* as an Other in turn. Such a relationship, however, is absent in Levinas's account: "That I am also essentially the other's other, and that I know I am, is the evidence of a strange symmetry whose trace appears nowhere in Levinas's descriptions" (WD: 128). Without such a symmetry – what Hegel called the reflection between subjects or movement of *recognition* – "I could not desire (or) respect the other in ethical dissymmetry" (*ibid.*).

This "transcendental" violence between Same and Other, according to Derrida, arises in the way that the Other is constituted with reference to the Self; the Other is always an other for me, hence cannot be separated from its relation with the Same. Such "violence" can of course take the form of empirical violence, conflict and war; but this difference, according to Hegel, can also be sublated into the dynamic, restless, nature of spirit. The relationship between Self and Other thus opens up the possibility both of ethical recognition and of violent domination. From this irreducible imbrication between Self and Other, Hegel also drew the consequence that violence and conflict are an unavoidable aspect of the experience of self-consciousness: "Hegel himself recognised negativity, anxiety or war in the infinite absolute only as the movement of the absolute's own history, whose horizon is a final pacification in which alterity would be absolutely *encapsulated*, if not lifted up, in parousia" (WD: 129). Levinas, by contrast, attempts to keep this violent reduction of the Other to the Same quite separate from the non-violent relationship with the Other that would embrace alterity. For Derrida, however, such a separation cannot be maintained without suppressing the manner in which Same and Other are constituted in thought and language (namely, with reference to the Other as the Other of the Self, and the Other as disclosed against an understanding of Being).

Having followed Hegel to this point (along with Husserl on the constitution of the Other as an *alter Ego*; and Heidegger on the pre-understanding of *Being* as a condition of encountering Others-in-the-world), Derrida then marks his critical distance from Hegelian dialectics. As we know, Hegelian dialectics recognizes difference as *negativity* that can be dialectically superseded. Levinas, however, wants to preserve the difference of the Other without subsuming it within the Same in the manner of Hegelian dialectics. Derrida too wants to preserve this difference but regards it, at least in this essay, as opening up a conflictual dynamic that can in principle never be overcome. But this also means that Hegelian negativity cannot be simply overcome; it is radical difference itself that signifies the possibility of conceptual distinctions and oppositions in general. For Hegel, the concept of a *pure* difference, without reference to identity, is impossible to articulate fully in language, since to do so is to deploy concepts that involve just this interplay of identity and difference.

As we have seen, this was precisely Deleuze's wager: to think a *non-conceptual difference* without reference to identity, that is, negativity. This dream shared by Levinas and Deleuze – Levinas desiring the pure alterity of the Other independent of the Same; Deleuze striving after a thought of pure difference without negativity – is what Derrida rejects as the dream of *empiricism*: the attempt to think *pure difference* without recourse to conceptuality. For Derrida, this is "the *dream* of a purely heterological thought at its source", a dream that vanishes "as soon as language wakes up" (WD: 151). As Hegel showed in the *Phenomenology*, sense-certainty's attempt to say what it means results in a dialectical reversal (the attempt to say the pure, singular "here, now" necessarily involves recourse to linguistic universals). So too with Levinas's account of pure alterity, which necessarily has recourse to the language of Being in its attempt to say the pure alterity of the Other: "As Hegel says somewhere, empiricism always forgets, at [the] very least, that it employs the words to be" (WD: 139). The problem with separating the Same from the Other is that their very meaning is bound up with the language of Being. The radical difference between thought and being is also a sameness that always escapes our attempts to articulate it in thought or language. It is a play of difference – or what Derrida will call *différance* – that must be thought differently, if we are to escape the metaphysical–conceptual machinery of which Hegel is the undoubted master. How to find a way beyond Hegel? Derrida tackles this question – obliquely – in his famous reading of Georges Bataille's rewriting of the Hegelian master/slave dialectic.

Derrida on Bataille on Hegel

Derrida's 1967 essay on French thinker Georges Bataille (1897–1962), "From Restricted to General Economy: A Hegelianism without Reserve", is a fascinating engagement with Hegel. The question at issue is whether it is possible to "escape" Hegelianism, as Deleuze and Levinas claim, or whether Hegelianism subsumes and integrates precisely that which opposes it. This essay exemplifies Derrida's "deconstructive" approach to philosophical texts, which combines critical interpretation with a performative writing that mimics and thereby undermines the text in question. Deconstructive readings are also parasitic, in this case upon Bataille's writings on Hegel, which claim to move beyond Hegel's system while at the same time deploying Hegelian concepts.

A few words about Derrida's concept of deconstruction are necessary at this point. To put it simply, deconstruction is an operation that involves a *reversal* and *displacement* of the hierarchy in a conceptual opposition (for example the opposition between speech and writing). This reversal is supposed to show that the minor, suppressed term is in fact essential for the identity or meaning of the major, primary term (writing is not just a transcription of speech; rather, as the possibility of repeatable traces or marks, it makes possible the transmission of speech). The meaning of the terms within this inverted opposition is then displaced, inscribed within a more "general" context of meaning and non-meaning so as to foreground the differential relationship between them (speech and writing in the narrow sense are made possible by "general writing" or the differential system of traces or marks). Derrida describes deconstruction as related to Hegelian dialectics, as thinking "*after-Hegel*", but with the crucial difference that it does not constitute a higher unity or rationally structured progression (see Derrida 1981: 77–9). Here again there is a striking proximity between Adorno's negative dialectics, Merleau-Ponty's hyperdialectic and Deleuze's dialectical philosophy of difference. Instead of the Hegelian movement of dialectical negation, however, Derrida points to the non-totalizable movement of *différance*: the differential process of differing/deferring between marks or traces that makes signification possible, as well as "impossible" – unavoidably prone to slippage of meaning, disruption of sense, infinite recontextualization and so on.

Mastery and sovereignty: from restricted to general economy

Let us turn now to Derrida's reading of Bataille's reading of Hegel, and the contrast between a "restricted" and a "general economy" of meaning. Here the word "economy" has multiple senses: that of a circulation of meaning or values, a system of what is "proper" or one's own, the movement of desire in psychoanalytical terms, but also the production, exchange and circulation of wealth. The narrower sense of economy as involving the exchange of goods in pursuit of a profit (restricted economy) is contrasted with the profligate expending of goods or values without return (general economy). Derrida's subtitle is therefore ambiguous: "A Hegelianism without Reserve" means both that Bataille offers an unreserved Hegelianism and that Bataille goes beyond the bounds of Hegelianism as such. The point is to show the ambivalent relationship between Hegelian dialectics and Bataille's "anti-Hegelianism". As I have mentioned, Derrida is very aware that Hegelian discourse is most powerful when confronted by anti-Hegelian discourse: Hegelian reason, which encompasses itself and its other, has produced a philosophical discourse that includes within itself "all the figures of its beyond, all the forms and resources of its exterior" (WD: 252). Hence the importance of those thinkers (like Bataille) who attempt to subvert Hegelian reason through that which exceeds its systematic unity and closure.

The strategy that Bataille proposes is to push Hegelian discourse to its point of exhaustion or collapse. The question then becomes the following: "how, after having exhausted the discourse of philosophy, can one inscribe in the lexicon and syntax of . . . the language of philosophy, that which nevertheless exceeds the oppositions of concepts governed by this communal logic?" (WD: 253). This is a succinct summary of the problem of post-Hegelian philosophy more generally: how to think beyond Hegel's dialectics, which attempts to rationally integrate any such otherness into the expanded dominion of reason. For Bataille, the only way to exceed Hegel is to "laugh at philosophy (at Hegelianism)": to mimic and thereby subvert the system precisely through those elements that remain unassimilable to it (laughter, erotic excess, religious ecstasy, pornographic literature and so on). As Derrida cautions, however, the challenge of subverting Hegel by laughing at the ruses of reason can be done "only through close scrutiny and full knowledge of what one is laughing at" (WD: 253).

Following Kojève, Bataille's reading of Hegel (as evident in his essay "Hegel, Death, Sacrifice") foregrounds Hegel's famous master/slave dialectic. What Bataille draws from Kojève is the centrality of the encounter with *death*: the master is willing to risk his own life, while the slave, by contrast, desires conservation of life instead. One accedes to mastery or lordship, to freedom and recognition, by risking death for the sake of freedom as independence. Hegelian lordship turns the risking of one's life into a moment in the "constitution of meaning" of rational self-consciousness; the struggle for recognition is indeed, as Kojève argued, a moment in the history of self-consciousness developing towards rational freedom: "To stay alive, to maintain oneself in life, to work, to defer pleasure, to limit the stakes, to have respect for death at the very moment when one looks directly at it – such is the servile condition of master and of the entire history it makes possible" (WD: 255).

Bataille then proceeds to rewrite Hegelian lordship through the notion of "sovereignty". The difference between these two concepts,

Derrida observes, will amount to the difference between *meaning* and a certain kind of *non-meaning*. According to Bataille, Hegelian dialectics can be said to act in the service of a *restricted economy* of life, one oriented towards the circulation, reproduction and enrichment of meaning. In this respect, the Hegelian economy of (conceptual) mastery also reveals a *comic* aspect: the Hegelian *Aufhebung* wants to profit from loss, to enrich itself by negating otherness. Hegel is truly a "speculative" philosopher (Derrida puns on the term's economic meaning), trying to profit from negativity and loss through dialectical speculation. In doing so, however, Hegel misses the *general economy* that subtends the restricted economy of meaning and can only ever be indirectly invoked (WD: 257). Bataille's notion of "sovereignty" is thus an attempt to exceed Hegelian dialectics by finding the "blind spots" of Hegel's system – laughter, eroticism, non-sense, ecstasy, expenditure without reserve, absolute negativity – and thus to subvert its conceptual mastery from within Hegelian discourse itself.

Derrida describes Bataille's strategy in relation to Hegelian discourse in terms that also characterize *deconstruction*: the sovereignty (of Bataillean or Derridian "writing") "cannot be inscribed within discourse, except by crossing out predicates or by practicing a contradictory superimpression that then exceeds the logic of philosophy" (WD: 259). In this sense, Bataille's strategy is a proto-deconstructive approach to Hegelianism: an attempt to find the undecidable elements of Hegel's philosophical system, everything that it must suppress in order to constitute itself as reason. Bataille's notion of sovereignty therefore does not break with Hegelian dialectics but rather takes it to a point of breakdown or exhaustion, thereby disclosing the suppressed elements of the conceptual economy of reason. This subversive strategy of deconstructive displacement opens up the restricted economy of meaning to the general economy of non-meaning; that which makes meaning (and non-meaning) possible, but which also uncovers "the limit of discourse and the beyond of absolute knowledge" (WD: 261).

Hence the "impossibility" of Bataille's task: to say in the language of servility (of meaning) that which is not servile but *sovereign* (beyond meaning). The very attempt to do so, however, reverts to the economy of meaning and thus to Hegelian dialectics: Bataille's "sovereign" strategy of writing "risks *making sense*, risks agreeing to the reasonableness of reason, of philosophy, of Hegel, who is always right, as soon as one opens one's mouth in order to articulate meaning" (WD: 263) – a criticism that Derrida also levels at Levinas's attempt to articulate the pure alterity of the Other. The only way to say the unsayable, so to speak, is by means of ruses, stratagems and simulacra. Bataille's strategy of sovereign writing thus pushes towards an experience of the "transgression" of reason and of the limits of the economy of meaning. In so doing, moreover, it opens up another experience of difference, an experience of *absolute difference*: "a difference which would no longer be the one that Hegel had conceived more profoundly than anyone else: the difference in the service of presence, at work for (the) history (of meaning)" (WD: 263). This difference between Hegelian conceptual–speculative difference and Bataillean sovereign or absolute difference marks the difference between the restricted and general economies of meaning (and non-meaning).

For Derrida, this is the most important aspect of Bataille's attempt to subvert Hegelian discourse and open it up to a dimension of radical difference. Bataille's "sovereign writing" is a strategy to evoke this absolute difference, this radical negativity that makes the entire dis-cursive–conceptual system slide, opening it up to sovereign silence or non-meaning. This sovereign writing remains irreducibly paradoxical: it cannot govern itself, or anything else, lest it revert to Hegelian con-ceptual mastery. It must subvert its own will to mastery, precisely in order to remain "sovereign" in Bataille's peculiar sense. As the ultimate subversion of Hegelian mastery, Derrida claims, Bataille's sovereignty must *renounce recognition*, and no longer seek to be recognized (WD: 265). In direct opposition to much German neo-Hegelianism, Derrida, following Nietzsche, Deleuze and Bataille, points to the need to *over-come the desire for recognition* in order to subvert the servile economy of consciousness and meaning, that is, the modern metaphysics of subjectivity or philosophy of representation.

This renunciation of recognition, Derrida contends, points to the emergence of two distinct forms of writing: the writing of conceptual mastery (Hegelian dialectics), which remains servile in its need for meaning; and "sovereign writing" (Bataille and Derrida) that exceeds discursive mastery while also subverting itself by way of an unlimited loss of meaning. Such "sovereign" or deconstructive writing remains unintelligible from the restricted philosophical viewpoint; it is a duplicitous operation, mimicking concepts in order to subvert them, a non-principle and non-foundation. Following Bataille, Derrida points to the possibility of such a deconstructive "general writing" that sub-verts the closure of metaphysics and history (so powerfully articulated by Hegel). Sovereign or deconstructive writing takes Hegelian thought seriously by exceeding or simulating absolute knowledge. Echoing Heidegger's reading of Hegel, it thereby absolves itself of Hegelian absolute knowledge, "putting it back in its place as such, situating and inscribing it within a space which it no longer dominates" (WD: 270). Derrida here appropriates Bataille's subversion of Hegelianism by assimilating sovereignty to deconstruction: the space of a general economy of meaning (and non-meaning), which becomes a general economy of writing, of *différance*.

Undoing dialectics: absolute difference

Having come this far with Bataille, however, Derrida then reverts to a more Hegelian perspective concerning the difference – if that is the right word – between restricted and general economies. At the moment of transgression, Bataille assimilates sovereign writing to the speculative character of Hegelian *Aufhebung*: the movement of determinate negation that both cancels and preserves, lifting the subordinate element into a more complex unity. Derrida, characteristically, points to a footnote in which Bataille suggests that sovereign writing remains akin to Hegel's speculative concept of the *Aufhebung* (WD: 275). Yet the latter, according to Derrida, remains within the restricted economy of meaning, that is, within philosophical–conceptual discourse and the Hegelian closure of absolute knowledge. Derrida's deconstructive move thus comes to the fore at this point: Bataille betrays the radicality of his quest for a sovereign writing by claiming that it is already encompassed by the Hegelian *Aufhebung* – thus confirming Hegelian dialectics in its speculative movement and in its power to sublate even the most radical opposition.

Despite this, Derrida insists that Bataillean sovereignty does uncover a radical or absolute difference, a sacrifice of meaning without speculative return that remains the blind spot of Hegelian dialectics. As Derrida remarks: "To this extent, philosophy, Hegelian speculation, absolute knowledge and everything they govern, and will endlessly govern in their closure, remain determinations of natural, servile and vulgar consciousness. Self-consciousness is servile" (WD: 276). Deconstructive or "sovereign" writing, on the other hand, marks the space – or rather the difference – between the restricted economy of Hegelian dialectics and the general economy of an unnameable difference. The difficulty is that there is no direct way of articulating such a difference without having recourse to the restricted economy of meaning, that is, to the system of philosophical discourse exemplified by Hegelianism. There is no way to engage in such a gesture of deconstructive writing, or operation of sovereignty, without having recourse to the economy of meaning articulated in philosophy. This means that Bataille, paradoxically, remains thoroughly Hegelian, while at the same time showing how Hegelianism might be subverted or displaced. Any "deconstructive" attempts to articulate this unnameable difference must acknowledge the extent to which we can do so only from within the limits of philosophical discourse – in this case, the limits of Hegelianism.

Beyond Hegelianism?

I have not been able to do justice to Derrida's extraordinarily rich engagement with Hegelian texts in his essay on Bataille's reading of Hegel. What I would like to point out in conclusion is that his deconstructive engagement with Hegel remains thoroughly indebted to Kojève's interpretation, primarily because this also provided the basis of Bataille's unorthodox approach. As some critics have argued, Derrida's deconstruction of Hegelianism might well be pertinent to Bataille's Hegel, but it may be less plausible in regard to Hegel's speculative thought, which is at once more dialectical *and* deconstructive than Derrida will acknowledge (see Flay and Butler in Desmond 1989). Moreover, despite the qualifications that Derrida insists upon, one could argue that Derrida too remains caught up within the performative paradoxes implicit in his deconstructive reading, or sovereign writing, of Bataille's Hegelianism. Given Derrida's affirmation of Bataille's attempt to think an absolute negativity or difference – so radical that it could no longer be *aufgehoben* by speculative rational discourse – we could ask how Derrida's deconstructivist appropriation of such a perspective deals with the radical *nihilism* Bataille's project entails (the negation of meaning without reserve). Hegelian discourse would pass through this radical negativity in order to integrate into a more comprehensive philosophical conceptuality that encompasses its other. Derrida, however, resists such a Hegelian perspective in favour of an unbounded sacrifice of meaning and signs without return. Such a move arguably requires acknowledging a positive moment of concrete intersubjectivity (or of contextuality, which Derrida will thematize elsewhere) in order to avoid radical scepticism or active nihilism in the "restricted economy" of politics.

In Derrida's later "ethical" and political turn, there is something of an acknowledgement of this difficulty: Derrida moves away from his earlier Hegelian critique of Levinas and acknowledges the dependence of deconstruction upon the Levinasian ethics of the Other (Derrida

1999). Indeed, Derridian deconstruction harbours an ethics of absolute responsibility grounded in our relationship with the finite mortal Other in his or her radical singularity. This is already partly evident in the "Violence and Metaphysics" essay, which acknowledges the profound questioning of the philosophical tradition posed by Levinas's ethics of the Other, despite its sharp critique of how Levinas remains ensnared within metaphysics (see Critchley 1999). This acknowledgement of the Levinasian ethics of the Other suggests that Bataillean sovereignty, construed as a figure for deconstruction, must be mediated by an intersubjectivist recognition of the Other (which Derrida says must be "given up" in radical sovereignty).

Derrida will pursue a similar deconstructive strategy in his extra-ordinarily challenging text, *Glas* (1986/1974), which juxtaposes the transgressive erotic fiction of homosexual outlaw poet Jean Genet with Hegel's philosophico-political discourse on the family, civil society and the proper role of the state (see Critchley in Barnett 1998). In *Glas*, which explores what "remains" after absolute knowledge – indeed after the "death knell" of Hegelianism as such – Derrida stages a performative conflict between the Hegelian system (the sexual and political economy of the family, civil society and the state) and that which exceeds it or exhausts it as its radical other (Genet's poetic–transgressive narratives about homosexuality, criminality and love). The pages of the text of *Glas* are thus divided into two columns, the left being devoted to Hegel and the right to Genet, such that the page cannot be read in an orthodox linear fashion; the unity of the text (indeed of philosophy) is thereby destabilized in a manner that paradoxically exceeds the Hegelian system by staging an encounter between it and its radical other. Derrida uses a dazzling array of literary, philosophical, poetic and historical references to weave a thoroughly heterogeneous text – full of interpolations, marginal comments, texts within texts, interrupted sentences and syntax – that performs a deconstruction of Hegelianism in both the letter and the "spirit" of the text. This deconstructive juxtaposition submits Hegel's conceptual system to the kind of performative destabilization that Bataille also attempted to achieve with his literary works and philosophical speculations. Nonetheless, as Derrida admits, we cannot escape the power of Hegelian discourse simply by engaging in a radical negation of reason, since deconstruction remains parasitically dependent upon this restricted economy in the very act of subversive displacement. The dialogue with Hegel, as Derrida remarks, will therefore remain "interminable", since it articulates the dialogue of reason and its other that defines philosophy as such.

I conclude with the observation that Derrida's ambiguous relationship with Hegelian dialectics, as is fitting for a philosophy of difference, remains open-ended, refusing conceptual closure. Deconstruction can be thought of as a mimicry of Hegelian dialectics, repeating but also displacing it by a deconstruction of its limits, opening it up to a radical difference that remains resistant to dialectical integration. In this sense, Derrida joins Deleuze, as well as Adorno and Merleau-Ponty, in responding critically and creatively to the challenge of Hegelian dialectics: transforming it from a metaphysics of identity, a closed system of thought, to a thinking of difference, an opening up of thought to its other. As Catherine Malabou writes in her marvellous book *The Future of Hegel* (2005), Hegelianism remains a thought of the future, a thinking of time and transformation – of *plasticity* – a thinking still to come. It is an originary thinking, in Heidegger's sense, always arriving to meet us from out of the future.

Summary of key points

Deleuze: from anti-dialectics to dialectics of difference

- Deleuze's core objection to Hegelian dialectics is that it integrates difference and plurality and so is incapable of thinking individuation and becoming.
- Deleuze's Nietzschean reversal of Hegelianism proposes a pluralist ontology of bodies as expressions of differential relations of force: in any body, the dominant forces are defined as *active*, the dominated forces as *reactive*.
- Hegelian dialectics, for Deleuze, remains a *restricted* form of critique that dialectically negates its other, and thereby expresses "reactive forces" of conservation and preservation.
- Against Hegelian dialectics, which overcomes alienation via the comprehension of our experience, Nietzschean genealogy overcomes nihilism by inventing new concepts and possibilities of existence.

Deleuze: from contradiction to non-conceptual difference

- Hegelian dialectics subsumes difference into representational thinking by pushing it to the level of contradiction, integrating contradictions into encompassing forms of synthesis, that is, to the infinitely large.

- Hegelian dialectics thus subordinates difference to identity, yoking it to the "fourfold root" of representation: *resemblance* in perception, *analogy* in judgement, *opposition* of predicates, *identity* of the concept (DR: 262 ff.).
- Instead of conceptual difference as difference inscribed within the concept (as with Hegel), Deleuze argues for a conception of "difference in itself", for *non-conceptual difference.*
- Dialectic from Plato to Hegel is marred by two difficulties: (1) the construal of difference as negativity and its "maximalization" as opposition and contradiction; and (2), the attempt to reduce the form of the philosophical question to the propositional form ("S is P"), which blocks the thinking of difference.
- Whereas for Hegel philosophy can only retrospectively comprehend our historical experience, for Deleuze philosophy is provoked by the encounter with difference and by the creative response to problems and ideas generated by this encounter.
- Deleuzean dialectics remains directed towards expressing the multiplicity of overlapping forces that compose a tendency towards individuation or becoming; but it also affirms the creation of new possibilities of thought and experience.

Derrida's "Hegelian" reading of Levinas

- According to Derrida, Hegel articulates a comprehensive version of the "metaphysics of presence"; but Hegel also provides a conceptual framework that can be drawn upon for deconstructing the metaphysical tradition.
- Levinas's immediate encounter with the Other, Derrida argues, is conceptually mediated; the concepts of the Other and the Same are mutually dependent, so the attempt to separate and prioritize one over the other is inherently questionable.
- Derrida challenges the "empiricist" dream shared by Levinas and Deleuze (Levinas desiring the pure alterity of the Other; Deleuze striving for a thought of difference without negativity): both articulate "the *dream* of a purely heterological thought at its source", which vanishes with reflection on language.

Derrida on Bataille on Hegel

- Bataille's gambit against Hegelian reason is to subvert it through that which exceeds its systematic unity and closure (madness, eroticism, laughter, excess).

- Hegel's dialectical movement of *Aufhebung* is in the service of a *restricted economy* of life that restricts itself to the circulation and reproduction of meaning.
- Hegel thereby misses the *general economy* that subtends the restricted economy of meaning. Bataille thus proposes the notion of "sovereignty" as expressing the "blind spot" of Hegel's system – laughter, eroticism, non-sense, absolute negativity – and thus attempts to subvert its mastery from within.
- Deconstructive or "sovereign" writing marks the difference between the restricted economy of Hegelian dialectics, and the general economy of an unnameable difference, which Derrida will associate with the neologism *différance*.
- There is no direct way of articulating such a difference without having recourse to the restricted economy of meaning, that is, to the system of philosophical discourse exemplified by Hegelianism.
- Deconstruction can be thought of as subverting Hegelian dialectics by a deconstruction of its limits, opening it up to a radical difference that resists dialectical integration.

conclusion

The future of Hegelianism

It would be tempting to conclude this book by suggesting the possibility of a partial *Aufhebung* between the German critical theory and French poststructuralist perspectives on Hegelian thought. The book's central thesis on the adventures of Hegelianism has been that contemporary European philosophy, in particular much twentieth-century French and German philosophy, has been decisively shaped by the simultaneous critique and appropriation of key Hegelian themes and concepts. Continental philosophy might even be facetiously called a series of footnotes to Hegel. As I have tried to show, the critical theorists' emphasis on Hegel as philosopher of modernity and theorist of intersubjectivity and recognition can be productively contrasted with French existentialist and poststructuralist critiques of Hegelianism in the name of singular existence, pure difference and radical alterity. The conflicting relationship between critical theory and poststructuralism, moreover, can be traced, at least in part, to their differing emphases in the appropriation of key Hegelian themes (singularity, difference and a rethinking of dialectics in the case of French Hegelianism; modernity, intersubjectivity and recognition in the case of German Hegelianism). At the same time, we find a certain convergence or resonance between Adorno, Merleau-Ponty, Deleuze and Derrida on the question of rethinking Hegelian dialectics as an open-ended, pluralist dialectic of difference, singularity, multiplicity and so on.

Certain Hegelian themes have played an essential role in the development of both French and German strands of European philosophy, above all the figure of the unhappy consciousness, the master/slave dialectic, and the struggle for recognition. Moreover, the Hegelian concept of *dialectic*, as we have seen, has proven extraordinarily productive, from Marxism and phenomenology to critical theory and deconstruction. The powerful challenge of Hegelian dialectical thought, which attempts to integrate reason and its other into a more comprehensive totality, continues to generate productive responses that strive to think difference, singularity, individuation and becoming on their own terms. This is true in the case of the various existential and phenomenological reactions against Hegelianism (as with Heidegger and Sartre); recent attempts to propose a post-Hegelian thinking of intersubjectivity adequate to modernity (with Habermas and Honneth); or in the strategies of deconstructing or transforming Hegelian dialectics from within its metaphysical economy (with Adorno, Deleuze and Derrida). The sheer richness of contemporary Hegelian and anti-Hegelian thought suggests that Hegel's claims to have developed a comprehensive philosophical system – one that would encompass its negative or other – are not as outrageous as they might first appear.

On the other hand, it would be risky to suggest that something like a Hegelian "synthesis" of French and German strands of Hegelianism is now at hand, for the simple reason that Hegelianism remains a living tradition of thought that is not yet at an end. It should be clear, moreover, that I have not presented anything like a "comprehensive" account of the various strands of Hegelianism, but have had to stylize my presentation, foregrounding certain philosophers and texts while ignoring others in order to present a reasonably brief account of this rich philosophical tradition. Thus, for example, I have not discussed French psychoanalyst Jacques Lacan, whose work has had a profound impact on poststructuralism and French feminism (in the work of Kristeva and Irigaray, for example). Lacan's famous rereading of Freud explicitly drew upon Kojève's reading of Hegel's master/slave dialectic, and the dialectic of desire and law, which in Lacan's rendering decentres the subject with respect to the symbolic order of language. Lacan was one of Kojève's most famous students, and the influence of Kojève's reading of Hegelian themes is unmistakable in Lacanian psychoanalytic theory of the desiring subject (see his famous essays, "The Mirror Stage" and "The Subversion of the Subject and Dialectic of Desire in the Freudian unconscious" in Lacan 1977).

Moreover, Judith Butler and Slavoj Žižek have reworked key psychoanalytic and Hegelian themes that have brought Hegel back into contemporary debates on subjectivity, desire and politics. Butler's first work, *Subjects of Desire* (1988), was a study of the Hegelian concept of

desire and account of subjectivity that was taken up by French existentialism, Lacanian psychoanalysis and French feminism, but also criticized by Deleuze, Foucault and Derrida. Butler has also analysed
the master/slave relation from the perspective of a psychoanalytically
informed theory of (gendered) embodiment, arguing that the slave is a
labouring body whose body is subjugated by the idle, disembodied
master; the unhappy consciousness, in turn, is alienated from its
embodiment as a finite, desiring, but also rational being (see Butler
1997: 31–62). Finally, Butler has recently returned to the famous
Hegelian interpretation of Antigone (a figure of enduring interest
for feminists). Antigone is a figure of radical otherness, Butler argues,
whose transgression is not, as Hegel claimed, an articulation of the contradiction between feminine–familial and masculine–political spheres.
Rather, she is a liminal figure of radical otherness whose fate is also an
interrogation of kinship and sexual relations that challenges Hegel's
account of gender relations, family, civil society and state (Butler 2000).

Slavoj Žižek has also recently come to prominence for his neo-
Hegelian/German idealist reading of Lacanian psychoanalytic theory
as providing the foundation for a theory of ideology adequate to the
complexities of global capitalism. Žižek explicitly deploys Hegelian
dialectics in his work on subjectivity and politics, albeit in an unorthodox psychoanalytic interpretation that is also neo-Marxist in inspiration. Throughout his work he consistently foregrounds the connection
between Hegelian thought and psychoanalysis and develops a psychoanalytically informed theory of subjectivity, ideology and cultural–
political criticism (see Žižek 1993, 1999). In this respect, we might say
that the integration of Hegelian insights from both poststructuralism
and critical theory within Butler's and Žižek's works points to a partial
"sublation" of aspects of the French/German philosophical divide. This
is further evinced by the recent debates *between* Butler and Žižek over
subjectivity, politics, and universality in modernity (see Butler *et al.*
1999) (Žižek remaining more Hegelian–Marxist in orientation while
Butler is more Nietzschean–poststructuralist). Such debates again
point to the productive tension between French and German versions
of Hegelianism, and suggest future possibilities for the Hegelian-
inspired theorization of subjectivity, politics and modernity.

From a different philosophical tradition, another exciting development I have not been able to discuss is the return of Hegel in
Anglophone philosophy. This is evident in the appropriation of
Hegelian themes by contemporary "post-analytic" philosophers such
as Robert Brandom and John McDowell (see Rockmore 2005: 100–38;

139–56). The revisiting of the Kant–Hegel relationship, for example, has been a striking feature of recent debates in epistemology over realism and anti-realism, naturalism and idealism, epistemological holism, and the concept–intuition relationship (see Brandom 1994, 2000; McDowell 1996, 1998). For social and political philosophy, there has also been a noteworthy return of the Kant–Hegel debate in recent arguments between defenders of Rawlsian liberalism and advocates of communitarianism inspired by Charles Taylor's neo-Hegelian approach (see Taylor 1975, 1983). Finally, the recent interest in "non-metaphysical" readings of Hegel (for example, Pippin 1989; Pinkard 1988, 1994) is another development that has brought Hegelianism back into the philosophical discussion, primarily by reading Hegel through Kantian and pragmatist lenses, foregrounding Hegel's critical credentials as a post-metaphysical thinker, and developing his account of the sociality of reason-giving practices. These contemporary "non-metaphysical" readings of Hegel suggest the possibility of a *rapprochement* between Continental and analytic traditions, which parted ways not least because of opposing views on the question of Hegelianism.

I have attempted in this book to show how French Hegelianism highlighted the themes of the unhappy consciousness, the relation to the Other, and the question of dialectics and difference, to the neglect of the more "German" Hegelian themes of modernity, intersubjectivity and recognition. German Hegelianism, on the other hand, foregrounded the problem of modernity, the critique of reification, and developed theories of intersubjectivity and recognition drawing heavily on Hegelian sources. At the same time, it neglected the more "Nietzschean" aspects of Hegelianism: the tragic–existentialist themes of alienation, difference, singularity and radical otherness, which were given an anti-Hegelian accent in poststructuralist critiques that still remained indebted to Hegelian dialectics in complex ways. In my opinion, the integration of these conflicting "Hegelian" aspects of poststructuralism and critical theory, along with insights from analytic neo-Hegelianism, into a critical Hegelian theory of knowledge, subjectivity and sociality remains an important task for the future.

The legacy of Hegelianism continues to shape the philosophical present and to open up future possibilities of thought. My argument has been that the history of French and German Hegelianism can be understood as a series of productive misinterpretations and original appropriations that continue to bring life to Hegelianism as a pluralistic philosophical movement. French Hegelianism appropriated the unhappy consciousness, the master/slave dialectic, and attempted to rethink Hegelian dialectics in relation to the philosophy of difference; German Hegelianism emphasized Hegel's theory of modernity, his defence of rationality, and combined both through the theory of recognition and social intersubjectivity. A clearer understanding of the plural and conflicting nature of Hegelianism, I suggest, might enhance productive dialogue between these often conflicting perspectives in contemporary European thought. Hegel famously remarked that philosophy always comes after a form of life has begun to grow old; the Owl of Minerva only begins its flight with the dusk. Hegelianism is defined, rather, by its responsiveness to forms of life in transition; it wagers that the Owl of Minerva will return with the dawn.

Questions for discussion and revision

one Introducing Hegelianism idealism

1. What does Hegel mean by "phenomenology"?
2. Is Hegel's notion of "spirit" another term for "consciousness"? If not, how and why does it differ?
3. Describe the basic movements in Hegel's account of the master/slave relationship.
4. What does Hegel mean by the "unhappy consciousness"? Why is it "unhappy"?
5. What, according to Hegel's account, is the relationship between the basic categories of "Being" and "Nothing"?
6. Is history a rational process in Hegel's view? If so, in what way "rational"?
7. What does Hegel mean by "civil society"? How is it related to the political state?
8. What was the relationship between the views of the British idealists and the emergence of analytic philosophy?

two Adventures in Hegelianism

1. What was the basic difference between the "Left" and "Right" Hegelians? Why did they emerge as two opposing Hegelian schools?
2. What did the "Right Hegelians" think was the proper relationship between religion and philosophy? How did this compare with the "Left Hegelian" view?
3. Outline Feuerbach's basic criticism of religion. Do you agree with his critique?
4. Describe the two aspects of Kierkegaard's existentialist critique of Hegel.
5. What did Kierkegaard advocate as an alternative to Hegelian thought?

6. What was Marx's view on the significance of Hegel's "dialectical method"?
7. Discuss what Marx meant by the "proletariat". What was its political significance?
8. Describe the four aspects of "alienation", according to Marx. Is this still a relevant analysis today?

three Reification and metaphysics: Lukács and Heidegger

1. What was Lukács's basic criticism of Hegel's concept of alienation?
2. Describe what Lukács's meant by the concept of "reification". What is its significance for modernity?
3. What is the relationship, according to Lukács, between the commodity form and modern philosophical thought? Is his view plausible?
4. Why does Heidegger think an enquiry into the meaning of "Being" is important?
5. Why does Heidegger talk of "*Dasein*" rather than "human being" or "subject"?
6. What is wrong with Hegel's conception of time, according to Heidegger?
7. Heidegger presents a "Cartesian" reading of Hegel. What does this mean? Is it a plausible interpretation of Hegel's conception of self-consciousness?
8. What is the connection, according to Heidegger, between modern metaphysics and technology?

four Enlightenment, domination and non-identity: Adorno's negative dialectics

1. What do Adorno and Horkheimer mean by the "dialectic of enlightenment"? In what ways is this still a Hegelian account?
2. What is the relationship between myth and enlightenment, in their view?
3. What, according to Adorno and Horkheimer, is wrong with our relationship with nature in the modern world? Do you agree with their claims?
4. What do Adorno and Horkheimer mean by the "culture industry"? What effects does the culture industry have on modern subjects?
5. Outline one objection to the analysis of modernity presented in the *Dialectic of Enlightenment*.
6. What does Adorno mean by the "non-identical"? What is its significance for modern thought and culture?
7. What does Adorno mean by "negative dialectics"? How does it differ from Hegelian dialectics?
8. Discuss one objection to Adorno's project of "negative dialectics".

five Modernity, intersubjectivity and recognition: Habermas and Honneth

1. Why does "modernity" become a philosophical problem? What is Hegel's significance in this context?

2. Discuss the key features of the Hegelian notion of "subjectivity" in modernity. What is the significance of subjectivity for understanding modernity?
3. Why is the shift from a model of "consciousness" to that of "intersubjectivity" important, according to Habermas?
4. What are the three media of intersubjective action and communication, according to Habermas's reading of Hegel? Why are these important?
5. What is the significance, according to Honneth, of Hegel's account of a "struggle for recognition"?
6. What are the three basic spheres of recognition, according to Honneth? Why are these important for the development of autonomous subjectivity?
7. What are the types of practical self-relation associated with the three spheres of recognition? Why are these important for social agency?
8. What is the relationship between "misrecognition" and the emergence of social movements? Why is this important for social and political philosophy?

six French Hegelianism and its discontents: Wahl, Hyppolite, Kojève

1. Jean Wahl emphasized the role of the "unhappy consciousness" in Hegel's thought. Describe the basic features of his "existentialist" reading of Hegel.
2. What account of human time does Alexandre Koyré present in his account of Hegel? What is its significance for understanding history?
3. Jean Hyppolite emphasized the centrality of the "unhappy consciousness" in his reading of Hegel. How did Hyppolite's interpretation attempt to combine existentialist and Marxist themes?
4. Discuss Hyppolite's later "Heideggerian" account of language and being. Does this conflict with his earlier account of Hegelianism?
5. What is distinctive about human desire, according to Kojève? Do you agree with his view?
6. How does Kojève's version of the master/slave dialectic differ from Hegel's? What is the ultimate outcome of the struggle for recognition between masters and slaves?
7. Discuss one objection to Kojève's account of the master/slave dialectic.
8. What does Kojève mean by the Hegelian idea of the "end of history"? Is his diagnosis relevant today?

seven Between Marxism and existentialism: Sartre, de Beauvoir, Merleau-Ponty

1. Sartre criticizes Hegel for his "epistemological" and "ontological" optimism. Outline Sartre's two basic criticisms of Hegel. Are these convincing objections?
2. Why does Sartre maintain that we must return to the Cartesian *cogito*?
3. Why are human relationships inevitably conflictual, according to Sartre? Do you agree?

4. Why does the problem of oppression become important in de Beauvoir's analysis of freedom? How does her approach to oppression differ from that of Sartre? Whose view is more convincing?
5. What does de Beauvoir mean when she talks of Woman as "the Other"? How can women deal with their status of being "the Other"?
6. Why does de Beauvoir describe gender relations under patriarchy as akin to the Hegelian master/slave dialectic? Is her analogy persuasive?
7. What does Merleau-Ponty claim concerning the relationship between Hegel and existentialism?
8. What is Merleau-Ponty's "Hegelian" objection to Sartre's claim that mutual recognition is impossible? Is his argument convincing?
9. What does Merleau-Ponty mean by "hyperdialectics"? Why is it significant for the relationship between dialectics and difference?

eight Deconstructing Hegelianism: Deleuze, Derrida and the question of difference

1. Deleuze argues that Hegel and Nietzsche are incompatible. Why is this so? What is Deleuze's view of the significance of Hegelian dialectics?
2. How do "reactive" forces triumph over "active" forces? Are there difficulties in Deleuze's account of the relationship between active and reactive forces?
3. What does Deleuze mean by non-conceptual difference or "difference in itself"?
4. What is Deleuze's basic criticism of Hegelian dialectics? What alternative model of dialectics does Deleuze propose?
5. What are the basic features of Derrida's deconstructive critique of Levinas's account of the metaphysical relationship with the Other?
6. In what way, according to Derrida, is Levinas "more Hegelian than he knows"?
7. What is the difference between Bataille's "restricted" and "general economy"? Why is this significant for confronting Hegelian dialectics?
8. What is Derrida's point in suggesting that Bataille's reading of Hegel ends up as a "Hegelianism without reserve"? What implications does Derrida draw from this for the project of deconstructing metaphysics?

Further reading

This book has studied a range of thinkers connected with the complex movements of Hegelianism. While there is no one comprehensive overview, there are some very good introductory texts that can usefully supplement my rather selective account. A good place to start is Tom Rockmore's *Before and After Hegel: An Historical Introduction to Hegel's Thought* (Berkeley, CA: University of California Press, 1993). Rockmore introduces Hegel's thought in its historical context, and provides a helpful overview of the key philosophical responses to Hegel. Karl Löwith's *From Hegel to Nietzsche: The Revolution in Nineteenth-Century Thought* (New York: Columbia University Press, 1991) is a classic in the history of philosophy and will repay careful study.

The best English-language study of nineteenth-century Hegelianism is J. E. Toews's *Hegelianism: The Path Toward Dialectical Humanism, 1805–1841* (Cambridge: Cambridge University Press, 1980). For a more succinct account, see Toews's article "Transformations of Hegelianism, 1805–1846", in *The Cambridge Companion to Hegel*, ed. Frederick Beiser (Cambridge: Cambridge University Press, 1993). Robert Stern and Nicholas Walker's article "Hegelianism" in the *Routledge Encyclopaedia of Philosophy* (London: Routledge, 1988, vol. 4, 280–302) provides a fine overview of nineteenth-century Hegelian schools as well as their more interesting offshoots.

For a fascinating discussion of British idealism and its relationship with analytic philosophy see Tom Rockmore's *Hegel, Idealism, and Analytic Philosophy* (New Haven, CT: Yale University Press, 2005). Rockmore also discusses analytic neo-Hegelianism (particularly Brandom and McDowell). There is a recently published volume, *Hegel and Contemporary Continental Philosophy*, ed. D. K. Keenan (Albany, NY: SUNY Press, 2004), that assembles a great selection of readings that I have not been able to discuss in this book.

Hegel

The explosion of interest in Hegel over the last three decades has resulted in a plethora of scholarly studies. Among recent texts I can recommend Stephen Houlgate's *An Introduction to Hegel: Freedom, Truth, History* (Oxford: Blackwell, 2005). Houlgate's edition of *The Hegel Reader* (Oxford: Blackwell, 1998) is essential reading for any serious student. The essays in *The Cambridge Companion to Hegel* (ed. F. Beiser) are recommended for authoritative discussions of key aspects of Hegel's thought. Highly influential but often contested is Charles Taylor's *Hegel* (Cambridge: Cambridge University Press, 1975), and his shorter study, *Hegel and Modern Society* (Cambridge: Cambridge University Press, 1983). Stanley Rosen's study, *G. W. F. Hegel: An Introduction to the Science of Wisdom* (New Haven, CT: Yale University Press, 1974), is the pick of the "metaphysical" interpretations of Hegel, explicating Hegel's challenge to Platonic metaphysics in an elegant and persuasive manner.

The most influential "non-metaphysical" interpretations include Terry Pinkard's *Hegel's Dialectic: The Explanation of Possibility* (Philadelphia, PA: Temple University Press, 1988) and Robert Pippin's *Hegel's Idealism: The Satisfactions of Self-Consciousness* (Cambridge: Cambridge University Press, 1989). Robert B. Williams has done good work to foreground the concept of recognition in recent Hegel scholarship; see his *Recognition: Hegel and Fichte on the Other* (Albany, NY: SUNY Press, 1992), and his *Hegel's Ethics of Recognition* (Berkeley, CA: University of California Press, 1997). Paul Redding's *Hegel's Hermeneutics* (Ithaca, NY: Cornell University Press, 1996) provides another fruitful "non-metaphysical" approach to Hegel's project. There are also good introductions to individual Hegelian texts: Robert Stern's *Hegel and the* Phenomenology of Spirit (London: Routledge, 2002) is very helpful, as is H. S. Harris's impressively succinct *Hegel: Phenomenology and System* (Indianapolis, IN: Hackett, 1995).

Hegel and Heidegger

This is a fascinating philosophical relationship that has not received the scholarly attention it deserves. David Kolb's *The Critique of Pure Modernity: Hegel, Heidegger, and After* (Chicago, IL: University of Chicago Press, 1986) is a fine study of the relevance of the Hegel–Heidegger relationship for contemporary thought. Dennis J. Schmidt's *The Ubiquity of the Finite: Hegel, Heidegger, and the Entitlements of Philosophy* (Cambridge, MA: MIT Press, 1988) is another illuminating study. Two interesting recent texts are Karin de Boer's Heideggerian critique of Hegel, *Thinking in the Light of Time: Heidegger's Encounter with Hegel* (Albany, NY: SUNY Press, 2000), and Catherine Malabou's "deconstructivist" reading of Hegel, *The Future of Hegel: Plasticity, Temporality, and Dialectic* (London: Routledge, 2005). Two essays that offer well-argued criticisms of the Heideggerian reading of Hegel are Denise Souche-Dagues's "The Dialogue between Hegel and Heidegger" in C. Macann (ed.) *Martin Heidegger: Critical Assessments Vol. II: History of Philosophy* (London: Routledge, 1992), and Robert R.

Williams's "Hegel and Heidegger" in W. Desmond (ed.) *Hegel and his Critics* (Albany, NY: SUNY Press, 1989).

Hegel and Adorno

Adorno's *Hegel: Three Studies* (Cambridge, MA: MIT Press, 1993) is well worth studying in depth. I would also recommend J. M. Bernstein's excellent essay, "Negative Dialectic as Fate: Adorno and Hegel" in T. Huhn (ed.) *The Cambridge Companion to Adorno* (Cambridge: Cambridge University Press, 2004), 19–50. For a good introductory study see Hauke Brunkhorst's *Adorno and Critical Theory* (Cardiff: University of Wales Press, 1999), which has a helpful account of non-identity and negative dialectics. For critical reconstructions of Adorno and Horkheimer's *Dialectic of Enlightenment*, it is hard to beat Habermas's chapter, "The Entwinement of Myth and Enlightenment: Max Horkheimer and Theodor Adorno", in his *The Philosophical Discourse of Modernity* (Cambridge: Polity, 1987), and Honneth's "The Turn to the Philosophy of History in the *Dialectic of Enlightenment*: A Critique of the Domination of Nature", in his book, *The Critique of Power* (Cambridge, MA: MIT Press, 1991).

Hegel and critical theory

The best book for an overview of Lukács's theory of reification and its relevance for the Frankfurt school is still Martin Jay's *Marxism and Totality: The Adventures of a Concept from Lukács to Habermas* (Berkeley, CA: University of California Press, 1984). The crucial Habermasian texts are the "Labour and Interaction" essay from *Theory and Practice* (Boston, MA: Beacon Press, 1973), and the early essays on Hegel in *The Philosophical Discourse of Modernity*. For Honneth's reading of Hegel and his transformation of the concept of recognition, see Part I of his *The Struggle for Recognition* (Cambridge: Polity, 1995), and Honneth's short text, *Suffering from Indeterminacy: An Attempt at a Reactualisation of Hegel's* Philosophy of Right (Assen: Van Gorcum, 2000). Herbert Marcuse's *Reason and Revolution: Hegel and the Rise of Social Theory* (Boston, MA: Beacon Press, 1960) is still an interesting read. The late Gillian Rose's brilliant *Hegel contra Sociology* (London: Athlone, 1981) argues for the importance of Hegel for a critique of social theory and for constructing a new critical theory of the subject.

French Hegelianism (Wahl, Kojève, Hyppolite)

Unlike German Hegelianism, which has been rather neglected, French Hegelianism continues to generate fascinating studies, particularly in the wake of poststructuralism. A highly readable account can be found in Vincent Descombes's *Modern French Philosophy* (Cambridge: Cambridge University Press, 1980). Judith Butler's first book, *Subjects of Desire: Hegelian Reflections in*

Twentieth-Century France (New York: Columbia University Press, 1988) is a fine study of French approaches to the Hegelian themes of desire and subjectivity. Another helpful book, with more historical detail, is Michael S. Roth's *Knowing and History: Appropriations of Hegel in Twentieth Century France* (Ithaca, NY: Cornell University Press, 1988). More recently, Bruce Baugh has written an excellent historical study, *French Hegel: From Surrealism to Postmodernism* (London: Routledge, 2003), challenging the received view that Kojève was the godfather of French Hegelianism. Baugh argues that the "unhappy consciousness" was the leitmotif of French postwar philosophy, and that some of Wahl's "existentialist" criticisms of Hegelianism were appropriated by Deleuze and Derrida.

Sartre, de Beauvoir and Merleau-Ponty on Hegelianism

There is a good essay by Robert R. Williams criticizing Sartre's reading of Hegel: "Sartre's Strange Appropriation of Hegel" in the *Owl of Minerva*, vol. 23, no. 1 (Fall 1991), 5–14. Kimberly Hutchings's chapters on de Beauvoir in her book *Hegel and Feminist Philosophy* (Cambridge: Polity, 2003) are excellent for understanding de Beauvoir and the possibilities of Hegelian feminism. I can warmly recommend Jack Reynolds's *Understanding Existentialism* (Chesham: Acumen, 2006) for very helpful introductions to Sartre, de Beauvoir and Merleau-Ponty.

Deleuze, Derrida and Hegelian dialectic

Recent Deleuze scholarship has been exploring the idea that Deleuze has a more complex relationship with Hegel than previously thought. Daniel W. Smith's article, "Deleuze, Hegel, and the Post-Kantian Tradition", in *Philosophy Today* 44 (Supplement), 2000, 119–31, is well worth reading on this score. James Williams's fine study, *Gilles Deleuze's* Difference and Repetition: *A Critical Guide and Introduction* (Edinburgh: Edinburgh University Press, 2003), explicitly argues for a Deleuzean dialectics comprising related moments of critique and creative transformation. I would also recommend Catherine Malabou's "One or Several Wolves" in P. Patton (ed.), *Deleuze: A Critical Reader* (Oxford: Blackwell, 1996). Malabou stages an original deconstructive encounter between Deleuze and Hegel, arguing against Deleuze's reductive containment of Hegelian dialectics, and suggests that a productive "block of becoming" between Hegel and Deleuze might be possible. Bruce Baugh presents a strong defence of the Deleuzean critique of Hegel in "Transcendental Empiricism: Deleuze's Response to Hegel", *Man and World* 25 (1992), 133–48. Simon Lumsden defends Hegel's conception of subjectivity against this Deleuzean critique in "Deleuze, Hegel, and the Transformation of Subjectivity", *The Philosophical Forum*, vol. 33, issue 2, Summer 2002, 143–58. Deleuze's early review of Hyppolite's *Logic and Existence* is reprinted as an appendix to the English translation of *Logic and Existence* (Albany, NY: SUNY Press, 1997), 191–5. It can also be found in Deleuze's *Desert Islands and Other Texts 1953–1974* (New York: Semiotext(e), 2004), 15–18.

The Derrida–Hegel relationship is immensely complex given Derrida's sustained engagement with Hegelian thought. There are the well-known essays "Violence and Metaphysics" and "From Restricted to General Economy" in *Writing and Difference* (Chicago, IL: University of Chicago Press, 1978); "The Pit and the Pyramid: Hegel's Semiology" in *Margins of Philosophy* (Chicago, IL: University of Chicago Press, 1982); and the extraordinary deconstructive reading of Hegel and Genet in *Glas* (Lincoln, NE: University of Nebraska Press, 1986). For our purposes, the most interesting secondary text is S. Barnett (ed.), *Hegel After Derrida* (London: Routledge, 1998), especially the enlightening essays by Simon Critchley and Heinz Kimmerle. With Derrida, I can recommend Malabou's *The Future of Hegel* as a text that brings Hegel "back to the future", opening up new ways of thinking between Heidegger and Hegelianism.

Key texts

Adorno, T. and Horkheimer, M. 2002. *Dialectic of Enlightenment*. E. Jephcott (trans.). Stanford, CA: Stanford University Press (German publication 1947).

Beauvoir, S. de. 1953. *The Second Sex*, H. M. Pashley (trans.). London: Cape (French publication 1949).

Beauvoir, S. de. 1976. *The Ethics of Ambiguity*, B. Frechtman (trans.). Secaucus, NJ: Citadel Press (French publication 1948).

Deleuze, G. 1983. *Nietzsche and Philosophy*, H. Tomlinson (trans.). New York: Columbia University Press (French publication 1962).

Deleuze, G. 1994. *Difference and Repetition*, P. Patton (trans.). New York: Columbia University Press (French publication 1968).

Derrida, J. 1978. *Writing and Difference*, A. Bass (trans.). Chicago, IL: University of Chicago Press (French publication 1967).

Derrida, J. 1986. *Glas*, J. P. Leavey and R. Rand (trans.). Lincoln, NE: University of Nebraska Press (French publication 1974).

Habermas, J. 1973. "Labor and Interaction: Remarks on Hegel's Jena *Philosophy of Mind*", in *Theory and Practice*, J. Viertel (trans.). Boston, MA: Beacon Press, 142–69 (German publication 1971).

Habermas, J. 1987. *The Philosophical Discourse of Modernity*, F. G. Lawrence (trans.). Cambridge: Polity (German publication 1985).

Hegel, G. W. F. 1948. *On Christianity: Early Theological Writings*, T. M. Knox and R. Kroner (trans.). New York: Harper (German publication 1907).

Hegel, G. W. F. 1969. Hegel's *Science of Logic*, A. V. Miller (trans.). Atlantic Highlands, NJ: Humanities Press (German publication 1811, 1812, 1816 (revised 1830)).

Hegel, G. W. F. 1977. *The Difference between Fichte's and Schelling's System of Philosophy*, H. S. Harris and W. Cerf (trans.). Albany, NY: SUNY Press (German publication 1801).

Hegel, G. W. F. 1977. Hegel's *Phenomenology of Spirit*, A. V. Miller (trans.). Oxford: Oxford University Press (German publication 1807).

Hegel, G. W. F. 1991. *Elements of the Philosophy of Right*. A. Wood (ed.), H. B. Nisbet (trans.). Cambridge: Cambridge University Press (German publication 1821).

Hegel, G. W. F. 1896/1995. *Lectures on the History of Philosophy. Medieval and Modern Philosophy, Volume 3*, E. S. Haldane and F. H. Simson (trans.). Lincoln, NE: University of Nebraska Press.

Heidegger, M. 1970. *Hegel's Concept of Experience*, K. R. Dove (trans.). New York: Harper & Row (German publication 1950).

Heidegger, M. 1996. *Being and Time*, J. Stambaugh (trans.). Albany, NY: SUNY Press (German publication 1927).

Honneth, A. 1995. *The Struggle for Recognition: The Moral Grammar of Social Conflicts*, J. Anderson (trans.). Cambridge: Polity (German publication 1992).

Hyppolite, J. 1974. *Genesis and Structure of Hegel's* Phenomenology of Spirit, S. Cherniak and J. Heckman (trans.). Evanston, IL: Northwestern University Press (French publication 1943).

Hyppolite, J. 1997. *Logic and Existence*, L. Lawlor and A. Sen (trans.). Albany, NY: SUNY Press (French publication 1952).

Kierkegaard, S. 1992. *Concluding Unscientific Postscript to* Philosophical Fragments, H. V. Hong and E. H. Hong (trans.). Princeton, NJ: Princeton University Press (Danish publication 1846).

Kojève, A. 1947. "Idea of Death in the Philosophy of Hegel", from *Introduction to the Reading of Hegel*, appearing in D. K. Keenan, 2004. *Hegel and Contemporary Continental Philosophy*, J. J. Carpino (trans.). Albany, NY: SUNY Press (French publication 1947).

Kojève, A. 1969. *Introduction to the Reading of Hegel*, J. Nichols (trans.). Ithaca, NY: Cornell University Press (French publication 1947).

Lukács, G. 1971. *History and Class Consciousness*, R. Livingstone (trans.). London: Merlin (German publication 1923/1966).

Lukács, G. 1975. *The Young Hegel: Studies in the Relations between Dialectics and Economics*, R. Livingstone (trans.). London: Merlin (German publication 1947/48).

Marx, K. 1977. *Karl Marx: Selected Writings*, D. McLellan (ed.). Oxford: Oxford University Press.

Marx, K. 1978. *The Marx–Engels Reader*, 2nd ed., R. C. Tucker (ed.). New York: Norton.

Merleau-Ponty, M. 1964. *Sense and Non-Sense*, H. L. Dreyfus and P. Dreyfus (trans.). Evanston, IL: Northwestern University Press (French publication 1948).

Merleau-Ponty, M. 1968. *The Visible and the Invisible*, A. Lingis (trans.). Evanston, IL: Northwestern University Press (French publication 1968).

Sartre, J.-P. 1958. *Being and Nothingness*, H. Barnes (trans.). London: Routledge (French publication 1943).

References

Adorno, T. 1993. *Hegel: Three Studies*, S. W. Weber (trans.). Cambridge, MA: MIT Press.

Barnett, S. (ed.) 1998. *Hegel After Derrida*. London: Routledge.

Bataille, G. 1990. "Hegel, Death, Sacrifice", C. Carsten (trans.) in *Yale French Studies*, no. 78, *On Bataille*. New Haven, CT: Yale University Press, 9–43.

Baugh, B. 2003. *French Hegel: From Surrealism to Postmodernism*. London: Routledge.

Beiser, F. 1988. *The Fate of Reason*. Cambridge, MA: Harvard University Press.

Bernstein, J. M. 2004. "Negative Dialectic as Fate: Adorno and Hegel", in T. Huhn (ed.), *The Cambridge Companion to Adorno*. Cambridge: Cambridge University Press.

Brandom, R. 1994. *Making it Explicit: Reasoning, Representing, and Discursive Commitments*. Cambridge, MA: Harvard University Press.

Brandom, R. 2000. *Articulating Reasons: An Introduction to Inferentialism*. Cambridge, MA: Harvard University Press.

Brunkhorst, H. 1999. *Adorno and Critical Theory*. Cardiff: University of Wales Press.

Butler, J. 1988. *Subjects of Desire: Hegelian Reflections in Twentieth-Century France*. New York: Columbia University Press.

Butler, J. 1989. "Commentary on Joseph Flay's 'Hegel, Derrida, and Bataille's Laughter'", in W. Desmond, *Hegel and his Critics*. Albany, NY: SUNY Press, 174–8.

Butler, J. 1997. *The Psychic Life of Power: Theories in Subjection*. New York: Columbia University Press.

Butler, J. 2000. *Antigone's Claim: Kinship between Life and Death*. New York: Columbia University Press.

Butler, J., Laclau, M. and Žižek, S. 1999. *Contingency, Hegemony, Universality: Contemporary Dialogues on the Left*. London: Verso.

Coole, D. 2000. *Negativity and Politics: Dionysus and Dialectics from Kant to Poststructuralism*. London: Routledge.

Critchley, S. 1999. *Ethics of Deconstruction: Derrida and Levinas*, 2nd ed. Edinburgh: Edinburgh University Press.

Critchley, S. 2004. "A Commentary Upon Derrida's Reading of Hegel in *Glas*", in D. K. Keenan (ed.), *Hegel and Contemporary Continental Philosophy*. Albany, NY: SUNY Press, 197–226.

Deleuze, G. and Guattari, F. 1994. *What is Philosophy?* H. Tomlinson and G. Burchell (trans.). New York: Columbia University Press.

Derrida, J. 1976. *Of Grammatology*, G. C. Spivak (trans.). Baltimore, MD: Johns Hopkins University Press.

Derrida, J. 1981. *Positions*, A. Bass (trans.). Chicago, IL: Chicago University Press.

Derrida, J. 1999. *Adieu à Emmanuel Lévinas*, Pascale-Anne Brault and Michael Naas (trans.). Stanford, CA: Stanford University Press.

Descombes, V. 1980. *Modern French Philosophy*, L. Scott-Fox and J. M. Harding (trans.). Cambridge: Cambridge University Press.

Desmond, W. 1989. *Hegel and his Critics*, W. Desmond (ed.). Albany, NY: SUNY Press.

Flay, J. 1989. "Hegel, Derrida, and Bataille's Laughter", in W. Desmond, *Hegel and his Critics*. Albany, NY: SUNY Press, 163–73.

Fukuyama, F. 1992. *The End of History and the Last Man*. New York: Free Press.

Heidegger, M. 1997. *Kant and the Problem of Metaphysics*, R. Taft (trans.). Bloomington, IN: Indiana University Press.

Henrich, D. 2003. *Between Kant and Hegel: Lectures on German Idealism*, D. S. Pacini (ed.). Cambridge, MA: Harvard University Press.

Houlgate, S. 2005. *An Introduction to Hegel: Freedom, Truth, History*, 2nd ed. Oxford: Blackwell.

Hutchings, K. 2003. *Hegel and Feminist Philosophy*. Cambridge: Polity.

Hyppolite, J. 1969. *Studies on Marx and Hegel*, J. O'Neill (trans.). New York: Basic Books.

Jay, M. 1984. *Marxism and Totality: The Adventures of a Concept from Lukács to Habermas*. Berkeley, CA: University of California Press.

Keenan, D. K. (ed.). 2004. *Hegel and Contemporary Continental Philosophy*. Albany, NY: SUNY Press.

Kimmerle, H. 2004. "On Derrida's Hegel Interpretation", in D. K. Keenan (ed.), *Hegel and Contemporary Continental Philosophy*. Albany, NY: SUNY Press, 227–38.

Kolb, D. 1986. *The Critique of Pure Modernity: Hegel, Heidegger, and After*. Chicago, IL: University of Chicago Press.

Lacan, J. 1977. *Ècrits. A Selection*, A. Sheridan (trans.). London: Tavistock.

Lawlor, L. 2003. *Thinking Through French Philosophy: The Being of the Question*. Bloomington, IN: Indiana University Press.

Löwith, K. 1991. *From Hegel to Nietzsche. The Revolution in Nineteenth-Century Thought*, D. E. Green (trans.). New York: Columbia University Press.

Malabou, C. 1996. "Who's Afraid of Hegelian Wolves?" in P. Patton (ed.), *Deleuze: A Critical Reader*. Oxford: Blackwell, 114–38.

Malabou, C. 2005. *The Future of Hegel: Plasticity, Temporality, Dialectic*. New York: Routledge.

McDowell, J. 1996. *Mind and World*. Cambridge, MA: Harvard University Press.

McDowell, J. 1998. *Mind, Value, and Reality*. Cambridge, MA: Harvard University Press.

Merleau-Ponty, M. 1973. *Adventures of the Dialectic*, J. Bien (trans.). Evanston, IL: Northwestern University Press.

Merleau-Ponty, M. 2002. *Phenomenology of Perception*, C. Smith (trans.). London: Routledge.

Pinkard, T. 1988. *Hegel's Dialectic: The Explanation of Possibility*. Philadelphia, PA: Temple University Press.

Pinkard, T. 1994. *Hegel's Phenomenology. The Sociality of Reason*. Cambridge: Cambridge University Press.

Pippin, R. B. 1989. *Hegel's Idealism: The Satisfactions of Self-Consciousness*. Cambridge: Cambridge University Press.

Popper, K. 1945. *The Open Society and Its Enemies*, volume 2. London: Routledge.

Poster, M. 1975. *Existential Marxism in Postwar France: From Sartre to Althusser*. Princeton, NJ: Princeton University Press.

Redding, P. 1996. *Hegel's Hermeneutics*. Ithaca, NY: Cornell University Press.

Reynolds, J. 2004. *Merleau-Ponty and Derrida: Intertwining Embodiment and Alterity*. Athens, OH: Ohio University Press.

Rockmore, T. 1993. *Before and After Hegel: An Historical Introduction to Hegel's Thought*. Berkeley, CA: University of California Press.

Rockmore, T. 2005. *Hegel, Idealism, and Analytic Philosophy*. New Haven, CT: Yale University Press.

Rorty, R. 1982. *Consequences of Pragmatism*. Minneapolis, MN: University of Minnesota Press.

Roth, M. S. 1988. *Knowing and History: Appropriations of Hegel in Twentieth Century France*. Ithaca, NY: Cornell University Press.

Strauss, L. and Kojève, A. 2000. *On Tyranny: Including the Strauss–Kojève Correspondence*, V. Gourevitch and M. S. Roth (eds). Chicago, IL: University of Chicago Press.

Sedgwick, S. 1997. "McDowell's Hegelianism", *European Journal of Philosophy* 5 (1), 21–38.

Smith, D. W. 2000. "Deleuze, Hegel, and the Post-Kantian Tradition", *Philosophy Today* 44 (Supplement), 119–31.

Taylor, C. 1975. *Hegel*. Cambridge: Cambridge University Press.

Taylor, C. 1983. *Hegel and Modern Society*. Cambridge: Cambridge University Press.

Toews, J. E. 1993. "Transformations of Hegelianism, 1805–1846", in F. Beiser (ed.), *The Cambridge Companion to Hegel*. Cambridge: Cambridge University Press.

Wahl, J. 1920. *Les philosophies pluralistes d'Angleterre et d'Amérique*. Paris: Alcan.

Williams, J. 2003. *Gilles Deleuze's Difference and Repetition: A Critical Introduction and Guide*. Edinburgh: Edinburgh University Press.

Williams, R. R. 1992. *Recognition: Hegel and Fichte on the Other*. Chicago, IL: University of Chicago Press.

Wood, A. 1990. *Hegel's Ethical Thought*. Cambridge: Cambridge University Press.

Žižek, S. 1993. *Tarrying with the Negative: Kant, Hegel, and the Critique of Ideology*. Durham, NC: Duke University Press.

Žižek, S. 1999. *The Ticklish Subject: The Absent Centre of Political Ontology*. London: Verso.

Index

absolute, the 10, 21, 34, 77–8, 152–3, 161
  Schellingian 9, 10
  Spinozist 9, 10
absolute knowing 11, 21, 49, 73–4, 105, 134, 192, 193–4, 196
abstract right 29, 30–31
Adorno, Theodor 28, 83, 84, 213
  negative dialectics x, 84, 88, 95–8, 120, 167, 168, 181, 190, 213
  non-identity thinking 83, 96
alienation 2, 4, 20, 31, 32, 46, 52–3, 55–7, 61, 83, 89, 107
  according to Hyppolite 130–33
  according to Rousseau and Hegel 63–6, 177
  according to Sartre 153
  existential 125, 127, 128, 130–33, 204
analytic philosophy
  Hegel and ix, xi, 1, 15, 33–5, 211
Aristotle 19, 22, 50, 71, 72, 181
art
  and aesthetic critique of modernity 97
  as commodity 92–3
atomization 4, 31
Auschwitz 28

Bataille, Georges 126, 144, 189
Bauer, Bruno 40, 45–7
Baugh, Bruce 126, 127, 128, 214
Beauvoir, Simone de x, 50, 125, 144, 147, 148, 149, 154–62
  account of oppression 154–6
  critique of Hegel 160–61
  ethics of ambiguity 159–62
  master/slave dialectic 156–8
  woman as the Other 156–9
becoming 23–4, 50, 71, 129–30, 172, 174, 177, 179, 180, 185, 202
being
  determinate 23–4
  and nothing 23–4
  pure 23–4
  question of (Heidegger) 69
Being and Nothingness (Sartre) 129, 148, 149, 155, 165
Being and Time (Heidegger) 51, 69–72, 129
Bernstein, J. M. 97, 213
Bosanquet, Bernard 32, 33
Bradley, F. H. 1, 32
Brandom, Robert 35, 203, 211
Butler, Judith x, 172, 202–3, 213–14